Adults Learning

Fifth edition

Adults Learning

Jenny Rogers

Fifth edition

Open University Press

Open University Press
McGraw-Hill Education
McGraw-Hill House
Shoppenhangers Road
Maidenhead
Berkshire
England
SL6 2QL

email: enquiries@openup.co.uk
world wide web: www.openup.co.uk

and Two Penn Plaza, New York, NY 10121–2289, USA

First published 1971
Second edition 1977
Third edition 1989
Fourth edition 2001
This fifth edition published 2007

A catalogue record of this book is available from the British Library

ISBN-13: 978–0–33–522535–4 (pb)
ISBN-10: 033–522535–7 (pb)

Library of Congress Cataloguing-in-Publication Data
CIP data applied for

Typeset by YHT Ltd, London
Printed in Poland by OZGraf S.A.
www.polskabook.pl

The McGraw-Hill Companies

Contents

Acknowledgements

Most of what I know about teaching and learning has been as a result of working with more experienced colleagues and with groups frank enough to give me high-quality feedback. My current colleagues at Management Futures are skilled designers and managers of learning and I benefit constantly from their wisdom. Without all these people there would be little for me to write about.

My interest in social psychology was first sparked as a postgraduate student at Oxford where I was lucky enough to encounter teachers such as Henri Tajfel, Michael Argyle and Peter Kuenstler. Their combined knowledge and enthusiasm woke me up from the trance of my undergraduate career. I have learnt enormously from every course I have attended as a participant, but the Columbia University course on organizational development run by Warner Burke stands out, as does my training in the Myers Briggs Type Indicator from Susan Block.

I owe gratitude to early colleagues at the BBC: John Robinson, Donald Gratton, Roger Owen and Sheila Innes for giving me the chance to deepen my experience as an educationist and to my long-standing friend Chris Longley for her personal support. As someone then new to the whole theory of adult learning, I learnt an enormous amount in informal conversations with a distinguished generation of British adult educationists such as Ralph Ruddock and Brian Groombridge. Later on, during my stint as a Commissioning Editor at the Open College, I also gained a great deal of knowledge about applied learning from both Richard Freeman and Martin Fischer.

The book would never have been written without the active encouragement and insight of my editor at Penguin, Richard Mabey. John Skelton at the Open University Press saw the book through several of its subsequent editions and his successor, Shona Mullen, has also been consistently encouraging.

Finally, I am grateful for my luck in having parents who constantly showed me that learning has intrinsic value. I also thank my family: my sons for their forebearance over the many hours of writing and rewriting this book through its various editions and most especially my husband, Alan. He knows why.

For Alan

Introduction

If you are one of the many tens of thousands of people involved in helping other adults learn, then this book could be for you.

When I wrote the first edition in 1971, I produced the book that I wished someone had given to me when I was new to teaching adults. Now, for this fifth edition thirty-six years later, that wish remains the driving force behind substantially rewriting the book yet again with several entirely new chapters and radically updated treatments of old ones. I now know a lot more about teaching and learning than I did in 1971, but the core principles of good practice seem much the same. The context has changed, the research is deeper and fuller, but the needs of adult learners are recognizably what they were then.

I envisaged the original target reader as someone who was an expert in a particular subject, but lacked knowledge of how to apply that expertise to working with adult learners. Probably I saw my core reader as working in adult education institutions of one kind or another – the old 'evening class' whose worthy tradition was firmly rooted in nineteenth-century philanthropic ideas of helping talented people climb out of the poverty imposed by their lack of access to education.

Since then, the whole teaching and training market has expanded tenfold. It's true that the original adult education colleges are still there, now charging in many cases what seem like market rates, along with the traditional subsidized courses. I have the London City Lit's brochure on my desk as I write. It is a dense, beautifully presented 192-page document, backed up by an equally professional website, so predictions of the adult education sector's demise seem to have been premature. There are also many more UK universities than there were 35 years ago and, cash-poor though they seem to be, and offering unattractively low salaries though they are, there are thousands more people working as teachers in higher education than was the case 36 years ago. But the most striking expansion has to be in the corporate sector where the need to train people in IT, in management development, in customer service – and dozens more topics – has led to a dramatic expansion in the numbers of professional trainers. The market for informal teaching is wider still. As I glanced casually at the newspaper recently, I read an item about how newly-literate prisoners are successfully teaching other prisoners how to read and write. Teaching also goes on every day in environments as varied as cruise ships, leisure centres, medical and nursing schools or community colleges.

The possibilities for learning and teaching seem literally unlimited. The quest for 'self-development' means that good old favourites like yoga classes are still going strong, but so too are the thousands of 'be-a-better-person' books. The ultra-rapid pace of change in companies of all sorts as they struggle to stay competitive means that training and development are now open to virtually everyone who is employed. 'Having a development plan' is no longer the preserve of people who'd been through a hippy stage in earlier life and had never quite got over it, but a sensible strategy for keeping your entire workforce flexible and up to date. Anyone who is a manager needs to accept that they must also be a coach. Leadership is now as much about coaching as it is about setting direction, and coaching is about helping people learn.

The media through which training is delivered are many times more varied than they were. Where once the only way to learn was assumed to be face to face or with a book, now it can be through blended learning, manuals, and increasingly by 'e' means, whether through the phone, video, the internet or by 'e-coaching'. Whatever the medium or the context, I still believe that the subject is a lot less important than the method or the means of delivery. The art of teaching adults is a broad-based and flexible one whose principles can be applied to a wide variety of situations.

It is a hard task to write a book about teaching and learning without sounding prescriptive or saintly – or possibly both. In the early editions, I did not attempt to explain how and why I had come to write it, perhaps because the experience was still too recent or perhaps because I was sensitive to the possible accusation that I was too young and inexperienced to be writing a book of 'advice' at all. The original book came out of two strands of experience: my own in the classroom and an early career experience with the BBC.

My first job as a young graduate was in a college of further education where teaching adults became an important part of a job which I had originally thought was going to be about the education of 16- to 19-year-olds. To survive and learn your craft in this environment your wits had to be sharp and your sense of humour well to the fore. As the youngest person in my 'adults' class working towards an English exam, I was the teacher but without any of the natural authority that age and experience confer. No wonder that I often felt I was engaged in a role-play rather than the real thing.

In the daytime in the same college, I found myself in some equally tricky situations. For instance, there was a class of 17-year-olds to whom I was 'teaching' economics, a subject I knew literally nothing about. The merciless teasing of my class taught me a great deal about the need to love your subject and the absolute necessity of burning to communicate your pleasure in it. Where the adult students were polite and reticent, the sparky young people I taught in the daytime never hesitated to give me candid feedback on my performance: 'Bit boring today – too much theory'; or, 'I liked that bit where we read the play instead of you talking'. They had gloriously direct ways of teaching teachers humbling lessons.

In effect my younger students trained me and I diligently and gratefully applied what I was learning to the adults' classes where the same forces were at work but far more subtly. After all, the adults did not have to be there. If the class was disagreeable, they could stop coming. The overriding impact of this experience amounted to one simple message. In teaching, the customer, not the subject, comes first and is always right, and the customer is the learner.

However valuable this experience was, it was considerably sharpened by my next job where I worked as an adviser on adult education to the BBC. If only every tutor could, as I did, sit anonymously in other people's classrooms. The 'mistakes' that we all fudge in our own efforts become burningly obvious when looking at someone else making them. I am reminded now of something I say to the people I train as coaches when alerting them to the dangers of disliking something you see in a client: 'If you spot it, you got it!'

Since no one in adult and further education really believed that the BBC knew anything whatsoever about teaching and learning, I was welcomed everywhere. 'It's only some girl from the BBC' I overheard one principal explain to one of his tutors, 'She just wants to sit in at the back'. So as an honorary invisible woman, I saw adult teaching of all types – probably several hundred classes in all – in the raw. I saw bold and innovative teaching that was years ahead of its time and that would still stand scrutiny today as outstanding. Equally, and perhaps more often, I saw tutors struggling because no one had apparently even attempted to show them solutions to the common problems of all teaching and learning: how to motivate, how to simplify without losing the integrity of the original ideas, how to help people learn.

One piece of good fortune fuelled my desire to pass on to others what I felt I now knew. In my first year at the BBC, I was asked to help evaluate a pioneering series called *Teaching Adults*. The series became a classic and introduced me to some of the best brains in the business. Some of them contributed to the book I edited for the BBC, *Teaching on Equal Terms*, but working on this project made me even keener to write a book of my own, hence *Adults Learning*.

It has been a satisfying book for an author, introducing me to many talented and interesting people and giving me the chance to work as a trainer of other tutors making similar journeys. The original publishers, Penguin, sold the rights to the present publishers, Open University Press. Over the years the book has been translated into many languages including Japanese and Mandarin and has sold well in excess of a quarter of a million copies – not bad for something perceived to be an ultra-specialist topic by its first publisher. One of my best moments ever as an author was seeing someone reading it on the Underground in London. I am sorry now that I did not follow my instinct and introduce myself to the reader, asking eagerly for feedback. Maybe this was just as well, as the Tube is full of crazy people and I don't think I looked very authorial that day.

In the years since writing the earlier editions, I believe I have become a living case study myself of why adult learning is still such a vital topic. I had had three different careers in earlier life – teacher, internal consultant on education and TV producer and all required concentrated learning in order to master the various skills that they needed. Since then, I have added several more careers. After working as a commissioning editor for the Open College, I became a manager, running a training department for the BBC. Then, feeling that spending my time on endless so-called working parties was not for me, I moved again. This time it was to start my own company, Management Futures, where we train, teach, consult and coach. So in addition to continuing to teach, I have also had to learn how to become an entrepreneur, management consultant, coach and director of a small company.

The safe career is now a fantasy for all of us. This is true for me, for my sons and for my clients. Like so many others, I have needed and wanted to learn new skills as I have shifted into the 'portfolio' economy. I have become computer and internet literate. I have added satisfying new hobbies to my life, including line-dancing and other forms of dance, an interest that involves a lot of intensive learning and which arouses much puzzled amusement among family and friends. I have continued my own formal development through courses on subjects as varied as personal image and mediation. I have written many other books, including three on human personality as seen through the lens of psychometric questionnaires and two books on coaching, also published by the Open University Press. Also, like so many of my contemporaries, I refuse to accept the possibility of the 'R' word. Retirement is not something I can contemplate. I am struck by the truth of one friend's recipe for a happy life: never get divorced, never stop learning, never stop working – and never spend Christmas with your family. The last perhaps is somewhat controversial, but I strongly agree with the other three.

As with its predecessor editions, this is not a textbook, though I know it is commonly recommended on teacher-training courses. You will not find a sober, pedagogical treatment here. I wanted to convey the essence of important ideas on teaching and learning but also to give some flavour of the authentic voices of tutors and learners, so this edition, like its predecessors, contains direct, anonymized quotes. I wrote the original book precisely because I was so maddened by the footnoted complexity and what felt like the perverse and cranky obfuscation of all the other material then available. There are now some excellent academic treatments of the same subject and I recommend some of them in the Further Reading suggestions which end each chapter.

My aim has been to write simply and accessibly. It has also been to write with a personal voice, so this is openly an opinionated book. The views I expressed in the first edition about the need to put learners at the centre of teaching, then considered to be radical and maybe somewhat barmy, are now mainstream and backed by far more proper research than was available when I originally wrote. Then, frankly, I was backing my hunches much of the time. However, even now, I emphasize what I have seen work for me and others through several decades of observation, thinking and practice in a wide range of settings. My hope is that it works for you, too, but in the end it is your choice. You will bring to the task, as we all do, a blend of understanding learners' needs with your own personal need, personal style, subject knowledge and experience. This book cannot offer you any easy, infallible guides to 'good' teaching. Teaching and learning are infinitely variable processes. You and your learners will have particular needs which only you can interpret. The suggestions I offer are meant to outline a range of possibilities from which you and your group can choose, rather than being a set of rules to which you must always adhere.

Carrying on learning is important to me and so is carrying on teaching. I and my company now train people in topics that I certainly never dreamed of when I wrote the first edition of this book, but I remain committed to my original vision that the principles of teaching adults are the same, whatever the setting, the medium, the types of learner or the subject. The effective teacher of adults has only one motto, and that is, 'Learners first'. How you might put that motto into practice is what the rest of this book is about.

1 Adult learners: what you need to know

Ask yourself what sticks in your mind as the outstanding pieces of learning you accomplished at school or college. My guess is that you are not very likely to nominate sitting spellbound at the feet of a 'great teacher'. My own main memory of school is of sitting in classrooms where teaching and not learning was the emphasis. If the teacher was a captivating character and able to hold my attention, the time would pass painlessly. Mostly, though, mediocrity prevailed and like so many of my fellows, I became an expert in a variety of displacement activities: daydreaming, skilfully passing notes to friends, doodling decorative hearts and names of fantasy boyfriends on my notebooks and otherwise dealing with the tedium that most of the timetable seemed to involve. The only activity in some lessons was scribbling down the teachers' words for regurgitation into essays, marked by the same teacher according to how faithfully we had reproduced what she had said. Lessons, with some noble exceptions, were the price to be paid for enjoying the real life of school – the social life of the breaks.

Rather than remembering wonderful lessons, it is far more likely that you will immediately remember your part in a particular school play, a project, a trip abroad, an experiment you successfully concluded on your own, the achievement of some sporting feat – all of them active pieces of learning where you were at the centre of the effort. From three years' study of history at university, my mind has wiped most dates, wars, monarchs and all the essays and lectures that went into recording them. If asked, for instance, as I have been by a homework-doing child, why William of Normandy invaded England, and why the industrial revolution started, I could not give a coherent response to either. Yet I can still recall much of the detail of a project in my final year at university when, as a special privilege, we were allowed to research and write up a subject of our choice.

This is the first essential principle of teaching adults successfully and it's a paradox. Teaching is about learning. As the American writers Postman and Weingartner wryly commented: '"Oh I taught them that but they didn't learn it . . ." is on the same level as a salesman's remarking, "I sold it to him, but he didn't buy it."'[1] You cannot do the learning for someone else. To say 'I learnt him' is not only grammatically wrong, it is also impossible. Therefore your task as a teacher of adults is to become a designer of learning.

In the learner's mind

Anxiety

Let's start with basics. Assume that most of your potential learners are anxious. The anxiety may not last, and, if you are doing your job properly, it will soon fade, but some anxiety is probably inevitable. Here are the authentic voices of adult learners talking about how they felt approaching learning:

> For months before this training started I used to dream about looking stupid on it. I was astonished at myself – a Cambridge First – being so worried about going 'back to school', but I used to think to myself, oh well, in another three months, two months, one month, it'll all be over.
>
> I opted to go on a special course for chief executives. The publicity emphasized that it would be very stretching – it was being run by a university business school. I know it was silly, but I felt that there was a severe risk of being out of my depth.
>
> I enrolled for a basic graphic design course at the local adult education place, but was very nervous about going – in fact I nearly didn't. I'd been working as a web designer already without any formal training and I really thought I was likely to be shown up as a fraud.
>
> My department is very keen on 'awaydays' but I dread them. It always seems to me that you are put on the spot and have to speak. What if I say something silly?
>
> I went on a leadership course which was led by people who had all been actors. It was run in a theatre with the idea that you could learn a lot about leadership by learning from acting techniques. To say I was frightened would be putting it mildly. I have always felt self-conscious anyway and I felt certain that other people would be far more confident and better at everything than I would be.

Memories of school

Why can we feel so negative about learning something new? There are several possible explanations. One is that in spite of all the training and development that now happens inside and out of employment, education is still seen as something that happens to children. To be back in a 'classroom' seems to revive memories of being at school and with it all the associated subservient status. As adults we are, after all, people who have acquired the status of maturity in our own and other people's eyes as partners, friends, employers or employees. Perhaps this status and self-esteem is less robust than it appears and is easily threatened when put back in the apparently subservient status of the learner.

This will be more of an issue when people's experience of school education has been disappointing, and even more so where education has involved the ritual humiliation so common in the worst of our secondary schools of all sorts, whether the fascistic rituals of the harsher sort of boarding school or the patronizing sneers of the graduate who is forced to teach children he or she despises at a so-called bog-standard comprehensive school. Don't underestimate the power of these memories:

> My parents thought they were doing a wonderful thing by sending me to a famous boys' school. What I learnt there was the corrupting power of authority. Of course there were some decent teachers there but so many of them were in it for the wrong reasons. Put me in a 'classroom' now, even one in a nice hotel with no sitting in rows or anything like that, and I'm right back there, still aged 13, terrified and determined to fight back in ways that won't get me into immediate trouble!

> Experience of school: constant failure. I was labelled not very bright at an early age because I'd had undiagnosed problems with my hearing. Even now, I see trainers/tutors as hostile to me and expecting me to be dim. I know how silly this is because I realize the kind of people I now encounter leading courses are the absolute opposite, but it takes me a long time to trust them.

> When I met my coach for the first time, the thought in my mind was that I was going to be meeting the headmaster. I just couldn't get it out of my mind.

> Whenever I go on a residential course, even a really good one, I know I'm going to have the same anxiety dream on the first night – strange bed, don't sleep very well. In my dream, I'm back at school and I'm doing an exam. I haven't revised and I'm going to be shown up. I wake up at the point where I'm faced with an examination paper which I can't answer.

Challenge to beliefs

Another possible explanation is that potential conflict is involved when an adult comes forward for learning. As adults we already have certain well-developed ideas about life along with our own systems and beliefs. To admit that we need to learn something new is to admit that there is something wrong with our present system. Many people, though they may perceive that they do need new skills or knowledge, feel so threatened by the challenge to their previous beliefs that they are unable to learn. I recently ran a short course on leadership for a group of media clients. It was soon apparent that I had a problem with one member of the group – or, perhaps to put it another way, he had a problem with me. I put forward some simple and commonly accepted ideas about 'emotional intelligence' (skill with people) being essential for effective leadership. He loudly challenged me on the grounds that I was suggesting an 'identikit' style of leadership that would 'take all the creativity out of the media'. Of course I was suggesting no such thing. What I was suggesting, however, was clearly a threat to his previous assumptions about leadership – and perhaps about his own behaviour, since emotional intelligence was not very apparent in the aggressive way he questioned me.

This may be why adult learners so often take refuge in the idea that what we are learning is really meant for someone else. Many years ago I was part of a group of teachers who had been pressed, perhaps clumsily, to attend a refresher course on basic teaching skills. Even though we all enjoyed ourselves and learnt a lot, it would have been impossible at the time to find a single member of staff willing to admit that the course was aimed at us. No, it was meant for 'very young' or 'part-time' teachers. To have admitted that *we* needed help would have aimed too sharp a blow at our ideas of ourselves as already competent teachers.

I have seen the same thing many times since working as a consultant to organizations. Senior management announces a reorganization. With the reorganization goes a need to acquire new skills, and training is offered as a way of supporting the change. In some organizations, childish resistance to this opportunity can take many forms. My colleagues and I have experienced all of the following: people who write letters or literally bring their in-trays to the group; people who tap away at their BlackBerries or mobiles; people who stalk out dramatically; people who arrive late and leave early ... the list is endless. The message is clear: we don't like or want this reorganization (fair enough), but also we don't need this learning; we're OK as we are. This will be particularly true where the new learning is also perceived to be a threat to identity. So, for instance, when the National Health Service introduced a much-hated 'internal market', doctors made no bones about their view that they were clinical specialists not business people. As one of my colleagues said at the time, 'If I had £10 for every time I heard the phrase, "this isn't a baked bean factory you know", I'd be a rich man!'

People who work on education programmes in developing countries have learnt the hard way that it is better to face up to the implications of these phenomena than to wait for them to catch you out. If you can run an educational event where the tutor is 'one of us' – literally a member of the community, you probably increase many times over the chances of your message being heard.

Let's not exaggerate the problems and let's accept that it will vary enormously from one person and one situation to another. A young graduate full of confidence with a degree newly in his or her pocket may bounce into a training course with little anxiety. A mature chief executive working on a course with his or her peers may soon lose whatever quivers of worry he or she has experienced beforehand. On the other hand, an adult non-reader may travel over city and county boundaries to make sure of finding a class where anonymity is guaranteed. However, my working assumption is that there will be some anxiety wherever there is real learning because real learning involves change, and that's difficult stuff for most of us.

Don't be fooled by the apparent confidence of the learner. One of my clients is a celebrity in his field and widely admired for his ability (known to some for being so clever that he is jokingly assumed to have two brains). He told me much later that he was so frightened at the thought of his first coaching session with me that he nearly cancelled it. And what was he frightened of? 'Ah', came the reply, 'it was fear of exposure. I felt sure that you would show me up as a fraud.' Since he had never met me, I think we can be sure that this said a lot more about him than it did about me.

Along with your assumption that there will be some apprehension goes a duty to defuse it as soon as possible. There is no case whatsoever for deliberately whipping up anxiety. Anxiety gets in the way of learning, because the person is preoccupied with his or her fears, and it gets in the way physiologically because it increases the amount of free fatty acids in the bloodstream and makes learning even more difficult. This is why ice-breakers, a bit of early fun and a frank acknowledgement of fear are all a good idea. I say more about this in the next chapter – on the first session.

Managing change

So if you take to heart all of these principles, you will be accepting that another way of looking at your role is to see it as the change manager for your learners. Change is at the heart of learning. If nothing changes then there is no learning. But essentially we will only change when what we want presents itself as a bigger reward than the cost of staying the same. So dissatisfaction is a great motivator – in fact, without it, change is unlikely. But if it is just at the level of a low hum of discontent, it may not be enough to prod us into learning. As a tutor you can learn from many years of research into change in organizations, all of which show clearly that the pain can be reduced by a series of precepts, which, though simple in themselves, often turn out to be hideously hard to implement. For tutors, there are a few which are worth a mention. Perhaps the most important is constantly to remind people of the rewards they will achieve by committing themselves to the effort of the change – the vision of how wonderful life will be when they achieve their end and to invite their comments and feelings at all stages of the process. At the same time, it would be unfair to minimize the hardships en route. I like the psychologist John Fisher's Process of Transition curve[2] as a way of understanding what is likely to be going on for your learners. Fisher suggests that we typically pass through eight stages of change. In learning terms this is how I interpret them:

Table 1.1

Stage	*Learner's state of mind*
1: Anxiety	Something new happens to create anxiety – perhaps the need to learn a new skill associated with a new job. The dominant state of your mind is, 'Can I cope?'
2: Happiness	Help is at hand – the course sounds good, there will be people there like you; your problems could be solved. You try not to worry too much about what could happen if this optimism is unjustified. *Lesson for tutors: prepare people in advance as far as you can by sending plenty of helpful information to shape expectations.*
3: Fear	Once the learning starts, worry about coping revives. It seems more difficult; other people may seem more adept or experienced. You may take refuge in a belief that faking it will be possible but will worry about whether such faking is sustainable. You may worry about what effect success or failure will have on you. For instance, if you fail, what will others say? *Lesson for tutors: do everything you can to anticipate and defuse this stage; see pages 7 and 54.*
4: Threat	As the pressure of the learning is stepped up, it can become clearer that existing beliefs or levels of skill are not good enough. The old rules no longer apply, but you may be confused about what the new ones are. Anger often accompanies this phase and it is often easier to project this on to someone else. So you may attack your tutors, alleging that they are inexperienced, speaking in incomprehensible jargon, incompetent, out of date or using inappropriate methods, or

alternatively, you may attack the other learners for their arrogance and stupidity.
Lesson for tutors: stay calm. It's not personal, though it may feel as if it is. Don't suppress the expression of learners' feelings, in fact encourage people to express them. Listen sensibly to feedback but be prepared to tough out this phase, especially if you know, based on past experience, that your materials and methods work.

5: Guilt

Now you understand what it is that you don't know. You may feel shame and guilt that you have been operating under misapprehensions for so long. Self-belief may be at stake – you have defined yourself as competent and now may be discovering that this has been an illusion.
Lesson for tutors: support and understanding are vital. Again, encourage people to express their feelings. Tell them that it's normal to feel like this and that it will pass. Encourage people to put their feelings of incompetence and helplessness into perspective: it is unlikely that they will have been getting whatever it is totally wrong.

6: Depression

It all feels overwhelming, the task seems endless and progress slow. You have reached a plateau. You have little energy and may feel stuck in a kind of paralysis. You procrastinate about the tasks that would progress the learning. At this stage you may decide to cut your losses and leave because in this way you believe you will save face.
Lesson for tutors: remind learners of their successes. Design learning which minimizes the chances of failure in the first place. Re-energize people through activities that are fun and low-risk.

7: Gradual acceptance

You begin to make real progress. The puzzle begins to fit together. You get encouragement from modest success and can see, at last, what it would be like to achieve mastery.
Lesson for tutors: feedback, feedback, feedback (page 58).

8: Moving forward

You are making faster progress and gaining confidence. Practice brings more confidence and with it, more success.
Lesson for tutors: offer affirmation, support and challenge. Discuss action plans for further learning (page 272).

The ladder of competence

This is another useful way of looking at the same phenomena. Think back to when you were a child and sat in a car with an experienced driver. It probably looked easy enough to drive a car because, more than likely, you were watching a skilled performance and any skilled performance looks effortless. Then when you began to learn to drive yourself, you suddenly found that it was all a lot harder than you thought. Learning to read the road, to steer, to look in the mirror, to signal, to park – no wonder you got flustered and worried about whether you'd ever learn to do it properly, especially since so much of it needs to be done simultaneously. After a great many lessons and even more practice, you take your test and pass. Now you do know how to drive, but you can't relax for a moment because any lapse in concentration could cause an accident, so you still feel anxious and uncertain. Finally after you have clocked up many more miles, you don't really have to think about it any more – it's automatic.

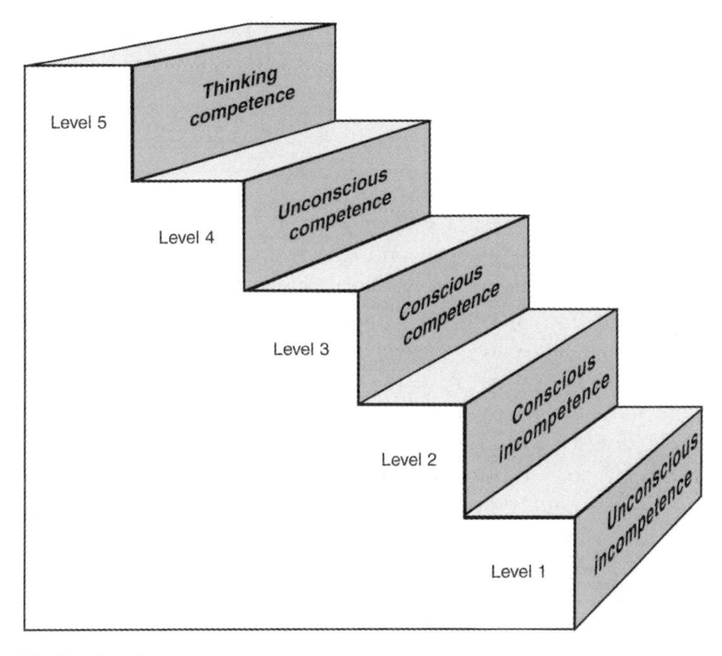

Figure 1.1 The ladder of competence

This process is usually known as *The Ladder of Competence*. Its originator is unknown though there have been many competing claims for authorship, among them from the US organization, Gordon Training International, founded by Dr Thomas Gordon in the early 1970s.[3]

The Ladder of Competence is an idea that is both simple and profound – obvious once it has been stated but not so obvious until then.

Level 1: Unconscious incompetence

At this level, the learner is like the child watching the experienced driver. As the learner, you have no idea what you do not know and you may deny that you need to know it – for instance, you may claim that such learning is irrelevant. Alternatively, you may believe that you already have all the skill and knowledge that you need, not seeing that you have fallen out of date, or possibly that you never were skilled in the first place. This is not a good place to be as a learner but it is where many of our learners will start. As a tutor, if you suspect that this is where your learners are, you will need to devise fair methods of initial assessment so that both you and they know where they stand. Be alert to the possibility that many tutors assume that most of the people they will be teaching are at Level 2 whereas actually many will be at Level 1. The shock of discovering that this is their level may be enough to drive some learners away. Your task is first to uncover the truth and then to support people through their dismay. It is always important to devise some way of separating aptitude and essential ability (potential) from existing skill. If you have a learner who has neither aptitude nor skill then both you and they may be better off honestly agreeing that your event is not for them.

Level 2: Conscious incompetence

Here, as a learner, you have been confronted with your ignorance or lack of skill, or both. Shock, despair and that feeling of never getting past this level may accompany this phase. You look at others who are outstripping you and wonder how they can do what they do. The task of learning feels gargantuan, a mountain you will never be able to climb. As a tutor your role at this stage is to reassure, to point out that this phase is both normal and essential. Remind people that it is better to know what you don't know than to live in the pitiable ignorance of Level 1. Alternatively, people may feel challenged in the best possible way by the learning journey ahead, but my experience is that they are more likely to be this at the point when their confidence and skill begin to build again. This is why the catch-them-doing-something-right approach is so important. Simplifying the task so that you maximize the possibility of right first time is the key to getting learners over this phase. In the terms of Benjamin Bloom's useful taxonomy (page 244), learners are at the stage of copying. Copying is slow, you are aware that you are following someone else's template, you don't feel completely in control, the script is running you rather than the other way around. Adults may find this even more agonizing than children do, but my guess is that probably children do too – we just don't notice it in quite the same way.

Level 3: Conscious competence

I have always found this phase the most interesting and challenging. Here people are saying things like

> If I try this my colleagues will say, 'She's been on a course'
> It feels clunky
> I'm so aware that I'm following a sort of painting-by-numbers approach and that feels unnatural and restrictive
> I can't quite make it seem like my own way of doing things

> It seems as if everything I'm doing is contrary to what I did before – it's like speaking a foreign language but you don't know the rules and everyone else does.

All of these comments are spot on. It does indeed feel clunky and unnatural because it *is* clunky and unnatural. Tell your learners, again, that this is all part of the expected scheme of things. Reassure them that it will get better. The key to success at this phase is to take it steadily, to follow the protocols, to learn each phase of whatever it is and to be patient about lapses because they are inevitable. One danger here is that as confidence begins to grow, the old default mode of Level 1 may begin to assert itself. Closely observed feedback is the key to averting this disaster. Many adults want to skip the discomforts of this phase. They want instant competence. In many cases this is an illusion, so beware of colluding with it. Instant competence usually just isn't possible because it takes a certain steady accumulation of supervised experience plus hours of practice to get beyond the fumbling slowness of progressing from Level 2 to Level 3 and from there to the genuine expertise of Level 4. For instance, learning a language or a musical instrument may take around 1000 hours of learning before you are at Level 2 and another 2000–4000 hours before you are at Level 3. If this is the case for your course, don't fudge it.

Level 4: Unconscious competence

This is the aim of all learning. At Level 4 you are operating like the experienced car driver who does not need to think about when to brake, signal or use the mirror. It is second nature. In the psychological jargon, you have *internalized* the learning and made it your own. You are confident. You have adapted the protocols and scripts and guidance of your tutors to your own unique style. You can and do experiment. You can and do play. You have created your own version of whatever was being taught and feel a degree of pleasure that this is so. You may have surpassed your tutors. You no longer have to think about what to do or why you do it. It's easy. Time passes quickly, you are unaware of the different parts of the skills you are using and if necessary you could teach others how to do it. You wonder, 'Why did this thing ever perplex me?'

Level 5: Thinking competence

There are dangers in reaching Level 4. One might be that of believing that you know everything anyone could ever need to know in this area. Another might be the danger of slipping into a habit of under-preparing for what previously seemed like an immense challenge.

I like the idea that Level 5 should be what we might call *Thinking Competence*. At Level 5 you are aware that your competence may be at risk of outdated-ness. You are conscious of the ever-present danger of complacency. You ask yourself,

> When that worked, why did it work? What didn't work and what might explain it? What do I need to be aware of? What may I be concealing from myself about what I don't know? Where might I experiment even further? Where is the leading edge in my field? Who is challenging my own accepted ideas?

This is where a professional supervisor may be useful, as is common in counselling and psychotherapy, coaching, nursing and medicine. Given the rapid expansion of knowledge, Level 5 seems like an essential part of keeping your skill fresh and relevant. It is why CPD (Continuing Professional Development) is a requirement in most professions where licensing is part of the deal – for instance, law and medicine. You may need to think about how to apply this to your own professional development as a tutor as well as to anything in terms of content that you deliver to your learners.

It is helpful to expose this model of learning to your group. Show them how it works and use it to explain how they are likely to feel at any one stage of their progress. Build careful strategies for tackling the related behaviours you are likely to see in any group whose learning you are managing.

Differing expectations

One associated issue may be that your learners have expectations about teaching method and that these are at odds with your own beliefs about the best way to learn. I had a vivid demonstration of this the first time I worked with doctors. This group was on a management development course. There were 24 of them in the room – a big group. My colleague and I had arranged the room 'cafe table' style – that is, small groups sitting at round tables. This was to maximize participation. Before we had even begun we had heard the grumbles. It was going to be difficult to concentrate; it was going to be impossible to take notes; they wanted to see us, not each other – and so on. And why was this? The answer was clear. Much medical education was then still conducted lecture-style where the purpose was giving information to a group which was expected to save its respectful questions until the end. Our assumptions about participation and learning from each other were stoutly resisted. What did they have to learn from each other? We were the experts weren't we? The value of our brief inputs of theory were, in our view, wildly overestimated, and the value of discussion greatly undervalued by the group.

You may see the same principles at work where there is a cultural mismatch between tutor and group. A colleague in our firm went to China to run a course. He met with polite bafflement at his attempts to run a participative programme. In the end his group indulged him, but he still feels that they did so only because obedience was owed him by virtue of his status as an expert.

You will not have to leave home to see the same phenomenon in some adult education classes. People often want something familiar. Here is one tutor describing this issue and how she coped:

> I was teaching French to children during the day using a very good audio-visual method. My adult class nobly agreed to try the same thing. I met my first snag in the first five minutes – no books. No books? They demand books, nicely of course. I say they cannot have books until they are familiar with certain sounds and patterns. Rebellion subsides. Second snag, five minutes later. Several of the class sneakily trying to write things down according to a phonetic script of their own. I explain about listening and speaking, they explain they must see things written down. We have this very polite battle lasting a few sessions. They begin to see the advantages. I begin to see that they need the reassurance of the written word. Eventually I do give out some written material and they sigh with relief as at the appearance of old friends. Pronunciation slips a bit, but general progress seems to be faster.

Now that the case for participation has been so widely and so well made, you may also see the reverse. I once ran a group where there was a somewhat doughy theoretical element to be taught and understood. I explained this at the outset. My group was disappointed. They wanted 'games'. I explained that games and the content of our course did not sit neatly together in my view. If they could come up with a relevant game then I would be perfectly willing to incorporate it into our event. That was the last I heard of games, but I was aware that my creativity and ability to design an interesting programme had been soundly challenged and that I was considered to have failed an important test.

Ageing

Even though we live in a society where the numbers of older people are increasing rapidly as a proportion of the total population, 'grey power' still has a long way to go before it is acknowledged as a real force. This is an ageist society where, for instance, many companies reject 50-year-olds as 'too old' and where it has only just, at the time of writing (2007), become against the law to state desired age ranges in a job advertisement. You may find that this prejudice has eaten into the self-esteem of your learners. However, be assured, and assure them, that research has demonstrated again and again that when learning is designed according to robust principles, age differences become less and less important. One classic experiment made the point in the 1960s. The psychologist Meredith Belbin, later to be celebrated for his work on team roles (page 94), was commissioned to retrain train drivers. He and his wife Eunice ran two experiments at the early stages of the work with matched groups of drivers. When offered active methods of learning where there was no time pressure, age made no difference at all to the drivers' performance.[4]

One large-scale study,[5] in which the same group of adults was studied over several decades, showed that scores on primary mental abilities increased slightly until the subjects were 40, then stabilized, only declining slightly after 60 and still to all intents and purposes in working order until the mid-70s. Other studies[6] have shown that it all depends what you measure. For instance, it may be true that younger learners are better at swift rote learning, but older people can make up for this in what is called *crystallized intelligence* through the more sophisticated judgement that may come with experience. More recent research has confirmed that the inevitability of decline in cognitive function with age is a myth. For instance, Professor Felicia Huppert of the University of Cambridge Interdisciplinary Research Centre on Ageing has commented[7] that risk can be reduced by deliberate efforts to remain physically, socially and mentally active. She points out that age-related loss of brain cells is far less than was once believed and also that new evidence suggests considerable potential for reorganization and plasticity. In fact, low birthweight seems to be a better predictor of cognitive decline in older adults than mere age. Professor Huppert's conclusions are that negative age stereotypes do impair performance because they encourage older adults to believe that they will fail. If you believe you will fail then you probably will. The issue for anyone teaching older adults is to make sure that you do not reinforce negative stereotypes – for instance through patronizing assumptions about 'making allowances' – but offer views which are based instead on positive assumptions. These will reflect the reality that a healthy, happy and active older age is far more the common experience than that gloomy vision of inevitable misery and degeneration.

Assuming there are no physical problems which affect brain functioning, my own experience as a tutor, and now as an older learner myself, is that age makes no difference whatever as long as people are motivated. Motivation is far, far more important than any other factor.

Motivation

Why it matters

It's so obvious really, but it must be stated. Unless you are motivated you will not and cannot learn. As a tutor you therefore must tap into and keep refreshing the motivation of your group, otherwise the whole process will collapse.

To learn, you must be motivated. To teach, you must uncover and sustain the motivation.

Some tutors feel that just being exposed to the subject is enough – people will 'learn by stealth'. Alas, this is not a sensible way to proceed. Can you, for instance, remember the telephone number of the last restaurant you phoned to book a table? Or your room number in your last holiday hotel? Most likely not. You probably learnt quadratic equations for Maths GCSE but can you explain the principle now? Think of the last foreign holiday you took in a place where no English is spoken. What words did you learn there, when you were hearing the language spoken all around you every day? Probably very few unless you were determined to try your hand at communicating in a new language and made a deliberate effort. Unless these are useful pieces of knowledge, being exposed to the information is not enough.

Lack of, or wilting motivation is one of the main reasons that learning fails:

> I ran a government training scheme. The people on the courses hated them. They saw them as a poor substitute for a job and were resentful about being obliged by threat of losing their benefits to be there. It was a real struggle.

> Basically they didn't know why they were doing the course. OK, the organization was introducing a new costing scheme but they were all cynical about whether it would actually happen because so many others had been proposed and then nothing had happened. They didn't see why they had to waste their time – they'd think about it when the new system was a certainty. It was grim. Stony faces, looking at watches and 'when's coffee?'

The upside of this downside is how wonderfully sustaining motivation can be. An adult who is determined to learn something is a fearsome force:

> My aim is to pass GCSE English because that is what my son is doing. I have been able to help him a lot and I suddenly realized I might be able to do it myself. I am absolutely determined to do it because I've always thought there was something special about English as a qualification. What has sustained me is the thought of actually getting that certificate. My tutor has been wonderful. She has praised us, nagged us and has kept dangling the thought of THE PASS at the end!

> People often ask me what keeps me going as everyone seems to know how hard it is to do Open University work on top of everything else that's going on in your life. It is very hard work but it's simple really.

> My stepmother and I did not get on very well and she made it clear that I was a financial burden, so university was out. She also implied that I was not bright enough. Although she's been dead for many years now, I know that one of my principal motivators is to prove her wrong on the second count and to feel, on the first, that this is something I deserve and owe to myself. I *will* do it!

There are some subtle differences here in how adults learn compared with the child equivalent. Being an adult and acknowledging that this is your status means that you have made the transition from others being responsible for you (however reluctantly you accept this, for instance as a teenager) to being responsible for yourself. This was the argument made so persuasively by Malcolm Knowles in his interesting book, *The Modern Practice of Adult Education.*[8] Adults are likely to have more insight than children into the actual processes of learning. They are likely to have more sense of discrimination about the methods they like and dislike and to be more able to support their arguments through evidence. Unlike children, adults are sharply aware that they want to use the learning they are acquiring and may want to do so immediately, whereas children may need to swallow their teachers' arguments about the curriculum being useful at some distant point in the future, or simply as an instrumental process that gets the student through an exam, itself a staging post to something else, also in the future.

When, as is increasingly the case, adults may have as many as eight different changes of career, they are also likely to have experienced training and retraining and to have been exposed to a wide variety of learning methods. Consumerism comes into play here as it does in every other area of life. Also, whether adults come to learning willingly or not, the truth is that, unlike children, they are free to leave. There may be unpleasant consequences of leaving – for instance a row with a boss, a failure to get promotion because of lack of a vital new skill or loss of government benefits – but they can leave the training if they wish. They are not prisoners. On the rare occasions when I have a reluctant learner in a group, I always point this out – very kindly and politely, but point it out I do. The presence of a grumbling cynic is destructive to a group; if people are so hostile to learning, and you have done your best to motivate them and they are still obdurate, it is much better for them to go.

All reasons for attendance are acceptable because any motivation is better than none. Adult learning is also time-bound in a way that is not the case for children. All adults will be able to think of attractive alternative ways of spending their time and your event has to compete with those:

> I have a towering in-tray. I'm trying not to think about it while I'm here.

What do I give up to get here? Watching *EastEnders*!

At the end of a long day there are great attractions to just sliding off to the pub with the others. It takes discipline to come here instead.

Extrinsic motivators

Adults bring a great range of motivations with them for learning. The simplest to understand are the so-called extrinsic ones – the learning that seems demanded by the learner's situation. Here are some of the most common:

- Promotion may depend on acquiring new skills or on passing an exam. For instance, in the police force, an exam system is an entry-level qualification for promotion – it does not guarantee a job.
- Entry to a new career may depend on acquiring the qualifications that go with it. So, for instance, a secretary wanting to make a career in human resource management will study for his or her CIPD (Chartered Institute of Personnel Development) qualification.
- More money may be offered to people who have a qualification.
- Change is a powerful motivator. Even people who declared themselves computer phobic now understand that a computer is more than just another kind of typewriter. IT literacy is fundamental to most jobs.

Intrinsic motivators

'Intrinsic' motivation is harder to grasp because it is not so visible. For example:

- Social motivation is a powerful propellant. Your learners may simply want the pleasure of being with other people. They may feel lonely and isolated. Learning may be their passport to essential socializing.
- Others come to learning because they see it as an important part of a new identity. They may want the yardstick of achievement: am I the kind of person who can learn Russian? Can I satisfy myself that I have the ability to get a black belt in judo? For these learners, the subject is important but so too is the proof they are obtaining that they can do something that they and the outside world think difficult.
- Some motives are straightforwardly to do with remedying some deficiency, real or imagined, which must now be faced.

> I read OK but writing was just a torment. When my son was 6 he began learning writing at school and he just couldn't understand why I wouldn't 'play writing' with him. He pestered me so much that I couldn't bear the shame of it any more. A local scheme found me a tutor and it was much easier than I'd thought. The worst bit was admitting to someone outside the family that I couldn't write.

This story and the many others like it was behind the modest success of the Adult Literacy Campaign of the 1960s and 1970s. Interestingly, the campaign found it much easier to recruit tutors than students, a difficulty which remains today. Any survey of functional literacy estimates anything between 10 per cent and 20 per cent of adults to be poor readers and writers.

> Messing up my A levels meant that I went straight into an accountancy office as a junior and then worked my way up to get accountancy qualifications. From there I got a succession of promotions, but always felt secretly a bit inferior to people who had degrees. So I set my heart on doing an MBA. To my colleagues, I presented it as something I needed to improve my CV, but actually it was all about how I felt about me! Getting that degree was fabulous and it made me realize that I had indeed been at a disadvantage before through the lack of that academic rigour in my thinking. I did get a promotion soon after, but I think it was more about increasing my self-confidence than about impressing my new employer with the letters after my name.

X and Y theories of motivation

Management thinking has much to offer teaching and learning. One astoundingly simple idea about motivation that has stood the test of time is Douglas McGregor's X–Y theory.[9] It is usually described in terms of management style, but since as a teacher you are also a manager – of a classroom – I believe it is highly relevant. People who lead, manage or teach using 'Theory X' assumptions believe that human beings cannot be trusted to work. They believe that we will avoid responsibility and effort if we can, therefore we must be controlled, directed, manipulated, force-fed and punished for disobedience. A more benign version of this style is also possible, characterized by condescension and faint praise, but where power and control are still essentially with the leader.

'Theory Y' leaders believe the opposite: that work is natural and that we work best when we take responsibility for ourselves. Creativity and play are important for problem-solving and the only way to do this is through engaging people, trusting them and giving them autonomy. Praise is more effective than criticism as a way to lead.

When you apply this to the classroom, it is possible to see that early mass education was largely a Theory X process. Iron discipline with harsh punishment for disobedience was the rule. Rote learning was the main teaching technique. Facts and not emotions were the focus, there were right and wrong answers and teaching was about talking, not about listening. Charles Dickens satirized this approach brilliantly in his novel *Hard Times* when he had the teacher, Thomas Gradgrind, a weak man who is also a bully, interrogate a class of young children on how to define a horse in order to impress a visiting government inspector. The only correct answer was a series of predetermined facts, none of which the children was likely to have known. Blame for what was going wrong got more attention than praise for what was going right. 130 years after the beginning of compulsory education, it is clear that learning professionals have largely embraced Theory Y as a better set of assumptions about motivation.

Another reason for the superiority of Theory Y is that, as years of research into organizations has proved, you get vastly better results. Everything you will read in this book about the methods that I believe will work is based on these beliefs. A piece of learning designed on Theory X assumptions is destined to fail. Adults, particularly, will fight back: through indifference or absence, through complaints and vehement protest, or just through skilful sabotage. My own last experience of this process as a learner was many years ago on a BBC management course where over a period of two weeks we were force-fed one complacent speaker after another, all of them men, who lectured us remorselessly, questions mostly not invited, on what to think and how to be. A game developed in the group where the focus of attention was on rearranging the detachable pin-board letters on our table-based name plates, but to do it in a way that the speaker would not notice. The prize, a large drink in the bar, went to the person who could rearrange the speaker's own name plate into some kind of – preferably scurrilous and clever – anagram, without him noticing. You can be assured that little or nothing of the speaker's fine thoughts was taken in and remembered.

Multiple intelligences

One further remarkable development about learning is that our understanding of what constitutes intelligence has deepened. Early theories were all really about verbal reasoning and the first tests, called Intelligence Quotients, IQ, tested this, much of it controversially, since the crude early tests were as much about culturally conditioned general knowledge as they were about cognitive reasoning. Since then, the American social psychologist Howard Gardner has offered us the attractive idea that there are actually multiple intelligences, not just EQ – Emotional Intelligence as popularized by Daniel Goleman[10] – but many more including Linguistic, Musical, Bodily-Kinaesthetic and Spatial. Knowing in which category or categories your curriculum belongs is an intriguing and useful line of inquiry. Too much of traditional education assumed that the only intelligence that mattered was verbal reasoning. For instance, the education of accountants assumed that they were essentially number-crunchers, so the only thing that mattered was their mathematical ability, whereas clearly if they are going to work directly with us, their clients, they need a high degree of emotional intelligence as well.

The pleasure of learning

Whatever analysis you make of the motivation of your learners, you will find that there are always some in any group who are simply there for the pleasure of learning:

> I have always loved learning. It gives me the kick other people might obtain from cocaine or booze. I have bought many part works and I own a set of encyclopaedias. I've joined many courses in and out of work. In my organization the head of the training department says I'm her favourite course junkie!

While it's important for you to know what the motivation is of your learners, remember that initial motivation is just that: the bundle of hopes and fears that people bring to the beginning of a piece of learning. It can be changed. In a successful group it grows and develops. In an unsuccessful group it shrivels and dies: this is a defeat for the tutor.

Maybe the truth is simpler. Learning is a natural part of being alive. As long as you are alive you can go on learning. To learn and master a skill, a piece of knowledge, to acquire a new outlook on a problem is a normal and fundamentally satisfying human process. For myself I am as proud of now being able to swim 1000 metres elegantly as I am to have passed an Open University examination. I am currently very pleased with myself for having at last mastered one particularly difficult dance and to be considered one of the more advanced students in my dance class. All these achievements have cost me time and effort. My true motivation is opaque to me, but does it really matter? I was ready for learning. I often find the process frustrating. I have been humbled by my inability to get past the blocks of my own mediocre performances, but I persisted. Now I take pleasure in knowing that all that effort was worthwhile. Surely this is what it is all about. Learning is part of a circuit that is one of life's most fundamental pleasures. Your role as a tutor is to keep the current flowing.

The essence of learning

> It has in fact been established that if we were to reverse the natural order of things and keep children away from school while sending their parents there instead, we could teach the parents the same thing for about a quarter of the expenditure in time and money.
>
> (John McLeish)

> I hear and I forget
> I see and I remember
> I do and I understand.
>
> (Chinese proverb)

Let's assume that your students are highly motivated. You understand that they might be feeling anxious and you have techniques ready to allay their fears. But this still leaves other questions. How do you guide learners through the substance of your subject? What are the best ways to engage their interest? Is it actually harder for adults to learn quickly than for children? Are there any special methods that should be encouraged or avoided with adults?

There are some simple rules of thumb based on research, experience and common sense which can help give answers to all these issues. First, remember again that it is important to distinguish between teaching and learning. You can be teaching away vigorously but your students are not necessarily learning:

> I have never in my life had such terrible teaching as on the course I did on industrial law. I swear the lecturer would never have noticed if the whole class had played noughts and crosses because once he'd started it would have taken an earthquake to stop him. His method was to introduce the topic, say 'Any questions?' and then before anyone could answer, plod on in a deadpan way non-stop for an hour and a half. The content was so dense that it was impossible to remember. He gave out some notes but these weren't much help because they seemed to cover different ground.

Here was a tutor who had prepared conscientiously, who probably left his classroom drained by the effort of talking for an hour and a half, but whose students had learnt nothing.

The learning cycle

This idea was first mooted by the US academic, David Kolb.[11]

Essentially, the concept is that for learning to be successful, you need to go through a cycle of learning:

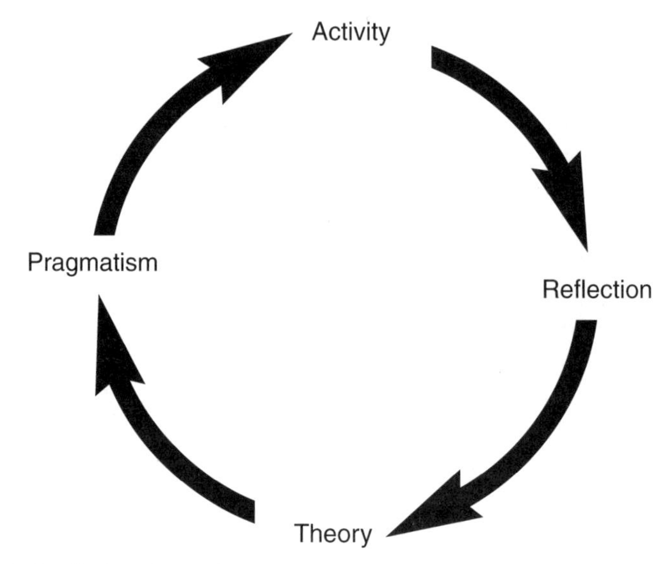

Figure 1.2 The learning cycle

- activity – doing something;
- reflection – thinking about the experience;
- theory – seeing where it fits in with theoretical ideas;
- pragmatism – applying the learning to actual problems.

David Kolb went on to develop his own descriptions of four learning styles, but I prefer the simplicity of the model developed by his British interpreters, Alan Mumford and Peter Honey.[12] What follows is based on their work.

Let's suppose that you want to learn how to design a garden. In the *activity* phase, you might, with a tutor's help, have a go at actually designing a small garden with a particular aspect and set of problems – let's say it is a small town garden with dry sandy soil, facing east and shaded by large sycamores from a neighbour's garden. This would involve you in making a number of decisions about materials, costs and planting. Having done that, it would be useful to *reflect* on it, standing back, getting feedback perhaps and observing how other learners have solved the same problems. You might then consider the *theory:* what rules of thumb there are for using particular materials or for dry, east-facing, shady gardens? At the *pragmatic* phase you might return to the original plan, revising your ideas in the light of everything else you now know and working out how to apply what you have learnt to your own particular situation. The cycle begins again when you return to activity – adding new features to your design.

The importance of the learning cycle is more than theoretical. We all have natural preferences for different styles. These may be slight or

Table 1.2 Likes and dislikes of different learners

Style	*Like*	*Dislike*
Activists	Doing and experiencing. Enjoy games, practical activities, anything that's new, energetic and involving, will take risks and volunteer to take the lead even when they don't understand the implications of doing so. Natural optimists.	Sitting around for too long; working alone; theorizing; having to listen to others droning on; having to wait a long time to see results.
Reflectors	Time to think, observe, take it all in first; love to watch others; need some solitude and above all, time. Like to ponder before speaking. Need to read and consider before giving a judgement.	Being hurtled from one activity to another, having no time to think; crammed timetables; lack of privacy, no time to prepare.
Theorists	To know where something fits in to overall ideas and concepts; analysis and logic; being stretched; abstract concepts; structure and clarity. Enjoy systems and seeing the connections of one idea to another; ask how an assertion is supported by research then ask questions about the quality of the research.	Frivolity, mindless fun; wasting time; not being able to question and be sceptical; lack of a timetable and proper structure.
Pragmatists	Practical problem solving; experimentation; chance to vary and modify other people's ideas; immediacy; relevance to 'the real world'; enjoy bending rules and seeing what happens; learning that answers the question 'How can I apply this?'	Anything airy-fairy and theoretical; learning that makes too many references to the past or the future and avoids drawing attention to NOW.

pronounced. Some people may be equally at home with all four styles, but mostly adults will have developed greater comfort with one over the other three. This will affect you as a tutor because your natural tendency will be to emphasize the styles *you* are comfortable with. It will also affect your group because they will have their own preferences and areas of comfort. So, for instance, if you as a tutor enjoy the activist style, you will want to run events which have a high degree of *doing*. You will build in a lot of variety – perhaps getting people working in small groups for much of the time with a lot of discussion. There will inevitably be people in your group whose preferences are for the reflective style. They may well find the relentless pace imposed by an activist tutor to be overwhelming because it gives them no time for their favourite style which is to think, stand back and reflect.

There can be strong likes and dislikes associated with each of the styles. Table 1.2 gives some brief descriptions.

Implications of the learning styles

The first challenge is to know yourself. Which of these styles are you naturally drawn to? Whatever your answer, remember that many of your learners will have different preferences. When designing learning (see Chapter 11), remember to touch on all four styles as far as possible, not just your own favourite.

Remember, too, that different subjects and circumstances will have their own imperative. For instance, if you are teaching people how to drive a car, there is probably no great place for theory – to drive a car successfully does not depend on knowing how the internal combustion engine works, though to pass the driving test you do need to know the Highway Code, a reflective activity. But mostly, learning to drive needs an activist approach. It cannot be learnt through reading books. If your subject is management development, you may be drawn by the attraction of the many US gurus and their books – a theoretical approach. However, your learners may only want the pragmatic answers: 'What can I apply from this to my own work and job?' 'What really works?'

Personality and learning

In the early 1990s a colleague introduced me to the Myers Briggs Type Indicator™, (MBTI) a personality questionnaire based on the work of the Swiss psychoanalyst Carl Jung. I became licensed to administer it and, later, so fascinated that I wrote two books on it.[13] There are thousands of other personality questionnaires and approaches to human personality and some of them have much merit. However, my personal favourite is the MBTI for its all-round versatility and also for the seventy years of research that has made it the classic it is today. To understand the full implications, you will need to take the questionnaire, either the standard MBTI itself[14] or one of many rivals also based on Jungian thinking, some of which are freely available on the internet. You will then need a debrief with a skilled and experienced practitioner and a permanent reference in the form of a set of Type descriptions. However, the essential ideas are relevant to teaching and learning as I briefly introduce them here.

The framework proposes that human personality can be explained along four bi-polar dimensions, known as *Preferences*. The theory is that although everyone can call on each of the eight preferences, we are all likely to have a preference for one side of each dimension. This is the dimension in which we are likely to have developed skill. All preferences are assumed to be of equal value:

Table 1.3

Getting energy		
Extraversion (E) Being with people, activity, breadth. *As learners: like variety, discussion and talking, being active.*	Or	Introversion (I) Reflection, needing privacy to think things through. *As learners: like to watch, listen, think and read.*
Taking in information: how we perceive the world		
Sensing (S) Trusting your five senses, liking things to be tangible, concrete, real, being comfortable with detail. *As learners: like rules, guidance and being told how; may enjoy rote learning; comfortable with detail and data; like to follow a protocol step by step; like practicalities and the here and now.*	Or	iNution (N) Liking ideas, theories and the intangible, seeing the big picture, don't want to be like others; jump in anywhere rather than step by step. *As learners: like to be autonomous, creative and individualistic. Like frameworks and theories. Attracted to the bigger picture, impatient with detail. Like the intangible, to consider what might be possible and what's in the future.*
Deciding		
Thinking (T) Deciding on the basis of logic and rationality; seeking truth, being tough if necessary. *As learners: like to critique and debate; sceptical; tough on self and others; competitive; spot the flaws before appreciating.*	Or	Feeling (F) Deciding on the basis of human values and relationships first, valuing harmony and collaboration. *As learners: like the human story, interested in relationships and emotions; enjoy working in groups in a non-competitive way; appreciative rather than critical.*
Living your life		
Judging (J) Liking to be decisive and in control; liking planning, predictability and order. *As learners: need to see a full plan; need definite goals and stages; responsive to deadlines.*	Or	Perceiving (P) Liking to stay adaptable, work at the last minute; need to have options. *As learners: like to follow their instincts; enjoy flexibility; don't like being too tied down to a rigid curriculum; last-minute workers.*

When you perm any of these preferences you come up with a four-letter Type profile – for instance ENTP, or ISFJ. There are sixteen possible profiles each with their own strengths, weaknesses and differing motivations. (See Figure 1.3)

One of the main lessons I have learnt from my own work on the Myers Briggs, and from having used it now with many hundreds of individuals, is that Type prejudice is deep rooted in all of us. As naïve subjects, we all tend to believe that our own way of experiencing the world is exactly how others experience it, and once we discover that this may not be so, we will tend to believe that our own way is also somehow superior to any other way. Research into Myers Briggs preferences and learning shows how much it influences both the way we learn and also how learning is presented to us by others. For instance, much traditional education was a Sensing–Judging process: a great deal of practical detail presented step by step in a planned and orderly way: *Follow this protocol and you will get to the right answer*. This would not have suited learners whose preferences were for Intuition and Perceiving. In higher education, which largely favours Intuition over Sensing, students with preferences for Sensing tend to take longer to get to the same point, and may not do so well as a result.

Personality preferences also influence motivation, so learners who share N and T (Intuition and Thinking) are likely to be driven by the need for competence. Those who share N and F (Intuition and Feeling) may be motivated by the wish to bring about social good; those who share S and F (Sensing and Feeling) by the need to bring about practical benefit for people, whereas people who share S and T (Sensing and Thinking) are likely to have efficiency and order as a motivator.

As with learning style preferences, this cuts both ways. Your own preferences will influence the way you learn and therefore most probably the way you design and present learning to others, but you will be presenting it to people who could be any mixture of the sixteen Types. These psychological preferences make a strong case for variety in method and approach as a given rather than just as an afterthought or happy accident.

Varying the pace

Imposing one pace on a group is not an effective way for them to learn. Perhaps you vividly remember, as I do, the intense boredom of schooldays where the main method of learning was hour after hour of being talked *at* by the teachers. At my school, as the 'top 5 per cent' we were initially 'creamed off' from our age group, and were then ruthlessly streamed again. Even so, there were wide differences of ability according to subject and aptitude. At gymnastics I was slow and cautious. I struggled in the middle bands in science subjects. In arts subjects I was often bored by waiting for others to catch up. If

ISTJ Thoughtful, courteous, responsible and perfectionist; needs to be in charge and wants efficiency. May feel is never off duty. Pays meticulous attention to systems and processes. Likes the clarity of sensible rules. Can be stubborn. May over-rely on detail and tend to dismiss the importance of people's feelings.	ISFJ Cordial, charming, patient; modest style fuelled by wish to help others through strong sense of loyalty to duty and liking for tradition. Observant of how others feel. Detail-conscious, steady and serious; delivers on promises. May need to guard against being exploited and feeling resentful.	INFJ Sensitive, patient, insightful and hardworking; willing to put effort into understanding the complexity of human relationships. Wants to contribute decisively to ideas that will affect people in important ways in the longer term. Can be dreamy and enigmatic and may find it difficult to put self first.	INTJ Inner energy, fierce independence and a preference for big-picture thinking go with calm and unflappable public face which disguises ardour for competence - for self and others. Impatient for improvement. Likes to organise. May have air of critical detachment which creates sense of being impossible to please.
ISTP Socially reserved; cool observer; needs variety; can come into own when the need is for quick thinking, practicality and coping calmly with a crisis. Needs to feel can meet the unexpected with ingenuity. Detachment, need for privacy and reluctance to communicate may create problems with others.	ISFP Kind, modest, attentive to others, with little need to impress or control. Loathes conflict. Needs to give service, but on own terms. Deeply loyal with quiet sense of fun; likes to offer practical support without judging. May make an art out of economy of effort and may annoy through holding back from communicating or explaining.	INFP Gentle, loyal and apparently pliant style may hide intensely idealistic and driven interior. Wants to live in harmony with values and expand potential of self and others. Has little interest in worldly possessions or controlling others. Endless quest for the perfect may lead to perpetual dithering or unnecessary guilt.	INTP Analytical, sceptical, cool seeker after truth. Tends to love the complex, theoretical and novel; resists authority and dislikes being in authority; constantly challenges the status quo through experiment; always ready to re-think. May need to learn that passion for the exact truth as sees it could alienate others.
ESTP Straightforward, cheerful, inventive, practical; has zest for life and loves a challenge as long as it results in immediate tangible action. Sees self as an adaptable realist who gets round the rules. Has accepting attitude to others. Enjoys trouble-shooting. May need to take care that expediency does not dominate.	ESFP Open, modest, generous and tactful; commitment to active fun, practicality and to valuing people creates disarming realism about self and others. Sociable, gracious, flexible and enjoys the limelight. Relishes the good things of life without apology. May need to take care that is not seen as frivolous or unfocused.	ENFP Enthusiastic, versatile innovator. Likes to improvise and help people solve problems through creativity and insights into how people tick. Must give and receive personal authenticity. Builds bridges and 'walks the talk.' May need to guard against 'butterfly' approach which exhausts self and others.	ENTP Energetic, brash, original; wants to be where the action is. Needs to be right and to be first. Loathes routine and detail. Likes to challenge conventional wisdom and values independence. May need to beware of unintentionally hurting others through love of argument and of having the last word.
ESTJ Crisp, decisive, courageous; wants to get things organised *now*. Needs to maintain stability and order through care with detail; has robust often hearty style with people. Down-to-earth, practical approach. May need to take care that in concern to get things done, does not overlook the need for tact and sensitivity.	ESFJ Friendly, brisk, talkative, loyal and practical; brings common-sense and warmth to dealings with people. Needs approval from others. Likes busyness, organising and socialising. Values working systematically and co-operatively. Sensitive to indifference. May need to give and take criticism in a more detached way.	ENFJ Tactful, diplomatic; natural facility with words and commitment to good causes that will make a difference to the world can inspire others. Loves encouraging others; believes passionately in equality. Sensitive to disharmony. May need to watch tendency to 'rescue' others or to allow idealism to become rigid.	ENTJ Energetic, clear-sighted, decisive, analytical; needs to turn ideas into action; loathes illogicality; needs to feel authoritative. Confident and articulate. Insists on looking at the big picture and enjoys robust discussions on improving standards and implementing change. Direct style can seem abrasive and may intimidate.

Figure 1.3 The sixteen personality types: in outline

the pace is fixed to suit the fastest it will demotivate the majority. If it is right for the middle band it will alienate both the brighter and the slower learners.

The more you can design learning so that people can work at their own pace, the more effective it is likely to be. This is not because competition is ideologically unsound, but because it doesn't work. With adults this is especially important. The older you are, the more likely you are to want to sacrifice speed for accuracy and the more likely you are to want information before making a response.

Scores of different experiments have shown that if adults are asked to learn something new under time pressure, the older they are the more likely they are to become confused and to make mistakes. Where no clock-watching is involved there is no difference in performance.

When no allowance is made for the increase in individual differences which age and experience bring, when decline in short-term memory is ignored and when tutors simply plunge on bearing the whole load of information-giving themselves, packing every moment with fresh and complex detail, then some situations of monstrous futility can develop:

> I came to nursing as a mature entrant and I nearly left it for the same reason. I could not bear the monotony of sitting for hour after hour where you were treated like children and where the facts came at you in a steady stream. No attempt was made to involve us in the learning: the only thing that mattered was passing the exams. It was like a convent school full of silly adults!

It is always better for adults to measure their progress against their own previous performance rather than to attempt frantic rivalry with their neighbours. People start with different kinds of knowledge and work at different speeds.

Relevance

While of course it is true that there are people who are drawn to learning for learning's sake, most adult learners are strongly motivated by wishing to acquire skills and knowledge they can use in practical ways. The nearer you can make the learning to the 'real' world, the more acceptable it will be and therefore the more quickly and effectively your students will learn. The obverse is true too. Offer adults learning that they consider irrelevant and they may well resist:

> To help me get through my accountancy exams, my firm paid for me to go to classes at a finance training specialist. I regarded it as a necessary evil. The content of the exams was so far removed from the

> way we actually did the job that the poor tutors had to follow the same silly 'rules'. They were constantly apologizing for it, saying that they knew we didn't need to know this or that thing, but it was on the syllabus and could appear in the exam papers. It had virtually no relevance to my job and I resented every minute I spent there.

Your skill as a tutor is to make the training resemble the real task, even if some of the distractions and complications of reality have to be stripped away:

> I wasn't sure how far you could 'learn' negotiating, but I went to the course anyway. It was excellent because all the exercises were based on exactly the sort of situations we meet every day. We started with simple two-handers and then went on to more elaborate scenarios using the same principles and finished with team exercises. Some people felt it was artificial because you didn't have all the information that you would have for real, but I felt that was actually a help. It allowed me to see the basic principles pretty clearly.

The importance of relevance holds good for any situation where adults are learning, even when the students are people whose intellectual capacities are well below the average. One tutor of adults with learning difficulties reported their indignation at having to practise handling money by using cardboard coins. She was forgiven this blunder only when the rightly despised cardboard was replaced by the real thing.

In the past, much vocational training ignored this need for realism and relevance. This led to the establishment in the UK of the Qualifications and Curriculum Authority, a body which sponsors National Vocational Qualifications (NVQs). These endorse the idea that it is only the skills needed for the job that should count as a qualification. NVQs have had mixed success. They have probably been more successful at entry level than for senior-level qualifications. However, the principle is sound, as is the movement to accredit prior learning. If you can demonstrate that you have competence, then you should get the qualification. And competence means you can produce the same excellent performance under the eagle eye of a trained observer every time.

Reinforcement and practice

Without reinforcement, skill and knowledge will fade quickly. The basic principles are easy enough:

1 Analyse the objectives of the learning (Chapter 11).
2 Find out what existing knowledge your learners have.

3. Break the objectives down into their component parts and set down success criteria for each.
4. Start with the pieces of learning that fulfil these criteria: they are basic building blocks; they are easy to learn.
5. Reinforce them through practice until people have thoroughly 'internalized' them – that is, they can do them accurately without conscious thought.
6. Slowly add more building blocks, making the learning more complex.
7. Reinforce through more practice.

Sounds easy doesn't it? In reality you will need immense subtlety to apply these principles. What is *enough* where reinforcement is concerned? How do you know whether you are going too fast or too slowly? What happens when you have a group which contains very mixed abilities? Is it possible to break down a skill so far that it loses its resemblance to the real thing?

The dance classes I attend as a learner are an excellent example. Such is my love of dancing that I go to classes wherever and whenever I can, and since I travel a lot I have sampled classes in many different places. I have probably been taught now by perhaps 50 different teachers over a ten-year period. All are teaching the same dances (they come and go in popularity just as pop music does) to similar groups of people. I see huge variations in effectiveness. Some teachers can barely be bothered to teach the steps, hurrying through the demonstration of a new dance, pleasing the minority in the group who are talented natural dancers but dismaying almost everyone else. You can spot these teachers by the large numbers of people who sit out a dance that is in any way complicated. At the other extreme are the patient plodders who break down every dance into tiny, slow sequences, going through it many times without music, reteaching every dance every week on the assumption that no one in the group will have remembered the steps. These teachers also lose people because the pace is too slow for many of their students. One such teacher in particular broke each sequence into such tiny, slow fragments that it lost its resemblance to the dance and became unrecognizable. The effect of this intended helpfulness was, paradoxically, to make the dance much harder to learn.

Only you and your group can judge what the answers are to such dilemmas. One of my own rules is never to compromise the integrity of the subject by oversimplifying. So, for instance, if I am teaching influencing skills, I do split the various techniques into identifiable parts which can be practised separately, but I emphasize that real situations involve using any or all of the techniques together and look for an activity towards the end of the event which will give people the opportunity to incorporate everything they have learnt.

If in doubt, ask the group. Look for feedback from how people are responding. In a dance class it is easy to see, even if the teachers sometimes don't spot it. People just don't do the dance well if they haven't had sufficient reinforcement and practice before trying the dance with the music. They will need to do it again if they are going to remember it properly. There will be similar tell-tale signs that you will spot with experience in your own groups.

If you have dropouts from a continuing course, follow up the non-attenders and ask what their reasons are for not coming (don't assume that this is anything to do with the course; it may not be). Ask for feedback specifically on how much practice and reinforcement people need. If you are overdoing it, step up the pace. If you are underdoing it, add more.

Catch them doing something right

It is important to design this phase of learning carefully for one simple reason. As adults, once we have made a mistake, it is much harder to unlearn it than it is for a child. It is as if once that trace has been made in the adult brain, it is difficult to replace. This is particularly the case with any 'kinaesthetic' skill – dance is again a good example. If I have literally put a foot wrong in learning a new dance, I find, infuriatingly, that my foot is making the same mistake over and over again, in spite of my brain telling it what to do.

As a tutor, your challenge is to design activities that give your adult students a high chance of getting it right first time. Wrong first time will more often than not mean wrong for some considerable time afterwards. This leads to discouraged, demotivated learners. Where you see a mistake, correct it straight away. The sooner you do this, the easier it will be for the learner to do better.

Using adult experience

The best-designed adult learning aims to minimize the disadvantages and maximize the advantages of the experience adults bring with them to learning. It can still be the case that trainers and tutors of adults bemoan the fact that their students are not the nice blank sheets presented by children. One of my clients, for instance, tried to instruct me to recruit only people under 30 as trainees for his new team on the grounds that people under 30 would not have had time to learn bad habits.

As adults we have had experience of the world and probably also some experience of the subject we have decided to learn. For this reason we will usually have a great deal to contribute, even if we are also much more likely to be sceptical and to challenge the 'rules':

> My most enjoyable groups have always been with women students who want to take up teaching after rearing their families. They simply will not accept pat theories and glib statements about child development because all the time they are asking, 'Did my children do that?', or, 'Was that true when my children were four?' Whereas a 20-year-old will write it straight down in her notebook, the mature woman always pauses to weigh and consider against her own and other people's experience. She always sees the ifs and buts. In these groups, by relating the students' experience to the general view, I feel we finally create a tremendously lively and complex picture of child psychology. They bring a depth and humour to rather dry theories which younger people could never attain.

That university teacher found her experience of teaching mature students rewarding precisely because she relished their wish to challenge. The same phenomenon can be unsettling if you are unused to it:

> I was working on a regeneration project which involved working with groups of people who had been unemployed for a long time. My role was to help them acquire job-search skills. I found out the hard way that you couldn't just give them rules. They constantly challenged me on the grounds that I didn't know what it was like, I'd never been unemployed and in their experience interviewers didn't behave the way I was suggesting. I knew that they needed my help but I wasn't getting anywhere. The penny dropped when I sat in with a colleague and saw how she handled it. I saw how she didn't make statements or lay down the law. She opened up the topic, asked for opinions and experiences and drew the advice out of that. It's much harder to do this than I'd thought and it took me several months to learn to do it as well as she did.

It is essential to solicit and use the experience of your learners. Failing to do so risks rejection of your message. More positively, by inviting comment you eventually arrive at a much richer and denser picture of the world and one that is therefore more relevant to real life. The more learners are involved and offer their own experience, the more they are likely to learn at speed.

This involvement is also important for another reason. Suppose you encounter the downside of adult experience: the stubbornly entrenched view, the commitment to one particular technique even if it is incorrect, the hidden gap in knowledge. Meredith Belbin again contributes some salutary lessons from his early work. When asking a group of trainees how many sixteenths they thought were in an inch, several said 'ten' and others thought there might be twelve. How are you to counter such mistaken assumptions if you don't know what they are? How are such students ever to learn if they are never obliged to hold their experience to the light so that they can see the holes in it for themselves?

Arousal

As adult learners we are more experienced and world-weary and we often need a good jolt to the system before we can start learning. This can be particularly true of groups meeting in the evenings, but applies more generally too. Most of us will be preoccupied, often still half thinking about other responsibilities, and in the evenings simply tired. For this reason an intensely involving first few minutes is always a good idea at the beginning of each major session whether first thing in the morning, immediately after lunch or in the early evening.

You will devise your own activities as appropriate to your subject, (see also ice-breakers, page 50) but here are some ideas from other tutors:

> Five minutes of warm up exercises – gets people stretching and changes the mood as well as being fun.
>
> I play a silly game called 'Bat and Moth' which involves people standing in a group and chasing each other. It has no purpose other than to get people moving!
>
> I start my maths classes with five minutes of mental arithmetic – fast and fun.
>
> I ask people to describe what percentage of their attention I have. Answers vary from 20 per cent to 95 per cent. I then ask what needs to happen to get to at least 95 per cent. It's fun and I get a lot of useful information too!

Such techniques are successful because they have certain elements in common:

- everyone in the group takes part;
- to do them at all you must be involved;
- they are fun.

The importance of short-term memory

This is one of the ways in which children and adults differ. As we grow older, our short-term memory capacity becomes less efficient and more easily disturbed. What seems to happen is that our brains receive information and scan it for meaning in order to decode it at some time in the future. If this scanning stage is interrupted, the information never passes from short-term to long-term memory.

In everyday living we experience this as a minor nuisance: for example, forgetting a twelve-digit telephone number as soon as we have looked it up. Where learning is concerned, any method that relies too heavily on short-term memory is doomed to failure. This means that lecturing and demonstrating on their own are poor methods to use with adults. The reason is that the words of the lecturer or demonstrator are perceived by our brains as a never-ending series of information slabs and each successive slab interferes with the storage of its predecessor. The result is the phenomenon we all know; the feeling that we have been fed a mass of information, all of it undigested.

This has important implications for all teachers of adults. It means that if you rely on any verbally conveyed method of giving information, you are unlikely to be helping your learners learn. You may enjoy it, your group may even enjoy it if you are a good performer, but they will probably not be learning. The core art of teaching adults is to find alternative ways of conveying ideas and information.

Learning as a constructive rather than a receptive process

Earlier assumptions about learning were that the human brain was essentially like a vast storage bin. You opened the lid and poured in facts. Education was about memorizing facts. Examinations were the process that tested how many facts you could recall when you had no books or other reference points to help you. Thus preparation for examinations took up huge amounts of time where canny establishments trained learners in information-retrieval under time pressure. Modern cognitive psychology has suggested that our brains work differently. Rather than proceeding as a linear process where facts are neatly stored, the human brain seems to work instead on the principle of neural networks of association. We mentally arrange and store knowledge in clusters of related ideas known as *semantic networks*. When we learn something new, we latch the new idea on to its nearest relative in an existing network. Learning is thus about incorporating or modifying existing ideas with new ones. It is essentially about recognizing patterns – in other words it is about problem-solving.

So if learning is about making connections and seeing patterns it becomes pointless to devise teaching methods which are about transmitting facts. This distinction is sometimes described as the difference between *surface learning* and *deep learning*. Surface learning is about remembering lists of data and collections of facts. It is about memorizing and regurgitating uncritically. Deep learning is about connections, patterns and logic. It will be about asking,

> Why did this happen? How could it happen again? What do I need to know in order to make sense of it? Where does it fit with what I already know? How should I be challenging this idea?

It is clear that adults can learn to learn. Experience of learning improves performance. People who have kept mentally in trim by maintaining a consistent diet of learning tend to do better than otherwise identical learners who have not. The reasons seem partly to do with practice and partly to do with confidence. Then, too, one of the benefits of working with adults is that they are alert to how they have learnt well and less well in the past. Delving into this and, of course, into the blocks, false assumptions and barriers it might be creating is all part of your job as a tutor.

You can speed this process where appropriate with some simple, well-designed activities intended to help people improve their learning techniques, for instance explaining the importance of learning styles and asking people to identify their own preferences, explaining the Ladder of Competence or introducing them to the MBTI. Using these tools increases the chances of learners being able to stand back from their learning and ask themselves what is going well, what is going less well, and what strategies they might use to build on strengths and overcome blocks. All of this will reduce the chances that they will project any frustration on to you, because understanding yourself and your own learning style is part of accepting that you are responsible for your own learning, not your tutor. Depending on the course and the subject, you can also achieve sensational improvements by showing people how to do note-taking, memorizing, rapid reading, creative idea-generation, essay writing, answering multiple-choice questions, and so on. If you are running a group where there is formal learning of any kind, it is often useful to build such help in the early weeks of the course. The work of the cognitive psychologists has also shown us that self-assessment is not just a feeble nice-to-have but an essential part of improving performance. Some of the most interesting work[15] about the process of learning has shown that outstanding learners have exceptional levels of ability in what is called *meta-cognition*. This means that they have self-monitoring and self-assessment skills of a high order where their own learning is concerned. Again, these learners concentrate as much on problem-solving skills as they do on acquiring factual information. They start by sharpening their understanding of their goals, look critically at where and how to research the data, constantly assess their own progress with a critical eye and have realistic ways of evaluating their ultimate achievements. These learners are alert to the possibility of not understanding a piece of material and will readily seek out alternative strategies – for instance asking for advice from a well-chosen skilled helper. They have a high level of awareness of their own problem-solving strategies. The good news for teachers of adults is that this ability seems to be something that adults are far more likely to posses than children. Also, it can be learnt as a set of skills in its own right. My own aim is to build such processes seamlessly into any of the training I deliver. For instance, I will commonly start each day of a four- or five-day course by getting learners into pairs to assess not only *what* they learnt the previous day, but *how* they learnt, what they struggled with and what their learning goal is for the day to come.

The discoveries of the cognitive psychologists are important. They tell us that the best designed learning will have problem-solving at its core because a learning task that is about solving a problem mirrors the process of learning itself. Instead of asking, 'What facts do my learners need to have?' the skilled teacher of adults asks, 'What problems do my learners need to solve?' In this way learning becomes as much about acquiring problem-solving skills as about acquiring knowledge.

Putting the learners at the centre

The most effective learning happens when we can fulfil these criteria:

- we really want and need the knowledge;
- we know how we will apply it;
- we will be rewarded one way or another for having it;
- we can draw on our own experience;
- we can learn at our own pace and style;
- we are encouraged to learn about where to find and then how to judge information;
- we are stretched and challenged;
- we are supported;
- we are treated as individuals with unique needs by whoever is helping us to learn.

Apply this list to any serious learning you have done in your life. For instance, if you are a parent, this is probably the most challenging role any human being can ever take on. How did you learn the role? Think about professional learning: where and how did you acquire your most useful skills? The answers are likely to be that in both these cases you learnt them on the job. The challenge for a tutor or developer is to accelerate this natural process a hundredfold by using the basic principles of learning described above. When you do, it is surprising how freeing it can be. For instance, both *action learning* and *problem-based learning* (Chapters 6 and 7) have taken these principles to their logical conclusions.

In *self-managed learning,* the same principles are at work. For instance, there are now several postgraduate degrees along the style pioneered by Ian Cunningham at Roffey Park in Sussex. These are run on the principle that there is no set curriculum. The courses whip away the security of being 'just' a student with all the dependency (and counter-dependency) this can produce. As a learner, you and only you are responsible for your learning. The framework can be startlingly simple:

- What do I know I know?
- What do I know I don't know?
- What don't I know that I don't know?

The course begins with the task of producing a learning contract. Each learner's contract will be different, but it will answer questions such as:

- What's my experience in this field?
- Where am I now?
- What do excellent people in this field do?
- If I want to be excellent in this field, what do I need to know?
- What literature is there in this field that I need to read?
- How will I get to my goals?
- How will I know I've got there?
- What evidence will I produce for the rest of the group and its tutors to prove that I have?

This first phase ends when every learner's contract has been assessed by every other learner – note, not just by the tutors. If it is too easy or too hard, it must be adjusted.

The second phase of the work will typically be about carrying out a project which will meet the criteria each learner has agreed. The final phase is assessment. Again, this will be done by the whole group, not just by the tutors.

This approach to adult learning is too radical for some. Its critics worry about 'soft options'; they yearn for the safety of the curriculum and teacher-in-charge power of the traditional learner–teacher relationship. However, these approaches put learners firmly at the centre, managing their own learning. This surely has to be the aim of anyone who is serious about real adult learning, whether as student or tutor.

Further reading

It can be difficult to get your head around the concept of learning. One of the reasons is that learning is invisible. We will never be able to capture exactly what it is, let alone answer all the core questions about it, such as, 'How does it happen?' 'What role does memory play?' 'When we transfer learning from one situation to another, how does this transfer happen?' In trying to answer these questions, many rival and complementary schools of thought have emerged – for instance Behaviourist, Constructivist, Humanist. Then there are the (mostly unsubstantiated) claims of the Neuro-Linguistic Programming (NLP) gurus among many others, as well as the contributions made by advances in understanding the physiology of the human brain. I have spared you the ins and outs of these theories, but it is a fascinating field. If it interests you, there is a useful summary of many of them in Alan Rogers's thorough book, cited below.

Boud, D. and Miller, N. (eds) (1997) *Working with Experience: Animating Learning*. London: Routledge.

Bruning, R.H. *et al.* (1999) *Cognitive Psychology and Instruction*. Upper Saddle River, NJ: Prentice-Hall.

Gardner, H. (1993) *Frames of Mind: The Theory of Multiple Intelligences*. New York: Basic Books.

Knowles, M.S. (1990) *The Adult Learner: A Neglected Species*. Houston, TX: Gulf.

Knowles, M.S. (1990) 'Fostering competence in self-directed learning', in R.M. Smith (ed.) *Learning to Learn Across the Lifespan*. Oxford: Jossey-Bass.

Merriam, S.B. (2001) *The New Update on Adult Learning Theory*. San Francisco, CA: Jossey-Bass.

Myers, I. (1995) *Gifts Differing*. Palo Alto, CA: Consulting Psychologists Press.

Rogers, A. (2002) *Teaching Adults*, 3rd edn. Maidenhead: Open University Press/ McGraw Hill Education.

Notes

1 Postman, N. and Weingartner, C. (1969) *Teaching as a Subversive Activity*. Harmondsworth: Penguin.

2 For more information on John Fisher and the Personal Construct Theory from which these ideas are taken, go to the Businessballs website: www.businessballs.co.uk

3 www.gordontraining.com

4 Belbin, E. and Belbin, M. (1972) *Problems in Adult Retraining*. London: Heinemann.

5 Schaie, K.W. (1994) The course of adult intellectual development, *American Psychologist*, 49: 304–13.

6 For instance, Merriam, S.B. (2001) *The New Update on Adult Learning Theory*. San Francisco, CA: Jossey-Bass.

7 *Positive Ageing*, Meyler-Campbell Annual Lecture 2005, unpublished.

8 Knowles, M.S. (1980) *The Modern Practice of Adult Education*. Chicago, IL: Follet Publishing Company.

9 Heil, G., Bennis, W. and Stephens, D.C. (2000) *Douglas McGregor Revisited: Managing the Human Side of the Enterprise*. New York: John Wiley and Sons.

10 Goleman, D., Boyatzis, R. and McKee, A. (2002) *The New Leaders*. London: Little, Brown.

11 Kolb, D.A. (1984) *Experiential Learning*. Englewood Cliffs, NJ: Prentice-Hall.

12 Honey, P. and Mumford, A. (1992) *Manual of Learning Styles*. Maidenhead: P. Honey Publications. Questionnaires are available on the internet which will identify your own learning styles preferences. For instance, www.campaign-for-learning.org.uk.

13 *The Sixteen Personality Types at Work in Organisations; Influencing with the Sixteen Types* (1997) jointly published by Management Futures Ltd and ASK Europe.

14 Available in the UK from Oxford Psychologists Press.

15 For instance, Glaser, R. (1991) The maturing of the relationship between the science of learning and cognition and educational practice, *Learning and Instruction*, 1: 129–44.

2 The first session

The first session is important. This is true whether it is the first session of a single day's event, the first meeting of an adult education class or the opening morning of a year-long course. It is in this session that vital first impressions are formed and motivation built or crushed:

> The organization ran a series of workshops for about 80 people at a time to explain the changes that were being introduced. The first session always consisted of a senior manager giving a welcome talk. The word went round about how hostile the audiences were and it was hard to persuade anyone to do the talk. I was organizing the conference centre where it all happened and I was acutely aware of what a difference this opening piece made. I saw dozens and dozens of them. The manager who could be relaxed, be straightforward and honest about what was going on, keep it short, make a few jokes – not too many, mind – always meant a much better day. Where we had the reverse, the day was finished before it had even started.

> The first night of the pottery class we didn't do anything at all, we just sat there while he gave us the whole history of clay. This wasn't what I'd wanted at all. He just talked and talked and talked.

> The whole event got off to a crackingly good start. There was no messing about. No going round the room saying who you were and what your reason for being there was. The trainers introduced themselves and then we were off within minutes. I had been dubious about whether to choose these providers but just from the plunge into the novel-feeling and subtle but demanding ice-breaker, I knew then that when they said they were *different* they really were.

The participants may be feeling nervous, but it is you who are on trial, not they. Even after many years of running courses and learning events of all kinds, I still feel a quiver of apprehension before meeting any new group. What will they be like? Will they like me? Will it go well? Are my assumptions about what they want and need accurate? Am I up to it? Have I got enough material? This apprehension is probably a healthy sign. I have heard actors say the same thing – that some stage fright means you give a better performance than when you feel none. Personally, I know that the day I routinely feel no tightening at all of the stomach muscles before meeting a new group will be the day that I decide it's time to stop.

This aerobics teacher describes well what the first session needs:

> I think of the first meeting as a kind of first date with a desirable partner who has to be wooed and courted. Shyness is out on my part while I have to recognize it on theirs. I mustn't be too overwhelming, but on the other hand I have to make what is on offer seem attractive. If it isn't a success, I know they'll disappear – endless polite excuses, but I won't see them again! Since they pay on each occasion and I get a cut, it matters to my wallet as well as to my pride...

Adults are rightly choosy. Whether it comes out of your pocket or out of an employer's budget doesn't seem to matter too much. If we don't like what we're getting, we will absent ourselves mentally or leave. Your plan to avoid this humiliating debacle will fall naturally into three phases: before, during and after.

Before the first session

This is the research phase. Find out as much as you can in advance about who will be in the group. Whenever I can, I will phone people in advance. This serves a number of purposes. First, it helps me cope with any nervousness I might be feeling, because when you actually talk to the people they almost always come across as helpful, pleasant and friendly. Secondly, it is good customer care. It shows that you are interested enough in participants' needs to take the trouble to contact them. Third, and most important, it gives me vital information about what they expect and want. I take notes during these conversations.

The questions I recommend are dead simple:

- *What can you tell me about why you are attending this event?* The answers here are always revealing. The question gives the sceptics the chance to voice their scepticism without feeling judged. It allows the enthusiasts to be enthusiastic. It also allows for occasional blinding honesty – the people who confess that they don't really know, but it's a week away from the office and they're looking forward to it.
- *What do you want to get out of it?* Replies here will tell you what people feel they must achieve. If you feel that these aims are over-ambitious, this is the time to say so. If, as is more usual, they are over-modest, this is also the time to say so.

- *What do you already know about the subject?* Or you can ask this question a slightly different way: *What other education, training or development have you had in this area?* This question gives you the chance to assess where people are in their learning. For instance, if you are running something suitable for beginners, you may well realize by asking this question that you have a bogus beginner in the group – someone who has already covered much of the territory you will be exploring. If so, probe their reasons for doing the same material all over again. Lack of confidence is the usual explanation. Where you feel that a participant is likely to be either bored or out of their depth, now is the time to say so, suggesting an alternative event or course.
- *What reservations do you have?* Note the way this question is asked. Not *Do you have any reservations?* Asking a question that begins *do, don't, is* or *isn't* will inevitably produce the answer the listener thinks you want to hear – in this case, *'No'.* Asking *what* reservations assumes that everyone is likely to have some, which is indeed the case. You need to know what these are. Common replies might be

  None that need trouble you!
  Afraid it will be a waste of time.
  Nervous about looking silly.
  Worried about my in-tray and what will happen while I'm out of the office.
  Hope we're not going to do role play because I hate it!
- *What else would it be useful for me to know?* This final question is immensely useful. By this stage of the conversation there is usually some trust and friendliness. Some people will say that there is nothing else you need to know. Others will use the moment to give you important additional information. In one such set of conversations I was told about the recent termination of a pregnancy and the agonizing guilt that this event had created, the death of a parent, a phobia about beef and a deadly quarrel some years back with a participant who was also going to be on the course.

Sorting out the housekeeping

Some years ago, I joined a course which met at our local concrete university. The first class was scheduled to start at 7.00 p.m. Unfortunately, the sign-posting at reception was inscrutable and the building itself designed to confuse, its grimy towers being linked by windswept ramps. I finally found the room after fifteen minutes of searching, but alas! The venue had been changed. A notice flapped on the open door announcing a different room, one I had passed several times already in my search. The tutor gave me a hostile stare as I climbed over benches to find a seat. He was annoyed because his introductory chat was being interrupted so many times by similarly lost latecomers – indeed, they kept sliding in until 7.45.

The course was not a success. Even though most people's fees were, like mine, being paid by their employers, the initial group of 22 was down to 10 by the fourth meeting.

Most such problems are entirely preventable by attentive housekeeping and good customer care:

- inform the receptionist;
- make sure he or she is welcoming;
- direct people with clear signage;
- double check the room booking;
- double check any audio-visual equipment;
- arrange the room so that it suits your purposes (see also pages 101–104).

Advance information to learners

Sometimes people just turn up on the spot and you can have no way of knowing in advance who they are. More commonly you will know. The more you can let them know about the event in advance, the better it will be for you and for them. It is especially important to plan how you can reduce precious contact time on the day that is devoted to bland, factual information by sending people this kind of thing in advance. Think about sending people any or all of the following:

- a welcome letter;
- a course outline;
- a description of the methods you are going to use;
- a map with instructions for finding the venue;
- details about food arrangements;
- additional costs, if any;
- dress code information;
- details of any equipment they need to buy or bring with them;
- reading lists;
- book list;
- brief CVs of tutors.

The more information people have about you, the methods, the content and what is expected of them, the fewer their shocks will be on the day and the better it will be all round. There is more on this on pages 32–35 as it links critically with the whole question of how you design a course.

Make a plan

You may feel that a plan is too formal, but I believe it helps. If you have a plan you can always abandon it if you wish, but without one, you are likely to feel unanchored and apprehensive. The simplest plan has three columns for time, activity and materials. Be realistic. Most activities will take longer than you think. See also page 250.

During the event

The first few minutes

The most useful comparison is to think of yourself as a host. A good host greets people warmly, introduces them to each other and tries to make sure that everyone has a pleasant time. Unfortunately, it is all too easy to fall short of this ideal:

> Got to the group on time, but no tutor to be seen – she arrived five minutes late, puffing and panting, but with no apology!
>
> We sat there in silence and semi-darkness – very uncomfortable. On the dot of ten, the tutor walked in, switched on another light and launched straight into a lecture. I had no idea who the other people were. In fact the tutor never told us his name either.

A better tactic is to arrive in plenty of time – at least an hour before the official start time. Remember that you need to allow time to rearrange the room if necessary. I never, ever, assume that the room will be laid out as I want it or that all the ordered equipment will actually be there and working. This is because mostly I have found that it rarely is, even when confirmed in writing, so I plan for plenty of time to arrange for furniture changes as well as for writing up anything on the flip chart or setting up PowerPoint. I want to get this out of the way well before the first people arrive so that I can give them my full attention when they do. Greet people warmly, shake hands, ask their names, and introduce them to one another. If you have refreshments available, always a good idea if the budget and venue run to it, pour people coffee or tea rather than leaving them to help themselves.

Introducing yourself

Always say something about yourself at the formal beginning of any event. A full-length biography is not what is required, but some information about you is essential. It need only take a minute or two, but should include:

- your name;
- your passion for your subject;
- your aims for the event;
- how you got from your original career to this event;
- what your credentials are – your authority for teaching the subject at all.

The swiftest and one of the most effective introductions I ever see of this sort is given by an actor with whom I frequently work. It takes about a minute and her intro goes like this:

> Hello, my name is X [first and surname]. I'm passionate about the whole subject of helping people give better presentations because I see all the time what a difference it can make to how we communicate. My aim today is to help you improve your presentation style and confidence. I started as an actor in the theatre and TV but now I do almost exclusively corporate work – I've been in it for six years, working with senior people in all sorts of sectors and industries. I specialize in working with people on their voices and I'm really looking forward to working with you today.

You must do this confidently. Rehearse it if necessary. Don't make the mistake of one unfortunate tutor on a one-day fitness course I attended at one of London's well-known adult institutes. She arrived late, looking flustered, and of course had not had time to rearrange the chairs, so we sat in higgledy-piggledy rows. She then astonished us all by saying, 'Don't take me as an example of fitness. I've put on weight recently.' I think it should go without saying that if you have to apologize for being a poor example of your subject, you should not be teaching it.

Formalities

Education and training in the public sector are increasingly plagued by intrusive processes that add little value to learning. An example is that in some courses, continued funding depends on appearing to have reached learning objectives. I use the phrase *appearing to have reached* them because so often it is clear that tutors are being forced to go through the motions. When I joined a dance class at an adult institute I was obliged, along with everyone else, to rate my existing learning on a five-point scale and at the end of the ten sessions to do the same thing again. The utter impossibility of describing, for instance, my ability in partner dances on such a scale was underlined by the overt cynicism of our teacher who begged us to conform because *this is the only way we can get our budgets*. When your first class is only an hour long, it adds little value to spend fifteen minutes of that time filling in forms. If it really is essential, again consider sending this stuff to people in advance so that it does not take up precious time on the day.

Learning people's names

If appropriate, have name badges prepared with people's names in letters big enough to be read easily at a distance – by you and by the participants. Never underestimate the importance of learning and using people's names as a way of making them feel that they matter to you and are part of the group. Not doing this is one of the main ways a group can fail:

> A colleague and I were running a course we have been doing for some time, so I suppose it was running the risk of seeming a bit stale – to us, that is. We were preoccupied on this occasion by some personal stuff – we were planning the launch of another course, very exciting and new and potentially very lucrative. Somehow we got very bound up in this and I think conveyed to the group that we were a bit over-pleased with ourselves. It was a big group, but normally I never have any trouble remembering people's names. This time I did. There were lots of women there of similar age and with very similar names: two Caroles, two Karens, a Caroline and a Carmel and we both kept getting them mixed up. We had very disappointing feedback from the group and thinking it over afterwards we both came to the conclusion that we had failed at this very basic level of acknowledging each individual.

There are a number of ruses you can use to help remember names in a big group:

- draw a seating plan for yourself and label each person as they introduce themselves;
- attach a private mnemonic to each person;
- use their names as early as possible and as often as possible.

Ice-breakers

Ice-breakers really help. They are vital for many reasons.

They oblige everyone to speak. Unless you speak you will not feel you are fully present at the event and all tutors want their participants to feel and be fully present, as no one can learn unless this is what is happening. Ice-breakers help people get over the shy stage as quickly as possible, and they help *form* the group – people begin to get to know each other.

Depending on which ice-breakers you use, you can find out further vital information about what the group wants and expects.

There are literally thousands of possible ice-breakers. Indeed, there are whole books and internet sites devoted to them. Most experienced tutors collect them from one another or as they see them used at events they attend as learners. What you choose will depend on how much time you have available – a longer course needs a more cohesive group so it will be worth a bigger investment of time. It will also depend on the subject. A solemn subject – a day's seminar on employment law, for instance – will not easily lend itself to a light-hearted ice-breaker. One important point about ice-breakers is that you should join in yourself. Never ask the group to do something where you remain aloof.

Here are some ideas for ice-breakers. They all work for me, depending on the event, and may for you:

- Ask people to sit in alphabetical order of first names and then to introduce themselves to the group. This obliges everyone to exchange names and also to move – both excellent tactics.
- Ask people to introduce themselves and then to sit in date order according to when they started their present job. Once sat down again, people introduce their neighbours. Works for similar reasons to above.
- Get people to mingle as at a cocktail party. Ask them to find two other people with whom they have something in common and then to introduce each other to the rest of the group.
- Draw two 'temperature charts', each with ten slots on the flip chart, one to represent people's level of apprehension, one to represent the importance to them of the event. Ten represents high and one represents low. Give everyone two sticky dots and ask them to place the dot on the appropriate place. Then ask them to change seats and sit first in order of levels of anxiety, asking each person to explain why they placed their dot where they did and what would help them get over their fears. Do the same with levels of importance. This has the advantage of confronting anxiety head on and letting people see that others share their fears. Let people return to their original seats, otherwise you will have all the confident people sitting together and vice versa. This is a time-consuming exercise so it works best where you have a small group and a reasonable amount of time available.
- Work in pairs, 'snowballing' to quartets. Ask people to state what they want from the event, and what they don't want, and then present a summary to the rest of the group.
- Sit in an open circle as everyone needs a clear view of everyone else. Ask everyone to find an adjective that starts with the same letter as

their first name and which also says something about their current state of mind or body, and then to introduce themselves to the rest of the group. For instance, Hoarse Helen had a very bad cold, and Jolly John was feeling relaxed. Each member of the group has to memorize the mnemonic and repeat it in turn before saying their own so all names get repeated many times. I have never found a better way of helping people to remember each other's names, though it is challenging, and possibly too exposing for some, to have to remember so many new names at once, even with the help of the mnemonic.

- Ask people to state their names, jobs and what they would be doing if they were independently wealthy and had no need to work. This is fun and memorable. I saw this ice-breaker done on a course for the senior partners of a major accountancy firm and several people replied that they were already independently wealthy and that what they were doing was the job they loved, so on this occasion, the ice-breaker fell a little flat.
- Form participants into birth order groups (first child, only children, middles and so on) and ask them to discuss and then report on what being in that birth order has done for their approach to whatever the subject of the course is.
- Active ice-breakers which involve physical movement of some sort – for instance, everyone stands in a circle and a ball is thrown from one person to another until everyone has been included and has said their name. Do the same thing again only this time ask people to repeat their own name and to say the name of the person to whom they are throwing. Another variant is to take a ball of string and pass it across the group from one person to another, making a web, each person saying their name as they go, then undoing it in the same order, again repeating names.

Even the notorious 'creeping death' can work in some circumstances. This is the ice-breaker where you start at one side of the room and work your way around with everyone saying their names and something about themselves or what they want to get out of the event. It's called 'creeping death' because most people are so nervous before speaking that they don't hear any of their predecessors and are so relieved afterwards that they don't concentrate on what follows either. However, there is sometimes a place even for this oldie. I saw it used very effectively on an event attended by 120 people. The young American speaker/tutor asked people to 'laser' their contributions – i.e. keep them to a few seconds, and ruthlessly interrupted anyone who showed signs of droning on. Most people quickly got the point and spoke for ten seconds or less. It was fun, involving and did the job surprisingly well.

You can learn from her technique here if you decide to run a version of this exercise. Model the amount of time expected by making the first contribution yourself. Tell people they only have two short sentences and interrupt immediately if any individual over-runs.

Choosing an ice-breaker

There is an art to choosing ice-breakers. These are some of the criteria you may want to consider:

The fit with the subject. There should be a good match between the style of the ice-breaker and the style of the subject or event.

The fit with the people. People who value their dignity may bridle at being asked to take part in what they deem to be a silly ice-breaker. High-spirited youngsters may dislike anything that could seem pompous and over-serious.

The fit with your own values and style. If the very thought of it makes you cringe, choose something else.

How well the attendees know each other. Where you are working with a group already known to each other you may be able to take more risks, or to design an ice-breaker which builds on their knowledge of each other. For instance, one popular ice-breaker asks each person to recount two things about themselves, one which is true and one which is false. The rest of the group has to guess which is which. Another asks people to describe two things they are most proud of that have happened in the last few weeks, one personal and one professional. Where part of the purpose of the event is to create intimacy, this one works well because it starts people off on a positive and personal note.

The amount of time you have available. Beware of ice-breakers which take up too much time on a short course. One of the worst offenders for me was an expensive course lasting just five hours of contact time where the first hour was taken up with each member of our group of 18 giving what felt like interminable accounts of their lives and what had drawn them to the event. This took up 20 per cent of the course time – for me, entirely unproductively – listening to other people rambling. Work it out for yourself if you are attracted by ice-breakers that involve each member of the group speaking separately – it's a simple question of arithmetic. If you have 10 people and each speaks for three minutes that is going to take up half an hour of the group's time.

The numbers in the group. As above.

The venue. A tiered lecture theatre will impose considerable restrictions on the kind of ice-breaker you can use. Heavy furniture may be in the way if you want to introduce an ice-breaker which involves everyone standing

up in a circle. Always inspect the venue first and take it into account when thinking about an ice-breaker.
Originality. Some ice-breakers seem tired because they have been over-used. Keep your stock refreshed by constantly swapping with other tutors.

Helping participants relax

Ice-breakers will usually help people relax, but you need to keep in mind that people may still be feeling apprehensive. Getting them to own up to the apprehension is always a useful tactic and you can achieve this by asking the question directly: 'Who is feeling nervous here?' Or, 'How are you feeling about this event?' Naming the fear usually means taming the fear.

Openly tackling the question of commitment and potential distractions is also useful. For instance, my colleague Jan Campbell Young often asks people to write down their major distraction on a piece of paper, to name it out loud to the rest of the group, and then to fold it up and place it in a bin, explaining that if people really want to, they can retrieve the 'distraction' later. (No one ever takes her up on this offer.) This symbolic naming and then parking of the distraction works for two reasons. One is that it acknowledges that we all lead busy lives and that our preoccupations are normal. The other is that it allows people to ask for help and support if one of their distractions has overwhelming importance, such as a seriously ill partner or some physical discomfort otherwise likely to intrude into the learning.

Introducing some laughter and pace is your next best tactic, depending of course on you and your personality and confidence. It takes a lot of experience to match the inspired clowning and energy of this enormously successful teacher of English as a Foreign Language, working with nervous and wary people of hugely mixed nationalities in a North London community centre. I included her account in the first edition of this book and have retained it for this one, even though the innocence of the multicultural experience it describes may seem a little unwordly in the so much more tense climate of today:

> We plunge right in at the first class. My main idea is to make them laugh with me. Anyone can understand action jokes even if they have no English so I'm constantly acting the jokes. I ask them their names and perhaps say a few words in their languages – Urdu, Spanish, Greek, Bengali – they usually understand and correct me.
>
> I always make sure that we do a lot on the first night, but it's usually very simple things like prepositions – under, over, in, out. To teach these things I get under the table, go out of the door, stand on the chair and get people to say, 'She's under the table', 'She's on the chair'.

> I always have plenty of real things to hand – bread, big jars of sweets – and we make up sentences about them: 'It's a sweet', 'It's a loaf'. By the end of the class, I make sure everyone has spoken at least once; usually I try to see that they've asked and answered a question. Quite often people who've been used to formal teaching in their own countries are very surprised by my methods. I know I shock some of them and they ask for books and grammar, but I concentrate on making learning enjoyable with quizzes and games. I aim to make sure everyone has a laugh and that no one sits quietly but also that they all make great efforts to speak to me and to each other. I hope to send them out of my first class buzzing with excitement. After a couple of classes, people frequently bring friends, neighbours and other members of their family to join the class.

Achievement

The first session should not be all jollity and nothing else. By the time the session ends, everyone should have achieved at least one piece of relevant learning. There are various reasons why this is desirable:

- people have joined to *learn* – if they only wanted social contact they would have chosen a purely social event;
- it helps to get them over the hump of anxiety;
- it gives them a fair taste of what is to come;
- it reinforces motivation.

These first tasks need only be small. At the same time they should be challenging and carefully designed to make sure that everyone can get them right. When carried out successfully, such tactics can have powerfully energizing effects, as this trainee television studio director reports:

> At the very first session we all had a go at directing a simple sequence of changing captions to music – 'A, you're adorable; B, you're so beautiful . . .' etc. Looking back it was exquisitely simple. At the time it was terrifying, but fun and achievable. Everyone had a go and more or less everyone went away on a high. We'd sat in the hot seat and got pictures on the screen!

The combination of fun, challenge and group support can mean that people achieve what seemed previously like impossible feats. Here is an account of a beginners' swimming lesson which did just that:

> In the first ten minutes every single one of us took our feet off the bottom. Okay, it was using a float, a rope or armbands, it wasn't real swimming, but considering that we were all non-swimmers and that several of us had serious doubts about our ability ever to swim it was amazing. Personally I was busting with pride that I'd got over a lifetime's fear. The boost to my morale was so tremendous that I actually swam a few strokes unaided during the second lesson and swam a whole width during the third.

These first tasks cannot be so difficult that they frighten people, but they must be true to the focus of the rest of the course. Don't introduce bogus exercises which will make learners feel patronized later. Keep the methods of the first session consistent with whatever you plan for later. Don't, for instance make this mistake:

> She kept telling us that the course was all about participation and that our contributions would be a valuable part of the learning. The trouble was that the whole of the first day was taken up with lectures. There was no participation to be seen anywhere.

This kind of difficulty can happen because participants are thought to need a dose of 'orientation' before the 'real' work of the course begins. If this tends to happen on your courses, ask yourself whether it is essential for it to happen face to face. Might the same 'orientation' be achieved more easily and less obtrusively by giving people a paper to read, an online exercise to do or a video to watch in advance of that first meeting?

Start and finish on time

Be wary of waiting for latecomers, however tempting it may seem. The people who have arrived on time will feel let down. Soon everyone will start coming late because 'the class never starts on time'. If you start late but finish on time, you may look as if you are cheating learners out of their due. If you 'make up for it' by finishing late, then your final few minutes are likely to be disrupted by people creeping out. Begin and end as you mean to go on: promptly.

Other useful activities for the first session could include negotiating ground rules, setting out your own expectations about the structure of the later sessions or curriculum – and so on. There is more about all of this in Chapter 5.

After the first session

Evaluate

Always ask yourself – and participants – how it has gone and how it could have gone better. It is common for feedback to suggest that participants have found the first session *slow*. This is usually because it is demanding to do everything I describe in this chapter and to accomplish significant pieces of learning. The psychological reason for the feeling of *slowness* is that often people are not yet fully committed to the event. Their minds are still distracted by everything else that is going on in their lives. So maybe some slowness is inevitable. If you are working with a colleague, sit down and assess the event together. Evaluation is a big topic (see Chapter 12) and it's especially important to review and evaluate the first session because there is still time to make changes which will improve the learning for everyone.

Further reading

Jackson, P.Z. (2001) *Making Your Training Flexible, Spontaneous and Creative.* London: Kogan Page.

RoAne, S. (2000) *How to Work a Room.* New York: Harper Collins.

The internet is the best source of ice-breakers. A search will produce many dozens of sites with useable and constantly updated examples.

3 Giving feedback

> The old saying that practice makes perfect is not true. But it is true to say that it is practice the *results of which are known* which makes perfect.[1]

Giving feedback, praising and commenting: these are all so important in learning that the topic deserves a whole chapter to itself. The principles are the same whether you are giving feedback in a traditional setting such as a classroom, over the phone as part of a coaching programme, or emailing comments to an online learner. Teaching adults is complicated enormously by the difficulty of appearing to criticize an equal. Not giving the right quantity or quality of feedback is one of the main reasons why adult learning fails, so it is worth thinking about how to get it right. There are two dangers: giving it in the wrong way and not giving enough:

> I went to a two-day workshop on how to give presentations. I was one of only two women so I felt conspicuous anyway. It was run by a management training consultant, but ' in-house'. I gave my first little presentation and I knew it was bad – I was so nervous I could hardly speak. The trainer's comments were devastating, they felt personal and cruel. I was utterly destroyed. I'm afraid I broke down and cried. The next day I just could not bring myself to go into work so I missed the second day. The whole thing was so mortifying it makes me cringe now to think of it. I learnt nothing; my terror of speaking in public was worse than it had ever been and my credibility with my bosses took a long time to recover.

> I get e-tutorials as part of my course with feedback on my assignments. My tutor rarely writes full sentences – in fact most of what he writes does not have verbs. A lot of the time I am completely in the dark about what he means because it's so cryptic and have to email him again, sometimes several times, to try to find out.

> My first experience of learning as an adult was a complete damp squib. I'd enrolled for a jewellery class at a very good London Institute. The tutor was a well-known craftsman but had no experience of teaching. He was a good demonstrator, but nothing more. I slaved over my little projects, but I never got a *crumb* of comment from him.

> He'd look at my efforts and would just say 'Hmmmm . . . yes' and pass on. What did this 'Hmmm . . . yes 'mean? 'Awful'? 'OK'? 'Boring?' 'Beneath contempt'? I never found out! I went on going to the class because the facilities were wonderful and the other students very friendly. We helped each other, but it would have been so much better to have had comment from him.

Feedback matters, because without it the learner is unlikely to improve. Imagine that you are one member of a group whose challenge is to complete some kind of task to a demanding standard. As the project progresses, your group does not receive any comment on whether or not it is hitting its quality targets. There is another group which does receive guidance. Who is most likely to be successful? Your group is going to continue haphazardly making the same errors over and over again. The other group will steadily improve.

Actually it is worse even that that. Because not having feedback leaves us in the dark, we can either seriously underrate our own talents and skills or else have pleasant fantasies about how wonderful our performance is. Organizational research has shown, for instance, that most of us believe we perform at the 80th percentile – a statistical impossibility. When we do find out how we compare with others, the shock can be intense. As the saying has it, *lack of feedback is inherently punishing.*

Adults come to learning in order to change and improve something. If performance does not improve, then all learners, but particularly adults, quickly lose interest: their motivation flags, and without motivation there can be no learning. Adults are rarely obliged to continue with a learning project against their will. By the time we have reached adulthood most of us are adept at slithering away from situations where we feel we perform badly.

Quality feedback is one of the basic rewards of learning because it is recognition and all human beings crave recognition. Feedback is therefore a critical part of learning, shown in Figure 3.1. as The Improvement Cycle. If as a tutor you break this cycle by failing to give the right kind of feedback then the learning will be unsuccessful – as happened in the presentation workshop I quoted earlier. What is especially sad about this example is that the learner blamed herself, whereas in fact the failure was the tutor's.

Just a little well-judged feedback can have a transforming effect. In an email to me after our joint experience of a rigorous course on mediation skills, one of my fellow learners, an experienced solicitor who already had considerable experience of the subject, made this comment:

> Easily the best part of this course, although a bit sobering at the time, was the detailed individual feedback we had from the Faculty member after the role plays. Knowing exactly what they were assessing helped of course [we had all been given the competency

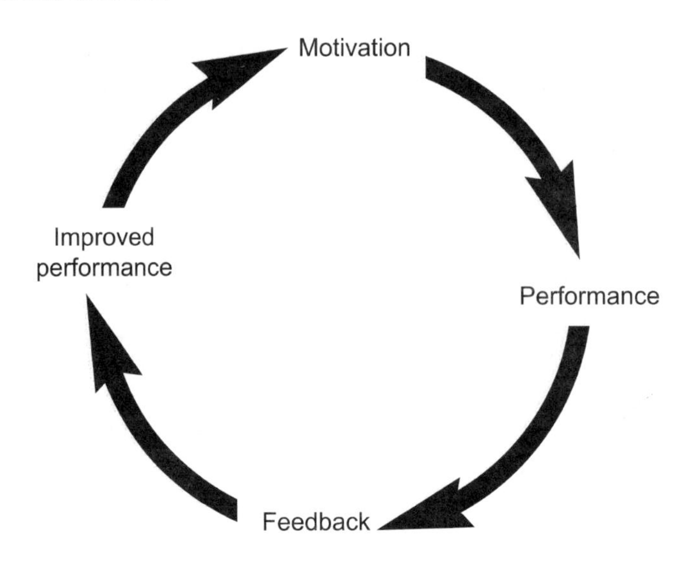

Figure 3.1 The improvement cycle

> breakdown well in advance] but I have never, ever had such detailed feedback and that includes my entire experience of education, my qualifying path to becoming a solicitor and my fifteen years in practice. It was given on the basis of close observation and also given in a calm and pleasant manner. It was never possible to say, ' But I didn't do that' because I knew I had! I was able to make enormous improvements between Day 3 and Day 4 and then again between Day 4 and Day 5 because so much of it was about micro-behaviours: the expression on my face when I said a particular thing, the exact phrasing of a comment, the length of a sentence, the fact that I did not shake hands with one of the parties in the mediation and the impact that might have had for real – and so on. It would have been impossible to have achieved the accreditation without it and it will have major impact on how I conduct mediations in my work. Without knowing it I had slipped into some bad habits. What a luxury to have someone observing you so closely where their only role is to help you improve!

The organization running this course, the Centre for Effective Dispute Resolution (CEDR) takes the whole business of giving feedback seriously, understanding how critical it is to the progress of participants towards eventual accreditation. Indeed, it takes feedback so seriously that it goes to the trouble and expense of having extra Faculty members present whose only role is to review how the feedback-giver is giving his or her feedback. As course members we were also asked for daily paper-evaluations of this particular aspect of the course.

The positive impact of skilled feedback can surprise even an experienced tutor:

> Although I was an OU tutor for many years, it never failed to amaze me what effect my comments had. It was quite common for students to ring me after they'd had their TMAs (tutor-marked assignments) back and to say things like 'You've no idea how many times I've read what you said'; 'I felt *thrilled* that you'd given me that mark'; 'I was thinking of giving up, but you've encouraged me so much I'm going to carry on'. Often I'd only written about 15 lines, but it was enough to make all the difference to a student who'd been wondering whether to give up or not.

When to give feedback

There is a simple rule about the optimum time to give feedback on learning: *give it as soon as possible*. Don't wait until either the triumph or the error is repeated. Give it immediately. The reason is that learning is like quick-drying paint. You only have a short time to correct the mistake or let it harden into a permanent error. If something is wrong, then put it right straight away. If all is well, then say so and say why. Then the learner can speed on to the next stage. If there is a mistake, help the learner put it right on the spot before the error has had time to become a standard part of how the learner performs whatever the task is and unlearning will take far more effort afterwards. The best time to give comment is while the effort of making the attempt is still fresh. Leave it until later and learners may have settled back into complacency, or into an environment – work or home – where your influence is more easily resisted:

> I was sent on a fair selection course. I thought I'd done OK, but I heard on the grapevine that the tutor thought I was being *difficult* and that she'd found my behaviour challenging. I was furious. For a start she'd told us that the course was confidential and there'd be no feedback to our bosses. To me it was all about political correctness – all I'd done was ask questions and also ask her to justify some of the sillier things she'd said.

How to give feedback

Here we come to the heart of the skill of teaching adults. As a tutor you are the peer of your learners. Indeed many of them may, in their non-learner roles, be the kind of people who may rightly make you feel humble. You cannot rely on being their superior in age, income, social class or occupation, only in your skills as a tutor or your knowledge of your subject. Because of this, it is your right and your duty to comment on their efforts. The challenge is how to do it effectively while leaving them with their dignity intact.

The power of the positive

It is often said that 'we learn by our mistakes'. I have often thought how thoroughly misleading this statement is. It would seem truer to say that we learn by our successes, *as long as we know why we are being successful.* First, we have to accept that as human beings our craving for praise and reassurance is utterly limitless. Praise makes us feel secure and confident, where negative criticism makes us insecure and self-doubting. But we can only learn from praise when we know what we are being praised for. This feedback is likely to help you repeat your success, for three reasons:

- it is given promptly;
- it contains encouraging words;
- it gives detailed comment on *how* you achieved an accurate result.

It's possible to assume that feedback is always about correcting mistakes, but in fact the most powerful feedback may well be the sort which tells us where we have got something right.

> That design really works for me because...
> That opening sentence is full of vivid language and drama. Keeping it short meant it really caught my attention.
> The contributions you are making in the group are really helpful. You are picking up on what others say and giving useful summaries of their points of view. It's creating a feeling of connectedness between one part of the discussion and another...

There is even a case for saying that by concentrating entirely on the positive the negative behaviour will simply fade away for lack of attention. *Catch them doing something right* could be an excellent motto (see also page 35). In a BBC career lasting sixteen years I can only think of three occasions when it was offered to me by a boss and I still vividly remember the impact of each one on my behaviour: hugely reinforcing and an instant growth in my confidence in two cases, and in a third, the calmly offered negative comments most probably made the difference between getting the next job I went for and failing at the interview stage. As a tutor and coach I do get a lot of feedback but this is largely because I constantly ask the questions that solicit it.

But in everyday circumstances, this is rare. Many years ago I worked with a colleague who was notorious for reducing trainees, both men and women, to tears of rage, frustration and humiliation. One of the reasons was his refusal, or inability perhaps, to give them feedback other than the occasional highly critical comment on their work. When I became his boss, I tackled him about it and he looked at me in genuinely blank innocence. 'Surely they know', he said, 'that if I don't say anything, I must approve . . . and that even if I do have a criticism, I'm giving them nine out of ten?' Alas, the opposite was true. The few comments he did make were assumed to represent dozens of silent criticisms held back only by intense restraint and dislike of 'scenes'. Some of the young trainees he actually held in highest esteem were the very people who believed he thought little of their work. If he had been able to catch them doing something right he would for certain have accelerated their learning ten-fold because positive feedback increases confidence and increased confidence leads to learners feeling able to take more risks, another essential condition for effective learning.

Giving learners access to the reasons for their success or failure is one absolutely fundamental rule for helpful feedback. Don't just say 'That was a good piece of work', or 'Well done'. This is appreciation but it is not feedback. Always give the reason: 'That was excellent because it was so neat', or 'Good – you looked confident, your nerves were under control and your voice was at just the right level'. One way of describing this ideal feedback is that it is *descriptive praise*. However, for feedback to stick and to be even more effective, this process has to be two-way:

> I see a number of people who are not formally trained tutors doing brilliant jobs. There's one chap who is superb: he is a good craftsman himself, but his trainees produce beautiful work in what seems like a very short time. When I watched him I realized that this is because all the comment on their work is a *dialogue*. First he sets the standard by showing them what perfect work looks like, and he even produces some 'shoddy' examples for comparison. Then he takes each trainee's effort and discusses it with them so that they are spotting for themselves what the problems and good points are, and how they happened, and then they are pointed to finding a way for themselves of putting it right.

This mixture of gentleness and ruthlessness can be difficult to achieve. It is pointless to put all the onus on the hapless student by demanding brusquely, 'Now what was wrong with that?' Many people will babble on guiltily in such circumstances without any real idea of the justice of their self-accusations. It is far better to establish a constructive dialogue which helps learners compare their own performance with the ideal and diagnose strengths and weakness for themselves. This puts responsibility where it belongs: on the learner, not the teacher.

It is usually best, too, to concentrate on only a few aspects of performance, whether good or bad. There is a limit to what most of us can absorb at a time without either intellectual overload or, if the comments are negative, damaged self-esteem:

> I was a tutor on a literacy scheme. I discovered early on that marking every single error in the writing was totally counterproductive: the students just couldn't take it, it was too dispiriting. Instead, I concentrated on about three significant mistakes each time. The improvement was usually staggering.

As well as concentrating on just a few mistakes at a time, make your feedback unambiguous and clear. In an effort to avoid being what they see as *hurtful* some tutors wrap up their comments in so many layers of qualification or anecdote that the main point is obscured. First, it is patronizing to assume that people cannot handle skilfully given feedback, so you cannot assume that the learner will be hurt. Secondly, if you put it the right way it will most probably be gracefully received. Furthermore, there is nothing more infuriating than to discover later that there was some obvious problem with what you have been doing and that it could have been readily put right, but no one has told you. For instance, it took me a long time to discover for myself that when you are learning to dance, you do it better and far more quickly if you don't look at your feet. I heard one of my teachers gently but firmly point this out to a beginner a few weeks ago and thought how lucky this person was to have someone prepared to intervene in order to save her many months of struggle.

If something is wrong, it is better to say straightforwardly what the problem is, to give the reason, and to leave it there. For instance, suppose you are training a new young manager in how to write a memo. Your trainee produces a reasonable effort, but it is too long. Your feedback is best delivered as some warm words of praise for whatever has been done well, and then a few succinct sentences saying that the draft is too long and why. You should avoid garlanding your comments with anecdotes about your own first efforts to write memos, funny memos you have seen in the past, or office gossip about the addressee. Enjoyable though this may be, especially for you, it will obscure the impact of your feedback.

There is one other common temptation which you should resist. If you see a mistake, don't march in, pick up the work and 'put it right' by doing a large amount of it yourself. As the expert, you know how to do it; it is the students who have to learn by doing it themselves.

Some tutors, rightly priding themselves on the standard of their own work, can find a beginner's mistakes too painful to contemplate, and will often seize the work and do the difficult bits themselves, sometimes under the impression that people are grateful for such professional additions. There may be occasional learners too placid to object, but most people feel cheated if someone else does all the hard work for them. They want the satisfaction and sense of achievement of learning to cope for themselves. They may find the tutor's well-meant interventions hard to endure, as in this art class run by a teacher whom the student had earlier described tactfully as having 'tremendous enthusiasm but lacking method':

> General instruction is given *ad hoc* ... moreover, in dealing with someone's problem, his enthusiasm leads him to paint half the picture himself, instead of merely demonstrating and suggesting and thereby letting the student feel that the picture was 'all their own work'. This makes everyone cross, but no one has had the courage to tell him we don't like it.

It is also better to leave the learner to work out the solution: you can suggest that the memo might be too long, but the details of how to achieve a better length should be up to the learner. Prescriptive feedback only postpones the problem to another occasion because it is your solution, not the learner's.

There are various other kinds of unhelpful feedback. One is the sort that is so generalized or vague that it leaves the learner completely stumped: 'You should try to be a bit more assertive . . .', or 'Your work lacks dynamism . . .', or 'It would be better if there were more light and shade in your performance'. All these are vague, waffly statements capable of dozens of different interpretations and unlikely to result in improved performance. Then there is the feedback that appears completely subjective: 'I like the way you paint clouds', or 'I prefer a different kind of analysis myself'. Learners will be much more likely to reject such comments as personal prejudice than if they are rephrased more objectively: 'There are lots of other ways to do x or y thing . . . one of them is . . .'.

Another trap is to offer feedback on aspects of performance that people are simply unlikely to be able to improve because of genetic inheritance, circumstance or personality: for instance criticizing a woman javelin thrower for not having the same powerful arm action as a man, telling someone that their regional accent is difficult to understand or ordering an essentially modest person to be boastful. Whatever feedback you offer, it should always be possible for the learner to act on it.

One principle is fundamental to the whole idea of constructive feedback: comment on the performance, not the person. All good tutors convey their liking and respect for their students and their longing for them to improve. This is the quality in good teachers that is most essential for success, hardest to pinpoint and impossible to counterfeit, but we all know it when we see it:

> He just burnt with a wish for us to know what he knew ... we *knew* we were the best class he'd ever taken and yet all his classes felt like that ... We all knew that we individually were the students he cared about ... and yet we knew he had no favourites!

> It was an extremely supportive atmosphere: very caring, very friendly, yet she was utterly ruthless with us. Sloppy effort was not allowed; the words 'I can't' were banned. Whatever criticisms were made, they were made knowing that she really urged you towards improvement and achievement because she liked you and had faith in you.

There is one simple test of 'pure' feedback. It should offer fact and description, not opinion and generalization. This applies equally whether you are praising or pointing out a mistake. Here are some examples:

> A learner has completed a role play where she has to ask a boss for a pay rise. You are running the role play. Genuine feedback is a comment along these lines: 'When you got halfway through, I noticed that you looked away from me and then began to wring your hands a bit. The effect it had was for me to feel as if you weren't going to push me for the rise'.

Note: It would not be genuine feedback to say 'You looked lacking in confidence.'

> A member of a learning set has been silent for most of the meeting. He has been looking away from the other members. The less he speaks, the more it begins to concern you. Your feedback to him is, 'X, we've been going now for nearly ninety minutes and I've noticed that you have only spoken once and that was very briefly when you told us about your new role. I'm beginning to get concerned about your silence and I wondered if you could tell us what is going on for you right now?'

Note: It would not be genuine feedback to offer any kind of reproach such as, 'Your silence is destabilizing this group', or interpretation such as, 'You're unhappy'. You cannot see inside the silent person's mind. You are simply describing the behaviour in as neutral a way as possible and creating a space for them to explain if they wish.

Raising self-awareness

The ideal kind of feedback is the sort that we give ourselves – as long as it is based on accuracy. We can only do this if our self-awareness has been raised. The writer Timothy Gallwey has contributed significantly to the debate here through his *Inner Game* books. Starting with a book on tennis,[2] reflecting his earlier career as a tennis coach and continuing the theme with his latest book *The Inner Game of Work,*[3] he puts forward the view that the role of the coach is to ask the questions which increase bodily and mental awareness, based on the principle that everyone has the resources to answer their own questions and to improve their own performance. The coach/tutor's role is to work with the learner to establish the critical variables in the task and then to encourage the learner to make accurate observations of his or her current performance against these variables. When these conditions are satisfied, Gallwey maintains that the person's performance will automatically improve because his or her body will adjust on its own. His books talk about the 'Inner Game' because he maintains that this is the game that matters – the mental state of the learner, ideally one of relaxed alertness where there is no concern about competitiveness and winning, but rather the expectation of success. Trying too hard interferes with performance. When the learner is concerned with the 'Outer Game', there is fear of failure. If the game is tennis for instance, the learner can become preoccupied with how to hold the racquet, how to stand, how to serve and to depend on the teacher for guidance and feedback. The essence of the Inner Game approach is that the learner gives feedback to him or herself, in answer to questions from the coach such as, *What did you notice? Where was your attention? What was going on in your head at that point?* We run a simple version of this technique on one of our courses where we ask people to throw a ball into a wastepaper basket as a way of showing the power of self-given feedback. The coach is assumed to know nothing about techniques of ball-throwing and is explicitly forbidden from offering advice even if they do have such expertise. The goal is to land the ball accurately every time, steadily increasing the distances between the thrower and the basket. The coach can essentially only ask questions such as, 'What was going on for you when you made that throw?' Or, 'What worked/didn't work then?' 'Where was your attention going?' 'What are the key elements that you need to manage here?' The answers will typically be:

> I was holding my breath – not helpful!
> Rocking on one foot gave me more momentum.

> Looking at the target really works.
> The key elements are how you stand, what's going on mentally, concentration, relaxation and eye movements.
> Expecting success – visualizing the ball going into the bin.
> Keeping my forearm loose but my upper arm a little stiffer.

Gallwey has taught tennis to people from scratch, using only this approach. It is powerful. On our courses, virtually everyone coached in this way can improve their performance dramatically within about ten minutes. In fact I am sure that this approach will work equally well with children. My 5-year-old granddaughter was able to throw with deadly accuracy after only five minutes of my coaching, to the amazement of her 9-year-old brother who truly believed that females were biologically incapable of throwing anything properly. For more on coaching, see Chapter 8.

The differences between feedback and criticism

I have found it useful over the years to distinguish feedback from criticism. This is not just a semantic difference. There is a great deal of difference in both technique and impact on others. A friend and I went to a salsa class run by a teacher who was himself a gifted performer and who also enjoyed his own high-camp act. During one of our classes, my friend was finding it difficult to learn one of the moves. He danced with her several times, watched by the rest of the class, showing her over and over again how to do it, becoming more and more frustrated by her apparent inability to learn while she became increasingly embarrassed at the unwelcome attention. Eventually he said in exasperation, 'Well, darling, you've certainly left your dancing shoes at home tonight!' He clearly could not see that what he was conveying was his own annoyance but at the cost of humiliating his student. As a tactic for improving her performance it was totally counter-productive. At a big yoga class, I overheard the following comment from the teacher to one of his students: 'You totally lack suppleness – you are hopeless!' That student left at the break having, I hope, told her teacher why. A different kind of comment, genuine feedback, will have a different impact – for instance, saying, 'You're locking your elbows and knees. That's making it difficult for your body to be as supple as it could be. Let the knees and elbows relax and you'll find that you can do it fine'.

Being on the receiving end of criticism is devastating. Over the years I have collected comment on what it has felt like. It's always the same, regardless of people's experience or seniority:

> It reduced me to tears.
> I hoped other people couldn't hear – it was so humiliating.

I reverted to feeling like a toddler being reproved by a parent.
Anger – it was so inappropriate – who did he think he was!

Table 3.1 lists the differences between feedback and criticism. As a tutor all your comments should be the sort in the left-hand column. It is often useful to teach this distinction to groups of learners. Much of the teaching and training I now do involves making sure that I am not the only person in the room with the licence and duty to give feedback. When your subject involves changes in behaviour it is excellent learning for everyone in the group to be able to give feedback. The more this task can be shared with others, the more feedback learners will get. Actually, it is a life skill, useful everywhere – as a consumer, as a parent, as a friend, as a partner.

Table 3.1 Differences between feedback and criticism

Feedback	*Criticism*
Designed to improve performance positively, focused on the needs of the feedback-receiver	A way of unloading anger and disappointment, focused on the needs of the giver. Driven by the need to punish
Calm	Angry, sarcastic, tart, dismissive, emotional
Concentrates on the positive wherever possible, certainly at first	Looks for the negatives, ignores or undervalues the positive
Tough on the performance	Tough on the person
Specific	Vague, generalized, uses words like 'you always' or 'you never'
Descriptive, focuses on facts	Evaluative, focuses on negative opinions
Owns your own opinion, uses 'I'	Attributes opinion to others: people say ... everyone thinks that you...
Asks open questions	Makes pronouncements
Focuses on the future; makes suggestions about positive alternatives	Looks backwards
Two-way – solicits the learner's opinions	One-way

I once had the opportunity to compare two tutors teaching rather similar courses at the BBC, and to see these different styles in action. The first tutor, Peter, had on paper a textbook-correct course. He was teaching us film direction. The objectives were clear, the curriculum looked interesting and perfectly paced. Humphrey's course on studio direction looked, and was, hectic, competitive and crammed with too many exercises in too short a time.

Yet students ended Peter's course rebellious, unhappy and disappointed by the small amount achieved. There were even rumours of fisticuffs. Humphrey's students, by contrast, gave him an end-of-course champagne party and forgave him the torture he had caused us by piling on work and stress. Why was this? The answer seems clear. Peter's course, for all its apparent perfection, was marred by his biting, sarcastic comments on our work, by his inability to remember our names or departments. Humphrey's comments on the other hand, though often severe, were never hurtful. He would recall our improvement from previous exercises, showed he never forgot our backgrounds, would offer generous praise for achievement, looked us in the eye, smiled, nodded encouragement and cheered our little successes. Even now, many years later, I still think of him warmly and feel grateful for the rigorous technical standards I acquired, thanks to him.

One aspect of Humphrey's technique holds good for any tutor: always offer some praise and offer it before the negative comments. However poor the performance, there must be some aspect which is praiseworthy:

> Our ceramics teacher was wonderful. He used to call us together two or three times in the course of the class and say, 'Look everyone, we all *must* see so-and-so's pot – it's so terrific – see the subtle glaze (or the slip, or the way the handle was put on). Isn't it *wonderful*! Just a teeny problem with the shape here – that's because of problems with X or Y – but *very* exciting!' I thought this was very clever. So-and-so glowed at the attention, learnt from mistakes, high standards were established, and a terrifically companionable atmosphere emerged. Somehow, by lucky chance, everyone's work achieved this spotlight over the course of the term!

Where a group combines commitment to high standards with a friendly, non-competitive atmosphere, another benefit emerges: people will begin to offer constructive and useful feedback to each other because they are following the example set by the tutor. It may even be possible to arrange exercises where they specifically do so by working in pairs and offering feedback to each other.

Although publicly given feedback can be useful with a secure and friendly group, in general it is safer, certainly at first, to give feedback privately. Comments on essays should be written for that learner's eyes only; thoughts on how to improve a skill are best delivered one-to-one and without eavesdroppers.

A vital part of any feedback session is agreeing what needs to be done to build on success and to correct any mistakes. This should be entirely a two-way process. Make any suggestions you have, then ask the learner what he or she suggests. Your own suggestions may strike the learner as too demanding and difficult, or sometimes not demanding enough. This could be an ultra-brief process or protracted, depending on the circumstances. As a learner in my large and busy dance class, I would be astonished and pleased to have more than a few seconds of my teacher's time. When I was qualifying to administer psychometric tests I expected, and got, ten-minutes' worth of comment and discussion whenever I fell into a difficulty.

Another way of achieving the same end would be to arrange a brief meeting to agree a couple of action points which would include further practice in areas of weakness.

The point of techniques like this is to make sure that the feedback has been heard and understood, and will be acted on in the future. It is easy to forget that what you think is crystal clear may not always be understood by the learner:

> I went to a residential weekend on photography. The setting was beautiful, the food excellent, the other students fun, but I didn't learn much. It was most frustrating. The tutor was eager to give me comments on my efforts, but he was in another sphere with digital jargon that I couldn't understand – it was all just a muddle in my mind. He would end by saying 'OK? Is that clear?' I'd just nod – I couldn't bear to say that it wasn't clear at all – I'd have felt even more of a fool. Then at the next session of course he'd look exasperated because I'd made the same mistake again and would say 'But I explained all this to you before!'

In checking for understanding, avoid closed questions which invite the answer 'yes' or 'no' – for instance 'Have you understood?' or 'Is that all right?' Closed questions do nothing to test whether the learner has really absorbed the feedback you have given. Look instead for questions beginning 'Tell me', 'How?' or 'What?'

Feedback from a distance

Learning at a distance has been around for a long time. Correspondence colleges have existed for well over a century and the Open University took the whole concept a stride forward when old methods of delivery were linked with television and radio. Now a plethora of electronic methods of delivery has been added (see also page 234). Whether you are an online coach, a tele-class facilitator or a traditional essay-marker, the one factor that will unite you is that you are not face to face with your learners at the point of giving the feedback.

All the usual rules of feedback apply, but there are also some special considerations. Face to face, tough feedback can be softened and made acceptable by the way it is delivered. The tone will indicate that the professional comment is meant to stand, but the smile, the gesture, the stance – will convey that no personal hurt is intended. The identical comment written baldly down on an essay could have a very different impact – indeed it could take an unusually tough and confident student to remain unscathed by it. A too-harsh written comment is at worst withering for the recipient, at best infuriatingly ambiguous. Face to face, at least there is opportunity to challenge a judgement on the spot; this is much more difficult at a distance.

The extremes are easily avoided. Few tutors would need to be told that it is inexcusably arrogant, not to say vituperative, to write, 'You are suffering from intellectual paralysis', as indignantly reported by one learner. Nor would many fall into the opposite trap of the university tutor who said ruefully of her own performance:

> I am so terrified of apparently giving insults that I hardly dare write anything critical. My marks are always too high until exams loom up – then I panic. I know it's not fair but I'm afraid of hurting my students by 'honest' criticism.

The true difference between teaching at a distance and teaching face to face is that much of the feedback has to be given in writing and every word must be weighed because that is what will happen to it when it is received by your learners.

It is particularly important to give reasons for your comments. These should be full and unambiguous. There is no place for the inscrutable ticks, mysterious interrogatives and baffling exclamation marks which may appear on a piece of work whose author the tutor will see in the classroom. Allusive comments are also unhelpful. Face to face, you can explain what you meant by the enigmatic words 'Jane Austen!' or 'See psycho-synthesis!' in the margin. Don't leave your learner guessing when you are limited to written words.

Offer feedback within a few days: the effort will be fresher in the learner's mind and your comments will therefore have more impact. Praise the positive, as you would when face to face, and be restrained about negative comments. A text, whether an email attachment or a traditional essay, which comes back disfigured by a rash of negative markings is horribly discouraging. When people's work is persistently full of mistakes, this always calls for investigation. Perhaps they have short-term special difficulties; perhaps they need intensive remedial teaching; perhaps they should not be on the course at all.

As with all good teaching, you must show that you understand and identify with the learner's point of view. A tutor who with strident triumph writes, *No! No! No!* on a learner's work shows insensitivity as well as bad manners. Adult learners are both easily put down by such comment and also inclined after an interval to reassert their own values and self-confidence: in other words, no learning can take place from such a negative exchange.

More subtly than this, you need to write comments which deliberately acknowledge that you have absorbed what the learner was trying to achieve. For instance, 'I see that you have thoroughly read X's book and I agree with your comments on his general theories. However, when you come to Z I think you should reread his section on Y where you may come to the conclusion that . . . Most authorities feel that . . .' A tone like this, which perhaps seems at first contrived and tentative, nevertheless allows the student to retain his or her self-esteem, flatters by showing that the tutor has taken him or her seriously and yet still allows space to reconsider the original judgement.

Be prepared to look underneath specific difficulties for underlying problems. Spotting symptoms is easy; knowing the cause is far more demanding. Students who naively paste in whole paragraphs from the internet without acknowledgement may not be unintelligent, devious or foolish. They may just be ignorant of the academic conventions of quotation. Similarly, people who have clearly only consulted one out of several suggested sources for an assignment may not be either lazy or stupid. They may simply not know how to fillet a source quickly.

Summary: how to do it

In summary, here are eight essential steps in giving feedback, whatever the setting or the means of delivery. If you follow these you will find that you will unlock potential in your learners faster than maybe either you or they believe is possible:

1. Ask permission. Say, 'May I offer you some feedback?' I have never yet had a learner refuse this request. Note that it is a closed question which expects the answer, *Yes*.
2. Describe what you noticed. Be specific. Stick to the facts. Useful phrases here are:
   I noticed that when you . . .
   When I read your phrase . . .
   When you got to point x in your explanation . . .
   About ten minutes in, what I heard was . . .
   What's happening here is that I saw . . .
3. Ask what the learner would like to have clarified.
4. Describe the impact on you or on the situation:
   The impact on me was that I felt . . .
   I got lost at the point where you . . .

What I noticed was that the rest of the group...
The effect seemed to be...

5 Start with the positive; whenever possible put more emphasis on that than on the negative.
6 Ask for the learner's view:
That's how it seemed to me, but what was going on for you?
How did it seem to you?
What's your own feeling here?
7 Agree next steps as a two-way conversation:
How would you like to proceed?
What would be a good next step for you?
Would you like another go?
What help do you need from me now?
8 Repeat the whole cycle frequently.

The power of asking for feedback

The feedback we ask for is many times more powerful than feedback that is given unsolicited. This is because when you ask for feedback you feel in control: you initiate the process and you can ask for clarification if there is something in the feedback that you do not understand. Whenever you can, teach your learners how to do this, showing them both how to give and how to receive feedback and build such episodes into the design of your event so that participants are constantly giving and receiving feedback as an everyday event. The best way to do this is to model it yourself. Ask constantly for feedback both formally while the whole group is together and informally in breaks and between sessions. Stress the personal nature of the question: you are asking for that one person's view at that point in the proceedings. Its status is informal – it does not have, nor should it, the mighty weight and responsibility of Counsel's Opinion. Useful questions are:

> I'm really interested in your feedback on how this is going for you...
> Could you give me some impressions?
> What's working for you so far?
> What's not working so well?
> What would you like to see emphasized?
> What would need to happen for this to be even more successful for you?

Giving feedback is a rare skill and much of the time what is offered is clumsy criticism. Nonetheless, inside the criticism there will be some useful learning. Follow this protocol yourself and teach it to your groups. You will notice that it is an exact mirror of the similar steps in giving feedback.

Useful steps in receiving feedback

1. Ask. When people are reluctant, stress its importance for your own learning and professionalism.
2. Stay non-defensive. Nod, smile, keep steady eye contact, stay calm. Avoid any self-justifying or explaining. You are just listening to the other person's view at this stage. You want them to go on talking and the surest way to shut them up is to start defending yourself. Similarly, do not start guiltily joining in and condemning yourself, if what you are hearing is negative. Nor is it appropriate to simper and dismiss apparent compliments. At this stage all you are hearing is the headlines.
3. Summarize the person's points to show how accurately you are listening and to make sure that you have heard it correctly.
4. Ask for clarification. When offered a generalization, ask for specifics: *Can you give me an example?*
5. Ask for the impact on the person or the situation as that person saw it.
6. Ask what they would like to have been different, if anything.
7. Offer your own view of what happened – but keep it brief.
8. Agree how you want to take it forward even if this is just to consider it along with all the other feedback you have received.
9. Repeat frequently.

As with all feedback, remember the truth of the saying that *feedback is not an instruction to change*. It will need to go in the pot along with everything else. But where you hear the same themes offered independently, ignore them at your peril.

Finally, be generous with the overall amount of feedback you offer. Most tutors, in common with most managers, grossly overestimate the quantity of feedback they give. To avoid misunderstandings of this sort, the guiding principle is that in every session you should find as many opportunities as possible for every learner to receive some feedback. This may simply be through a self-check list in a book, a how-did-you-get-on conversation with a partner, a private or public brief discussion on performance, written comments on an assignment, an action plan for further training or a semi-formal session on general progress.

In giving feedback to learners your own skill as a tutor is severely tested. The possibilities for misunderstanding are endless, the risk of being too direct or seeming personal ever-present, the temptation to say nothing, or to say too much, ever-looming. But without feedback, your learners cannot learn and as a tutor you cannot be said to be teaching.

Further reading

Gallwey, W.T. (2000) *The Inner Game of Work*. London: Orion Business.
Jackman, J. and Strober, M. (2003) Fear of feedback, *Harvard Business Review*, April.
Sherman, S. and Freas, A. (2004) The Wild West of executive coaching, *Harvard Business Review*, November.

Notes

1 Bartlett, F.C. (1947) The measurement of human skill, *British Medical Journal*, 1.
2 Gallwey, W.T. (1997) *The Inner Game of Tennis*. New York: Random House.
3 See Further Reading, above.

4 Understanding your group

I have written this chapter as an introduction to the ideas that I have found helpful myself because of their direct relevance to what goes on in an adult class or training room. I make no claims to comprehensiveness. It's an eclectic mix of theories, but all of them are classics that have stood the test of time. Most people teaching adults will do so in a group setting. Without at least some frameworks for understanding group behaviour, you might well be at best surprised, and at worst feel deskilled, when you encounter some of the phenomena I describe here. For specific practical ideas on how to manage some of the resulting behaviour in groups, you may want to consult Chapter 5, even if you do not consider yourself to be a facilitator as such.

Groups are powerful

Human beings are herd animals. We cannot truly live alone unless in exceptional circumstances. Although our superior consciousness and intelligence gives us the power to discriminate and weigh up our decisions, we are profoundly affected by the behaviour of the rest of the group, as are cattle, many birds, dogs and other species which mass together. When we are members of a group, our behaviour may well be significantly different from how we behave as individuals. We may go along with choices that we would not tolerate if we were making the same decision alone. We may take more risks. We may feel more vulnerable – or, alternatively, more protected. We may accomplish more than we ever could alone and feel grateful to the group who supported us through the transition – or we may feel shame that we were part of something we now regret. Group behaviour may be benign or malign in its influence, but it is rarely neutral. Few areas of social psychology have been as much studied as human behaviour in groups and yet to me there is still something mysterious and unpredictable about it when applied to any one group with whom I am working.

The Stanford Experiment

For startling light on the power of groups you only have to consider the legendary Stanford University Prison Experiment. It still has the power to shock. In 1971, nine young men who had volunteered for the chance to earn $15 a day as subjects in an experiment on prison life were 'arrested', blindfolded and taken to a makeshift 'prison', in reality a building on the Stanford campus. They were among 24 men out of 70 volunteers judged after a battery of psychological tests to be the most 'normal' and stable. The other 15 men became 'guards' with instructions to maintain control of the 'prison'. The experiment was designed and conducted by Philip Zimbardo, a professor of psychology interested in how apparently normal people could carry out abnormally cruel acts on other human beings, such as the terrible deeds of camp guards during the Holocaust. Within days, the 'guards' were behaving like real guards and had in effect dehumanized their 'captives', forcing them into harsh and degrading acts such as putting paper bags over their heads, encouraging them to betray fellow prisoners and making them clean out lavatory bowls with their bare hands. The experiment was stopped on the fifth day when Zimbardo's fiancée, Christina Maslach, appeared as a newcomer on the scene. As she explains, she was an outsider and was therefore able to see clearly what was happening in the name of science. Even so, she confesses to difficulty in persuading her academic colleagues – and Zimbardo himself, whom she later married – to stop the experiment on the grounds that it was clearly unethical. Here we see two parallel expressions of the power of the group. Both the experimental group of subjects and the group of academic psychologists who had devised the process were in the grip of group power.[1]

The experiment was repeated for a BBC television programme in 2001 and was halted after only two days as the same behaviours emerged. The behaviour of US troops in Abu Ghraib prison is only another and more recent example of the same shocking actions where one soldier led an Iraqi prisoner around on a dog leash and a group of Iraqi prisoners was photographed with utter contempt for their humanity and dignity in a naked pyramid. The soldiers present clearly saw nothing wrong at the time with what they were doing – they took photographs to celebrate it. In the Stanford experiment, the 'guards' begged the university team not to stop the experiment.

At the same time, it is obvious that so much positive human achievement has also been made possible through the power of the group. Acts of selfless courage, extraordinary feats of exploration, scientific discovery, glorious architecture, military victory, engineering feats – wherever you look, it is far rarer to find that the individual has accomplished his or her triumph alone than to realize that it was made possible through group effort.

The underlying reason for all of this, and it is so obvious that I hesitate to write it, is that our species has a profound fear of being separated from the herd. When homo sapiens emerged on the planet between 200,000 and 150,000 years ago, it was essential for survival to be part of a group and it still is. Since we have faced no significant evolutionary challenge since that time, the evolutionary psychologists – and I see no reason to disagree with them – claim that our brains are still hard-wired in the same way as they were in the Stone Age. In some respects you could say that with the exception of a death sentence, separation is the ultimate punishment for human beings. All torturers know this. To deprive a person of the company of others is often enough to send a prisoner over the edge of sanity. Solitary confinement is cruelty. It is why in descriptions of bullying there is invariably an account of the bullied individual being mocked, ignored and banished from the company and approval of peers. To look different, to hold a different opinion, to be *other*, is to invite exclusion – and exclusion is unbearable. Fear of it, and the negative fantasies we project when we believe it is possible, is what creates conformity in groups.

The road to Abilene

The mechanics of how all this happens has never been more clearly or more entertainingly described than by Jerry Harvey, an American academic and writer, an enthralling storyteller, both in person and on the page. His book, *The Abilene Paradox*,[2] describes another phenomenon to which you need to be alert. In the book, one of his essays (or, as he dubs them, *sermons* because really they are morality tales) is taken from his own family. On a hot, dusty day in Texas, there is a discussion about whether to drive the 50 miles to a restaurant in Abilene. Everyone agrees that they would like to go. The journey there and back is uncomfortable, the meal indifferent. Back at home, to be friendly, Harvey, as he confesses, 'dishonestly' comments that it was a good trip. One by one the family reveals that no one had really wanted to go. All had done so because they thought everyone else wanted to do it. The paradox is that everyone has done what no one really wanted, therefore wasting effort and achieving nothing. I recall a recent group of which I was a part where we spent a similarly disheartening day, energy gradually leaching out in desultory, synthetic discussion. Later, I discovered that we too had been on a trip to Abilene. Privately we had all felt that the discussion was wrong-footed and pointless, yet we had all taken part apparently willingly. Professor Harvey comments that it is not *disagreement* that needs to be managed in groups but *agreement*. If no one surfaces their discontent then a false consensus sustains the unproductive activity. It is all too easy for Abilene symptoms to wreck a learning group. Here is a simple example: as a tutor you assume that the group is inexperienced and will prefer to learn through a particular method. You don't really want to teach this way. Your students assume that you know best how to teach them. They don't really want to learn this way either but go along with you. The individuals in the group assume that in thinking this, they are alone whereas the truth is that everyone privately agrees that they would prefer something else. Result: a most unsatisfying experience all round.

Preventing trips to Abilene

- State your own assumptions about the course and its methods throughout.
- Ask for your learners' assumptions about what they expect; ask about how they want to learn.
- Ask what your learners feel about any differences that this conversation has exposed. By this I mean really ask. Don't just ask a closed question: *Is that all right?* (Expecting the answer, Yes). Ask, 'What do you all feel about this?' And then wait patiently for the answers.
- Observe, be super-alert, watch for the small behaviours that could indicate the beginning of disengagement.
- Gather feedback constantly (Chapter 3): build it into the course design.

The Asch and Milgram experiments

Another, even older, and also well known experiment was conducted by Solomon Asch in the 1950s and is also described in Harvey's book. A naive subject would invited to be part of a group allegedly part of a *vision experiment,* to discuss which line on a card was identical to one of three lines on another card.

Unknown to the subject, the other members of the group had been briefed to give the wrong answer. A third of the subjects agreed with this obviously incorrect response despite what their eyes were clearly telling them. Jerry Harvey's comment is that there was actually no overt pressure at all to conform. Instead, the third of the subjects who agreed with others in the group were simply demonstrating their fear of being separated from the herd. This is the same theme that Hans Christian Andersen explores in his fable *The Emperor's New Clothes,* where it took a small child to blurt out what everyone's eyes were telling them but which all were collectively denying. It is also why whistleblowers have a hard time.

As a teacher of adults you need to understand and harness the power of the group and this begins with understanding your own power. The Stanford experiment, and others like it, show the importance of leadership in groups. Those apparently nice, well-brought-up young men of the experiment all behaved as they did because someone in authority had told them that it was all right.

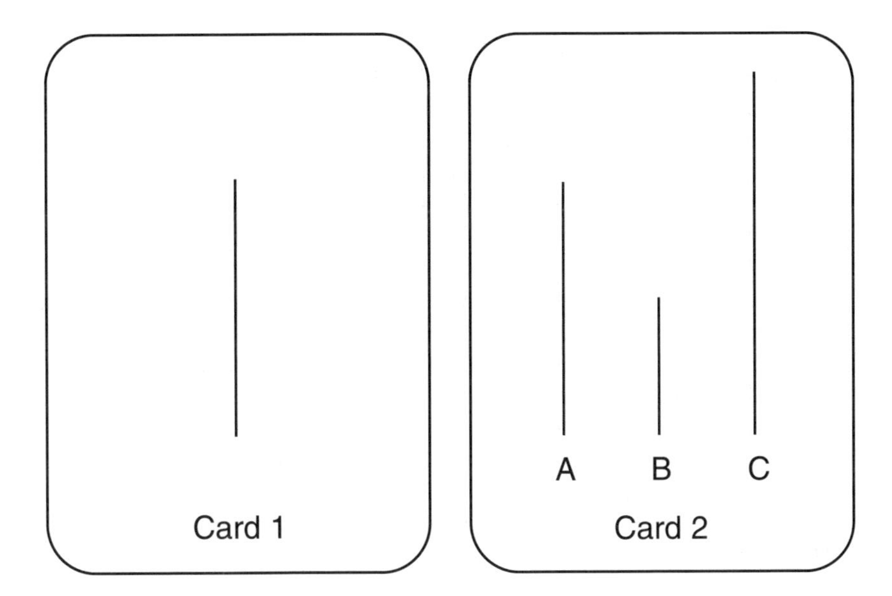

Figure 4.1 The Asch experiment

The same was true of an even more startling and equally well-known experiment run by Stanley Milgram[3] in 1965 where more than two thirds of a group of research subjects administered what they believed, wrongly, were severely dangerous electric shocks to another human being because an apparently authoritative person in a white coat had told them that it was permissible. As with Zimbardo's work, many of the subjects were deeply distressed afterwards when they realized how appallingly they had behaved. Some of the subjects in Asch's experiment tended to blame their eyesight rather than to accept that they had been manipulated by the desire to conform.

Please don't think for a moment that none of this applies to you because you are, of course, not running an experiment to explore the darker sides of human nature. If you are working with a group as its tutor then you have the responsibility to lead it. Harvey's, Zimbardo's and Milgram's work shows how much we need and how readily we respond to leadership. Asch's experiment shows how important it is to protect the unpopular minority view and to prevent collusion and premature convergence of opinion. As a tutor you are in a leadership role and potentially have power. The only question is how you choose to exercise it.

Your leadership style: the work of Kurt Lewin

Time and time again, other research work has shown how critical the style of leadership is to the success or failure of any venture, including learning.

In one of the most often quoted field studies of a type initiated by Kurt Lewin and his followers in the 1930s, the behaviour of three different types of leader was observed. A group of 10-year-old boys in youth clubs was in turn placed under three different types of leadership: 'authoritarian', where the leader was stern, bossy, encouraged competitiveness, punished those who misbehaved and made all the important decisions; 'laissez-faire', where they did virtually nothing – for instance, remained withdrawn from the boys unless directly asked a question; and 'democratic', where the children themselves decided what they would do, and regarded the leader as someone who could effect individual solutions to problems. All three leaders set the groups various handicraft tasks. In the authoritarian groups the boys were submissive and well behaved on the surface while the leader was present, but showed signs even then of submerged aggression, often 'mishearing' instructions or 'accidentally' damaging materials. Among themselves they were competitive and mutually disparaging. When the leader left the room they tended to abandon work instantly and to run about noisily. The laissez-faire groups did almost no work whether or not the leader was present. Under democratic leadership the boys worked well together without fear of one outdoing the other. There was little tension or aggression in the atmosphere, and, unlike the boys from the authoritarian group, some of whom broke up their models at the end of the course, all the work was regarded as 'ours' and treasured accordingly. The temporary absence of the leader made no difference to the amount of work the boys did. The genius of Lewin's work was to demonstrate convincingly that differences in group climate were not the result of individual differences – for instance in temperament or intelligence, but were the result of differences in leadership style.[4]

This work was later repeated with groups of MBA students at Harvard by George Litwin and Robert Stringer with similar results.[5] When I describe The Climate Lab (page 202) I am describing a modern version of the same study. It has demonstrated without any doubt that leadership affects climate, climate affects motivation and motivation affects performance. When the only variable is leadership, there are profound differences in the performance of the group. They apply as closely to how a tutor of adults runs a learning event as to how a manager runs a factory or to how a football coach runs a team. There are few clear and proven cause and effect relationships in human groups, but this is one of them:

Leadership
↓
Climate
↓
Motivation
↓
Performance

Your task as a tutor is to create the most effective climate for learning, and it starts with the leadership style you adopt. Here are some examples of how it can play out, all three of them descriptions from students in higher education:

> *The authoritarian style: a mathematics tutor*
> I know we were just kids as far as he was concerned, only 20-year-olds, but did he have to treat us as if we were in the kindergarten? He would sweep into the lecture room, wait for a moment to make sure we were all looking at him, giving us a glare if he felt this wasn't so, reproach anyone who fidgeted, hardly ever invited questions and if you did dare to ask, you would get a brusque answer. He never looked at anyone directly, just stared around somewhere at a space just above our heads. Of course what happened was that under cover of apparently scribbling down our notes assiduously, we actually devised all sorts of games – for instance, maths bingo, where the game was who could first get *house!* for the number of times he said various of his favourite catch phrases. Or another was to take it in turns to see who could ask the most obscure question with a further game about how long the answer would be. Naturally attendance went down to a tiny number, but for those of us who stayed, it was an exercise in subversion. The awful thing was, I'm quite sure he was entirely unaware of what was really happening.
> *Characteristics of the authoritarian style: taking all the responsibility for outcomes, standards, procedures; punishing disagreement – for instance with sarcastic comments; refusing to consult or share power; downplaying relationships; making no personal contact with members of the group; insisting that it's your way or no way.*

> *The laissez-faire style: tutor on a teacher training course*
> The subject was Psychology of Early Childhood, and I believe our tutor was actually extremely knowledgeable, but she wanted to be loved more than she wanted to lead us. She hesitated to insist on anything. She really wanted us to take control of the whole thing, so all the time it was, *What do you want to do here? Is this all right?* She

hated any conflict. I was vague throughout about what the true aims of the course were. If we failed to show at the seminars, we were never asked why. She looked anxious the whole time. It was as if there was a black hole at the centre of the whole thing, it felt shapeless. The real leadership was in the hands of the most dominant member of the group, a mature student who actually ended up making most of the decisions about essay subjects and deadlines – even about our project work, but that drew protests from the rest of us and dragged our energy into fighting him rather than into the work. It was a most unsatisfactory experience.
Characteristics of the laissez-faire style: constantly seeking unrealistic consensus; refusing to insist; standing back; putting emphasis on positive relationships at the expense of achieving goals; hating running the risk of being disliked; avoiding conflict; feeling safer as a member of the group than as its leader.

The democratic style: tutor on a humanities course
This was the most outstanding person I met while at university. He was extremely clear what our goals were and kept emphasizing them – and this was more than just ensuring that we got the best grades we were capable of, though that was obviously important, too. For him it was about deepening our learning of his topic. He wanted us to know what he knew – and more. He kept saying that he expected us to outstrip him and that nothing gave him greater pleasure than to read an essay where a student had pleasantly surprised and stimulated his own thinking. His marking was transparent and fair – there was no quarter given if you were wrong or plagiarized someone else's work and there was constant recognition for getting things right. We had feedback all the time. He respected us as individuals yet there was no overt competition – if anything we competed against ourselves and helped each other. You felt stretched, yet it all felt achievable. I have never participated in anything before or since where there was such a creative buzz. It was rare for anyone to miss a seminar and altogether it was a privilege to have been taught by him. I got my best grade in his subject.
Characteristics of the democratic style: emphasizing goals; setting standards; encouraging creativity and individual responsibility; giving individual feedback especially the positive sort; encouraging productive relationships both between members of the group and yourself; defusing conflict through mediation; consulting; delegating appropriately.

Of course we would all prefer to be taught by the third of these tutors. Although authoritarian leaders can produce short-term results, the energy, as in the account above, ultimately goes into the negative process of protesting or subverting. In the group led by a laissez-faire leader who wants everyone to be happy and confuses being liked with being a leader, the group experiences dismay at the lack of leadership and energy goes into finding an unofficial substitute leader. Energy in the democratically led group is channelled into whole-group and individual achievement by pointing the group towards shared goals and aligning people to those goals through involvement. The striking truth is that what Lewin described as the democratic style is also highly correlated with superior performance.

Creating the climate for learning

In an interesting study[6] which applied the Litwin and Stringer concepts to primary and secondary school classrooms, Charles Bethel-Fox and Fionnuala O'Conor define a learning climate like this:

> The collective perceptions by students of what it feels like, in intellective, motivational and emotive terms, to be a student in any particular teacher's classroom, where these perceptions influence every student's motivation to learn and perform to the best of his or her ability.

As with every other study of this sort, there was a clear correlation between the climate created by the teacher, the closeness of this to the climate the students wanted and the performance of the students. It is unsurprising to me that what has been proven many times over to be correlated with the success of teams in organizations is also true of the learning climate created by teachers in schools. The same dynamic is at work. As Bethel-Fox and O'Conor say, 'Climate ... is a significant predictor of academic performance. Better teaching practices are found in classes with higher levels of climate'. This study worked from nine different climate dimensions, but for simplicity, I prefer the dimensions of the original work. What then, as a tutor of adults, should you consider in thinking about how to apply this to your everyday management of learning with groups? Table 4.1 shows the five key dimensions. How far would your students say that this is what you create?

Within these general guidelines on creating an appropriate climate, there will be more than one way of leading your group and this will depend on its maturity, the nature of the task and your own preferences.

My own framework shown as Table 4.2 is one that I put forward in my book *Facilitating Groups*.[7] I adapted it from a famous article[8] written in 1958 by Tannenbaum and Schmidt on leadership styles. Since facilitation is only another variant on leadership, it seems a useful way of looking at the process.

Table 4.1

Climate dimension	*Tutor behaviour*
Clarity	Constantly emphasizing the end goals of the learning. Making these goals seem attractive. Inspiring people by describing how learners will benefit from their achievements; being clear about the boundaries – of behaviour, of the subject, of the goals.
Standards	Creating consistently high standards – for instance being clear about what constitutes excellence, clarifying what is expected in order to satisfy an examiner; modelling excellence in your own thinking and behaviour; communicating the difference between an allowable individual interpretation and a mistake.
Recognition	Giving constant positive feedback when people do good work; spending time with individuals so that they have an unambiguous idea of where they are on their own learning journeys; correcting errors tactfully, swiftly and in a way that people can hear. Showing warmth and respect for individuality.
Responsibility	Creating the situation where everyone knows that they are responsible for their own learning; encouraging individual initiative and discouraging dependency on the tutor; asking for feedback from learners; encouraging creativity, measured risk and exploration; putting emphasis on learning how to learn as much as possible on the subject.
Teamwork	Creating an inclusive, open, trusting and cooperative learning environment where people can own up to difficulties without fear of being judged, support each other and are proud to be part of the group.

Table 4.2 charts the variation in the amount of power held by the tutor and by the group. As you move to the right of the table, the tutor's authority diminishes and the group's authority increases. There is no implication that all groups could or should move from the left to the right hand side. It all depends: on the circumstances, the aims, the composition of the group and the skill of the tutor. It also depends on where the group is in the typical life cycle of any human group.

Table 4.2

	Telling	*Consulting*	*Involving*	*Stepping out*
Tutor style	In charge of task and process Chooses venue, agenda, design of exercises and discussion Prescribes Gives information Manages the time Interprets the events and feelings of the group for the group Raises group's awareness of what is going on	Consults group on its needs Facilitates reconsideration of agenda Emphasizes consideration of group's needs May share leadership with some of the group	Group chooses how it will use tutor skills Group may rotate leadership, decide to change agenda, timings Tutor still likely to feel responsible for group process	Group manages itself Facilitator becomes a resource to the group Tutor may leave group entirely responsible for its own task and process
Dominant state of group	Dependency within a framework of positive regard for all members	Submitting to benevolent government	Interdependence	Independence
Pluses	Group feels safe Often right for early sessions May be very task-focused Tutors often like it because they are experts-in-charge	Gives group practice at taking responsibility within safe framework; good compromise between extremes	High performance; fun; purposeful atmosphere	Group cannot rebel as there is no authority figure; clear that group is responsible for own actions and learning
Minuses	Group does not take responsibility for own learning; may rebel; may feel childlike	Gloss of involvement is only skin deep; may be clear that tutor does not trust group to be adults; learning may be limited	Tutors may miss the buzz of being in charge; groups can get worried by their own freedom Minimal involvement by tutor may look like laissez-faire abandonment It takes time to get to this point and the group may not have this time	Responsibility may be too much too soon. Group may fall apart without leadership. Ambiguity may be too much for some members Control issues may surface and waste group's time

The group life cycle

> It was chaotic. Rival factions from different departments, standing up making speeches denouncing the others ... people sulking, threatening to leave – awful!
>
> I could have stood on my head at the beginning in that group for all the reaction I'd have got. I felt like coming in with a false moustache or a clown's nose to see if it would even have surprised them.

A group has its own life and behaves in its own way and this is different from the way the individuals inside it will behave. Being prepared for some of the problems is essential if you are to be its leader.

There are several useful theories which can help you understand that how groups behave can form a number of recognizable patterns. A classic of this sort was described in a well-known paper in the 1970s. Tuckman[9] and Jensen described a typical cycle of group life. Their theory is recognizably similar to the explanation suggested by the psychometrician, Will Schutz, the developer of the FIRO-B questionnaire.[10]

1 Forming

At the *forming* stage, the group is still uncertain. People are polite – there is a false consensus, a pretence that everything is all right. Members are wary of one another. Conversation remains at the level of what one of my colleagues calls 'ritual sniffing': 'What's your name?' 'What's your job?' 'Where are you from?' 'Did you have to travel far to get here?' In a learning group, people will look to you to provide a sense of safety. Politeness and a sense of distance will be the prevailing feeling. There are no cliques but also there is no sense of belonging. People are still figuring out whether or not they want to be in or out of the group. The most important question in the minds of individual learners is 'Do I belong here?' This stage is similar to the one Will Schutz describes as the '*inclusion*' stage.

Symptoms of forming-stage problems will include: unexplained absences; people arriving late and leaving early; an over-sober atmosphere; lack of genuine participation.

Useful tactics at the forming stage: being clear before the first meeting through joining instructions about what membership of the group involves; being overtly welcoming yourself; using ice-breakers (page 53); discussing a group contract (page 115); accepting that there is a limit to how far you can push against this process. Depending on funding and also on the time available, it can also be useful to hold some kind of preliminary social event. Hold your nerve: the inclusion stage will pass if you are giving the right leadership. Overt leadership from you is the name of the game at this early stage.

2 Storming

As the group's business progresses, it will reach the *storming* stage. This is the stage that Will Schutz calls *control*. The pseudo-consensus has broken down as people begin to realize that they don't all share the same assumptions and beliefs. People become bolder.

Symptoms of storming-stage difficulties will include: conflicts emerging, either between individuals in the group or between the group and its leader/ tutor. At this stage the preoccupation – of group and tutor – is, 'Who's really in charge here?' You can expect challenges to your leadership, even if they are the reticent ones of 'Excuse me, but I've done this before' or, 'I'm finding this harder than I thought'. Interpersonal conflicts may also break out between individuals or groups within the group. There may be fierce discussions about rules and rule-breakers – for instance, people who do not return promptly after breaks or who do not deliver on work between sessions. There may be objections about people who allegedly talk too much. The issue at stake is who makes the decisions and how such decisions are made. If people object, they are more likely to express their dissent at this stage than at the apparent calm of the forming or inclusion stage.

Handling storming-stage conflicts: It is a mistake to ignore the conflicts. If you do, they will return to haunt you later. Sometimes there will be direct onslaughts on your authority and you need to deal openly and confidently with these, too:

> I was teaching the techniques of job-searching to a group of long-term unemployed adults. This was tricky anyway because we are an area of very high unemployment. On the second day, the whole thing nearly collapsed. Mutterings about 'It's all very well for him – he's got a job' turned into openly hostile verbal attacks by one half of the group, while the other half sprang to my defence – 'Give him a chance – anything's worth a try'. I calmed the whole thing down with great difficulty and suggested that we started again. The ones who were angry were given a lot of time to say what it was about me that had caused such attacks and the rest were given their say, too. I retrieved it by the skin of my teeth – but it was a crisis, no doubt about that.

Other useful tactics to deal with the storming stage include: asking how many others share the concerns of whoever has raised the challenging question; having a break to take the immediate steam out of things; teaching the group listening skills and insisting that they are practised. At this stage, expect to take the role of mediator in obliging different factions to hear what each has to say. Restate the learning goals for the group. Remind them of why they joined it in the first place. Reassure them that some conflict is normal and healthy. Show them that expressing conflict does not mean terminal collapse. By staying calm yourself you will show the group that the storm will pass. There is more on all of this in the chapter on facilitating (page 107).

3 Norming

At the *norming* stage the group has settled down. A pecking order has been established, people know each other better, they have accepted the rules and probably developed little subgroups and friendship pairs. In a short course – say, of a day's duration – all these stages can be passed through with great rapidity:

> First session – quiet and cautious. Second session – glances of irritation exchanged at 'things people say'. Coffee break. Third session – the break in the clouds... they've talked during coffee and have discovered that other people are not so awful after all. Fourth session – purposeful: emergence of jokes, sense of where people are going. End of day – people are exchanging addresses and phone numbers!

Building on the momentum of the norming stage: Ask the group constantly for feedback on how they are finding the pace and be prepared to adjust it in the light of what they say; accelerate the amount of self-managed learning that people are undertaking; flex the structure of the group so that there is a constant mix of varying-size small group work and whole group interchange. You can begin the process of handing authority to the group at this point.

4 Performing

At the *performing* stage the group glides into action. It reaches its objectives. People know how to work together. Will Schutz calls this phase *affection,* characterizing it as a time when there is a high level of trust and rapport between the individuals in the group where the question is 'Am I liked and trusted here?' They will express interest in each other's personal lives and exchange information which it probably felt far too personal to disclose earlier. For people with a low need for expressing affection, it can seem as if it is all getting out of hand – they may complain that 'things have got too touchy-feely'. But generally speaking, this stage is characterized by a strong feeling of existing as a group with its own roles and rules. People may socialize outside the group. If you let them, they may well always sit in the same seats; they will enjoy group tasks and will carry group loyalty to great lengths. At this stage, the power of the group to support learning is considerable:

> I went to a two-day assertiveness course organized by my company. It was very well run, but the best thing about it was the amazing feeling that developed very quickly in the group. The other women were so terrific – for instance, if someone who had been really shy managed a more assertive role play, there would be spontaneous applause. People spoke warmly to each other about their efforts. I've rarely seen anything so inspiring... it made us all achieve feats that would have been impossible alone.

Your role at this stage is to ensure that the group has all the resources it needs: physical, psychological and intellectual. Model personal disclosure yourself, if it feels appropriate. Keep reminding them of the importance of teamwork. Be lavish with your positive feedback. A group does not reach the 'performing' stage by accident. It is the natural and positive way for groups to develop, but it happens because that is the way the tutor has nudged and pushed it. This sort of triumphant conclusion to a course is usually the result of a great deal of conscious effort and skill on the part of the tutor:

> Best of all, we had an end-of-session party to which we all contributed food and drink. Very enjoyable it was too! This was an unofficial meeting in our own time, but just before the end, R., who had spent most of the year making ribald jokes at my expense, presented me with an elaborately wrapped parcel containing an enormous box of chocolates and, on top, a beautifully written 'poem' dedicated to the group and listing in doggerel verse the various idiosyncrasies of the members – including one lady's habit of doing her revision in the lavatory! They insisted upon my declaiming this to them. It made a very suitable epilogue – with just the right touch of ironic banter – to what had been a very entertaining and I think mutually rewarding group.

Will Schutz's work adds a further gloss to the popular and readily understandable framework offered by Tuckman and Jensen. He suggests that groups can get stuck at one stage and that if the problems posed by each stage remain unresolved, the group will founder. Also, he points out that the group has to pass through the stages of inclusion, control and affection in that order – you cannot jump straight to affection.

He says that the process is dynamic, that is, never truly resolved because it is always open to change and external influences. So the arrival of a new person or departure of an existing member takes the group straight back to the Inclusion phase. For a simple comparison taken from family life, consider how the arrival of a new baby or a frail elderly parent alters the dynamics of what was previously a duo, trio or however many members the family

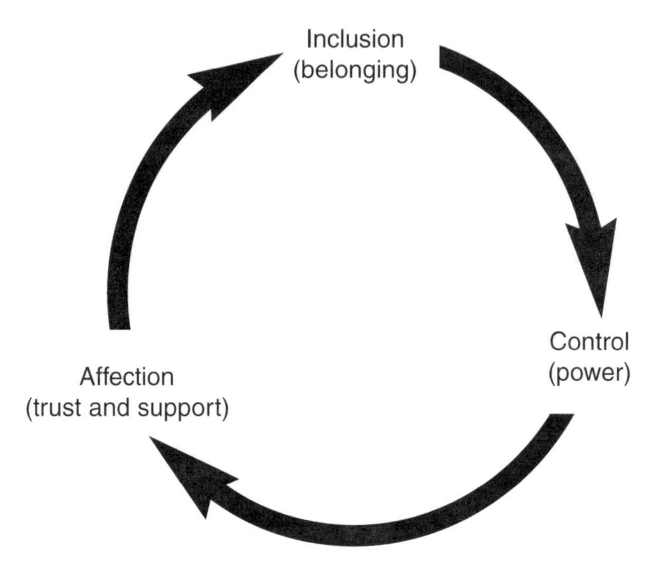

Figure 4.2 Will Shutz's Group life cycle

previously contained. Inclusion is immediately back on the agenda – who's in, who's out? Who now feels left out because of the new arrival? Which routines have to be altered? Whose needs have to take precedence? What does it now feel like to be part of that bigger group? How does it affect the comforting feelings of significance that the individuals in the group previously had? It is just the same in learning groups. This lecturer's shrewd and rueful observation sums it up well:

> We were on our eighth meeting when the Dean told me that there would be a new student joining us. This young man had switched courses. I was amazed at the impact this had on the group. Several people were openly resentful that he had disturbed our pattern – for instance that they were now a group of 16 instead of 15 and they 'hated' the fact that this made it 'impossible' for them to work in trios. Someone commented spitefully on his clothing – he was wearing well-polished formal shoes when everyone else was in sloppy old trainers and Birkenstock sandals. I had to point out that four groups of four could work just as effectively as five groups of three, but I just got hostile stares and was told that in each of the trios they had become friends and didn't want to change. I had to insist and it wasn't pleasant. If I had anticipated it, I could have emphasized that it was their duty to welcome him, might have appointed a volunteer buddy etc. etc., but I thought of all of this a lot too late.

5 Mourning/adjourning

A final stage is often added to this framework to include *mourning* or *adjourning*. This is the stage where the group faces the prospect of its own disappearance. Where a learning event has been intellectually gripping and emotionally stretching, we often feel reluctance to leave. The group has become safe, nurturing, a place where 'real life' has been successfully kept at bay, where maybe new discoveries have been made in the company of others making the same journey. It can feel horrible to contemplate the ending of the group. This is why so many people swap addresses, often knowing in their heart of hearts that they will not, as promised, keep in touch. It is always unlikely in the extreme that the group will ever reassemble exactly as it is at the final moments of a course, even where individuals do form lasting friendships.

What can you, as tutor, do about this? When your group has run well, the answer is probably nothing. The responsibility is for the whole group, not just for you. However, there are some simple ideas you may like to consider to ease the pain of separating. One is to offer a follow-up day where people can get together again to review their learning. Another is to have a closing ceremony of some kind. These are like ice-breakers in reverse. Little ceremonies that I like and have seen work well include:

> Getting people to stand up and form a circle. You then throw a soft object of some kind from person to person. The task is to say one sentence about the programme, which sums it up or which identifies the most important thing they will do differently as a result of attending. You continue until everyone has had a turn.
>
> On long programmes, have a gift ceremony. Everyone puts their names into a hat and each name is then picked out. You then buy a tiny present for the person whose name you have pulled out (strict cash limits apply) and give it to that person saying something about what they have contributed to the programme.
>
> Sit people in a circle and put a 'talking stick' on the floor in the middle (could be anything – a real stick, a flipchart pen, an object which has some symbolism for the group). Ask people to come forward one at a time, take the stick and say something about the meaning the event has had for them.

Relationships within the group

As well as patterns which can explain whole-group dynamics, you also need to think about relationships between individuals, including those between yourself and group members. Again, there are some useful theoretical ideas which can explain phenomena which would otherwise seem troubling.

Replaying family roles

Growing up in family groups gives all of us imprinted experience of what it is like to be part of a group. We learn roles there that we can be tempted to reproduce at any point when we are once again in groups. So our experiences of being children (less powerful) and how we coped with parents and teachers (more powerful) create patterns that can become permanent. So, for instance, if you were the petted youngest in a large family, you may easily fall into the role of indulged baby in a group. If you were the responsible first-born, you may find yourself always being the person who puts their hand up for extra responsibilities in a group. If you were the family clown and were rewarded for that with laughter and attention, then you may still be the person who relieves tense moments with a joke. If you were a middle child who found that it was enjoyable to lead an us-against-them revolt, children against parents, then you may be tempted to do the same in an adult group. As a tutor, your own attitudes to power and dependency will have been formed by experiences like this. Your own will be unique, of course, but ask yourself what connections there are for you between your feelings of confidence, or lack of it as a tutor, and your experience of growing up. I would be surprised if there were none.

Similarly, each member of your group will have their own patterns. These will appear in any learning group, though neither you nor they may know their origins. Where you see persistent patterns of behaviour in group members it is worth considering whether this kind of dynamic may be at work.

Meredith Belbin's team roles

When you are new to teaching adults, you may assume that because people have come together to share a learning experience, they must therefore be similar in temperament and style. Even worse, you may assume that they should somehow be similar. The work of Meredith Belbin[11] (see also pages 17 and 36 for his work on learning), a British occupational psychologist, shows how mistaken this is. In the 1970s Dr Belbin was working at Henley

Table 4.3

Role	*Characteristics*
Action-oriented roles	
Shapers	Challengers; motivated by wanting high performance, impatient and driven. Will want to get on with whatever the learning task is. Enrol Shapers as allies. They are influential and can set the pace for others. Shapers may be impatient of anything they see as soft or sentimental and a distraction from the serious business of learning. They may offend other learners through their brusqueness, particularly where they try to give feedback. Shaper feedback is more likely to come across as criticism of the person.
Implementers	Like to organize. Love efficiency and good at carrying plans through. May be a useful helper in chores such as contacting the group through emails between meetings. Will deliver course work on time and may offer help to you and others on how to get the best out of whatever resources are available. Implementers like routine. They may resist changes to the curriculum and methods.
Completer-Finishers	The perfectionists who love detail. May correct your flip chart spelling or point out inconsistencies in your handouts. Will present their own work immaculately. May annoy others through reluctance to share tasks or through appearing pedantic and being unable to see the bigger picture.
People-oriented roles	
Coordinators	Calm, self-possessed, orderly approach reassures the group. These are the people who will listen to others and may bring you early summaries of how the rest of the group is feeling as well as wanting to progress the group's goals. You want them on your side because you don't want an alternative leader to emerge too soon, if ever. Often opinion leaders. The excellent social skills of Coordinators may sometimes make them appear manipulative.
Team Workers	The bridge-builders. Team Workers are interested in others and enjoy connecting people. High levels of emotional intelligence mean that they are likeable and trusted. To get to the *Performing* or *Affection* stage of group development (page 90), it is usually essential to have a Team Worker in the group. Talk to them about what is going on under the surface of the group's business – they will usually know and may be able to alert you to any individual distress which you might not otherwise notice until much later. The Team Worker's hatred of disharmony may mean that they run away from conflict or from tough decisions or exaggerate the misery of others.

Role	*Characteristics*
Resource Investigators	The people with excellent networking skills. Motivated by the need to innovate. May be able to bring you suggestions for alternative speakers, books, ideas. Encourage them: you want them on your side but beware of being too swayed by their optimism and enthusiasm; tomorrow they may be on to something different. May become restless and bored if they perceive you or your course to be *dull*. When you get this feedback from a Resource Investigator, check it out with others before assuming that they speak for everyone.
Thinking-oriented roles	
Plants	Plants are motivated by ideas. There is nothing they love more than a new concept. Often well read and quirky in their taste, they will have much to offer a learning group, as long as you encourage and manage them. Don't be offended by their frequent challenges about whether you know this or that theory or book and beware of pandering to their love of theory if it is not appropriate for the whole group. Plants can be introverted and may retreat into silence if you let them or else, if on their special subject, may talk too much. Practicality is not their strong point.
Monitor-Evaluators	These are the judicious people who can always see both sides of any argument. In a facilitated discussion they will encourage the group to take a rounded view of the topic. They will insist on weighing up a decision, including looking at its possible downsides. Monitor-Evaluators may sometimes seem over-gloomy. They are naturally risk-averse, so watch out for their tendency to hold back from action.
Specialists	Specialists have deep knowledge of the subject. Their identity tends to be invested in being a technical expert. Your task is to ensure that this expertise is available to the rest of the group without swamping it. Specialists can be too narrow in their interests, so don't let them stay too narrow.

Management College to research what made for effective teams. He set up an experiment where small teams played each other at a version of Monopoly. The difference between his game and classic Monopoly was that there was bargaining between rounds. To his surprise, the teams composed of highly intelligent people of similar temperament lost the game resoundingly. Instead, success was correlated with difference in the temperament and style of team members. Belbin's subsequent theory of informal team roles is well known and it plays out in classrooms as much as it does in any other group and will be important where there is any degree of interdependency. Belbin defines an informal role of this kind as a tendency to behave, contribute and interrelate to others in a particular way – in other words, our behaviour will tend to be reasonably consistent, regardless of the setting. Each role has something unique that it contributes to the success of the group and also has what Belbin calls an *allowable weakness*. There are no better-than or worse-than roles. All have their value. He groups the roles into three: *action-oriented, people-oriented and thinking-oriented*. Table 4.3 shows the roles, with some suggestions about how you may expect to spot them among groups of learners.

Belbin's work emphasizes that difference in a group rather than similarity is what will tend to create effective performance. In the context of learning, his theory is a useful reminder that the same roles and needs are likely to be at play and that diversity is to be cherished rather than suppressed.

Transactional analysis

This is a thought-provoking set of ideas, originated by the psychoanalyst Eric Berne. He wrote a best-selling book called *Games People Play*,[12] which quickly gained popular success in the 1960s. It became so well known that many of the concepts of transactional analysis (TA) have passed the stage of being technical psychoanalytical terms and have become clichés. So phrases like *games-playing,* and *win-win* are now widely understood, even by people who have never heard of TA.

TA has much to offer tutors and trainers. This is a postage-stamp sized explanation of what it is. Berne suggested that at any one time we are all in one of three 'ego states'. He called these 'Parent', 'Adult' and 'Child'.

Parent state judges and tells. How we do this will depend on our own experience of being parented. Parent state has two variants, Controlling Parent and Nurturing Parent. Controlling Parent is bossy and uses words like *should, must* and *mustn't*. Nurturing Parent suggests, soothes and takes care of others. Both in their way are interested in control and responsibility. *Adult state* is unemotional and factual. It is detached, rational and logical and is the state we are in when we are problem solving. *Child state* also has two variants, Natural Child and Adapted Child. When we are in Natural Child state we are playful, creative and can enjoy life. Adapted Child is resentful, rebellious and insecure.

There is no assumption in TA that Adult state is the best state to be in.

The transactional part of TA is where it becomes most interesting to tutors. Any conversation is a transaction. Remember we are always in one state or another. So if you and your group are in logical problem-solving mode, everyone may be in matching Adult states, and that could be fine. However, if you are in Controlling Parent mode, you may, in TA language, 'hook' the Adapted Child in your group, producing resentful or subversive behaviour. A striking example of this was recounted to me by a colleague:

> I was running a course for senior people in a particular sector. They were an exceptionally boisterous group and got very drunk over

> dinner one night, making a lot of noise. We had the hotel almost all to ourselves, but there was one elderly couple also eating in the dining room. I was so embarrassed I felt I had to go and apologize to them for the noise. They were very gracious but I could see they were a bit put off by the racket. The next day I still felt very angry about what I saw as bad behaviour and before we started the morning's session I told them what I had done and also that I had been ashamed to be part of the group. There were a few minutes of silence, and then they really laid into me. Told me that I couldn't take responsibility for them, they weren't children, they were offended, how dared I. They reduced me to tears. I carried on, but with the greatest difficulty.

In this example, the tutor had gone into Controlling Parent State and had hooked the Adapted Child of several members of the group. As they became angrier and angrier with her, they also flipped into Controlling Parent and she went into Adapted Child. She described this incident as one of the most upsetting in a long career in this kind of work. It certainly illustrates how Controlling Parent is not often an appropriate state for a tutor. Nurturing Parent may be more so, particularly at the beginning of an event when the need to feel safe may be the predominant one in your group. It is worth thinking, too, about the value of Natural Child State. Groups often need to play and be creative – i.e. be in Natural Child State – and so do tutors. Staying in any one state the majority of the time is likely to be a limitation. For instance, if you rely too much on Adult State, you will probably strike your group as overly cool and detached. If you are in Nurturing Parent State too much you could come across as a mother hen, refusing to allow your chicks to grow.

Another useful concept from TA is the *I'm OK, You're OK* framework. I like to think of this in a slightly different way, as two axes. One runs from 'I value me' to 'I don't value me'. The other runs from 'I value you' to 'I don't value you'. When you put them together, they form a matrix with four options (see Figure 4.3).

Where you are on this matrix will probably depend on your early experience. For instance, if you grew up with loving parents who cherished you and encouraged you to cherish others, then you will value yourself and others – the ideal place to be, resulting in a confident, sensitive human being. If you grew up constantly criticized and told you were a failure and other people were cleverer, nicer and altogether better than you, then you will value others but not yourself. This will probably result in lack of self-esteem and constantly seeking to please others, keeping danger at bay through compulsive caring or avoiding responsibility. If you grew up believing that you were a person of no importance and that others could not be trusted

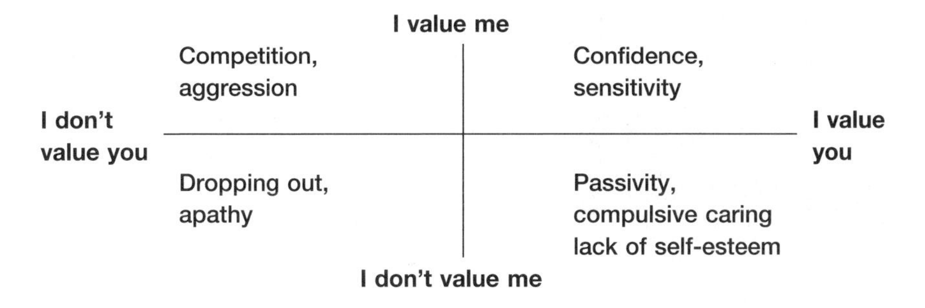

Figure 4.3 The value matrix

either, then you will be in the 'I don't value me' and 'I don't value you' area – a place where feeling powerless and out of control leads to abdicating all responsibility for yourself and others. The final position is where you value yourself but don't value others. This is often the result of a childhood where there was at least one dominating parent. The child eventually gives the dominating parent a taste of his or her own medicine and learns to discount the feelings of others through relentless competitiveness and aggression. Each of these can become life positions. Some questions to ask yourself about TA would be:

- Which ego-state are you typically in when you are running a group?
- Do you over-use some at the expense of others?
- Which transactions are typical for you? What are their typical consequences?
- Which of the life positions is typical for you? How does this affect your attitude to power in a learning group?
- How do you typically deal with participants who are at any position on the matrix other than 'I value me, I value you'?

The size of the group

There are some basic laws of group life which relate to its size. The larger the group, the fewer the people who will speak and the more decision-making is concentrated into a few hands. It runs roughly like this:

Table 4.4

3–6 people:	Everyone speaks.
7–10 people:	Almost everyone speaks. Quieter people say less. One or two may not speak at all.
11–18 people:	5 or 6 people speak a lot, 3 or 4 others join in occasionally.
19–30 people:	3 or 4 people dominate.
30+ people:	Little participation is possible.

A friend who was a distinguished adult educationist, with whom I discussed this phenomenon, told me that he had once been present at an international conference of 60 people. A lecture had been given by an eminent scientist who concluded by inviting questions from the floor. 'Do you know,' commented my friend, 'that the only three people who asked questions were *all* Nobel prize-winners!'

This is the simple explanation for non-participating behaviour in large groups: it takes far more courage to speak in a large than a small group. Here are the comments of first, a student nurse, and second, an MBA student:

> I can talk in a group of four, I freeze in a group of ten!

> It takes guts to join in a larger group discussion: there's that awful moment when out of the corner of your eye you see every face turned to yours. You feel everyone judging you, so the temptation is to stay mum.

The ideal size for a learning group is between 8 and 12. Anything smaller than 8 runs the risk that there will be too small a range of opinions and experiences. Increase the group much beyond 12 and you will inevitably find that it becomes difficult to draw everyone in.

Sometimes, however, you will find that you are landed with a larger group because administratively it is 'more convenient'. There are workable solutions to this problem.

> I plan sessions which alternate whole-group talk/discussion with lots and lots of role play in threes and fours.

> I give a general introduction lasting 10 minutes, then I split the group into smaller groups of five or six with a problem to solve. They report back to the main group for the final 15 minutes.

> Pairs working on mini projects, prepared in advance by me. . .

Beware, though, of introducing small-group work without designing it carefully and thinking it through:

> My heart sinks at a conference or the like, when the session leader says brightly, 'Now we're going to split into buzz groups for five minutes' and gives you some entirely pointless 'task'. You know it's meant to encourage participation, but so often it just seems a stale and meaningless device, and sometimes, I'm sorry to say, suggests that the lecturer can't be bothered to work out something better.

There is more on the implications of group size and its effect on what you can do with a group in the chapter on design (page 249).

The influence of the room

> The course venue was a small and hideous room in a hotel with no natural light, striped wallpaper and noisy air conditioning. You either shouted to make yourself heard over the fans or turned it off and began to feel terrible through lack of oxygen. We all had our elbows in each other's ribs because it was so cramped. The ultimate irony was that the course was on customer care!

> The room was a great big barn: high ceilings, bare floor, hard upright chairs. The only way to get people feeling more comfortable was to set out our chairs in a circle in one corner.

Manipulating the physical shape of your group – where and how participants sit – has an enormous influence on how they behave. The key factors for maximum group contact and participation are:

- keep the space between chairs to a minimum;
- remove redundant chairs;
- establish open 'eyelines' – let everyone be able to see everyone else without having to twist or turn;
- comfortable but businesslike chairs;
- a room that just fits the group, not too big and not too small (but too small is better than too big);
- tables or desks that fit the purpose – or none;
- thinking carefully about where you seat yourself.

There are hundreds of ways in everyday life in which the way we arrange and use the furniture in a situation is a symbolic way of showing how we feel in it, or of showing what the power and communication situation is. One chair round a dining table might have arms – it is a 'carver', and in many families this chair will always be taken by the most authoritative person and will be put at what becomes the head of the table. In most churches the parson's distinctive and influential role is stressed by the fact that he or she stands some distance apart from the congregation, who usually sit facing him or her in strict rows and are not expected to make any but a unanimous response. Quakers, on the other hand, who have no priests or pastors and who encourage contributions from anyone at a meeting, arrange their chairs in a hollow square with no special places. In an office one can expect the manager who leaves the desk to come and sit companionably beside a visitor to be friendlier than the manager who remains firmly behind it.

Exactly the same sort of symbolic representations are at work in learning groups. A group listening to a lecture will sit in straight rows facing a lecturer, who sits or stands apart. The arrangement of the seating emphasizes that the lecturer is a special person.

In a group where a little more discussion is expected, the tutor may still stand apart, but will face people sitting in two curved rows. In a craft group where the students are working individually and expect individual attention from the tutor, they will sit at tables dotted all over the room. Where they expect to help each other and work in small groups, several desks will be pushed together. In a discussion group where the tutor is no more than chairperson, the chairs might be arranged in a completely closed circle in which the tutor takes his or her place just like anyone else.

Large groups

Sometimes it is inevitable that you will be dealing with a large group. Again, how you lay out the room will influence the outcome. Some alternatives to sitting in rows are:

- Café circles where no more than six to eight people sit at smallish round or hexagonal tables. The problem with this is that some people will have their backs facing away from you unless you encourage them to rearrange their chairs to face you. Also, some venues may only be able to offer square tables.
- Two shallow semi-circles. The lack of tables makes this more informal than a standard lecture layout and it is usually easier for people to split into smaller groups for at least some of the time.

Desks and chairs themselves serve to emphasize roles and relationships. It is quite usual in most classrooms to find that the tutor's desk is larger and the chair more comfortable than the rest of the furniture in the room. It may be even perched on a platform – literally in a 'high up' place.

Tutors who abandon their chairs to stand in front of the desk, or perch on it, may be able to talk more informally with participants. When they are behind desks they emphasize their teacher role. In a circular or hollow-square seating arrangement, tutors who want to emphasize that they are just another member will take care to leave the special chair alone. When they resume the role of leader they will return to it.

You are sure to find that a group tries to emphasize your role as leader by creating physical space between you and them:

> I always arrived first to set out exactly the right number of chairs in a neat circle. By the time we began, I nearly always found that, mysteriously, a space had appeared between my chair and my neighbour's!

> I've noticed that people will go to considerable lengths to avoid sitting next to me. In one large group I teach, students will even form a second row rather than take the last 'free' spaces at either side of me.

It's up to you how you deal with this phenomenon. Let it pass unremarked if you feel it is of no significance, or even that it is a valuable way of emphasizing your leadership role. Insist on closing the gap if you are aiming for participation and equality.

Comfortable and uncomfortable chairs, large and small groups have other inescapable influences. Small chairs, apart from being extremely uncomfortable, may suggest a childish role. Hard, upright chairs may communicate an unpleasantly spartan and disciplined atmosphere. One of the most challenging groups I have ever run was in an open prison where I had been asked to bring my own group to form a discussion group with some pre-release prisoners. To add to our considerable nervous uncertainty of how to conduct ourselves in so unfamiliar a setting we had our first few meetings at one end of an enormous cold hut, sitting in a circle on hard wooden chairs, and generally gazing at our knees. Discussion was slow. The improvement when we moved to a small sitting-room with easy chairs was amazing. No doubt this was partly because we had by then been meeting for three weeks but the easy chairs in themselves seemed to suggest that we could all relax, and the social rather than educational associations were a positive advantage.

It does not need elaborate research to show how influential the seating is on the kinds of communication people make and feel able to make. Clearly, sheer physical distance is important. Someone sitting at the back of a number of rows is less likely to speak to the tutor than someone at the front.

For people sitting at the front, the difficulties of twisting round to address other people or even to see and hear other people will generally mean that most people listen to and encourage talk from the one person who has a good view of everybody – the tutor. In the opposite type of group, by sitting close to people and facing them, it is extremely hard not to talk to them, which is why contributions to conversation in a circle are usually divided pretty evenly between members. After only a short time the pattern becomes well known to all the members and hard to break. The longer a formal pattern continues, the harder it is for the shyest, most silent member to speak; the longer the garrulous 'circle' group continues, the harder it is for them to listen to a lecture. In other words, the shape of the setting first influences and then reinforces the typical way in which the group behaves.

You should feel free to manipulate the teaching space in any way you like, altering it frequently if necessary during each group meeting. My own rule of thumb is that I never expect to use the room exactly as I have found it on arrival. My assumption is that I will change it to suit whatever I and the group need. However, just occasionally you may find that this is impossible. This management development consultant recently recounted the following story to me:

> I was working in a glossy building, the headquarters building of an international bank. A colleague and I began shifting tables to rearrange the room and we were well on with this when three security men burst in and commanded us to stop. The building has glass walls and CCTV so they had seen what we were doing. Moving tables was forbidden – it was Against The Rules. When we used the same room two weeks later, there was a notice taped to the middle table saying Under No Circumstances Can These Tables Be Moved. This, of course, told us everything you needed to know about the culture in that organization – and did not make for an effective learning environment!

The tutor–leader

Many of the skills in dealing with groups come down in the end to the personality and skills of the tutor. These are remarkably similar to the skills that leaders need in order to be successful in organizations. Thinking back to my own schooldays and to the teaching I have encountered since, the outstanding teachers all shared an enthusiastic, open, relaxed style while teaching. Away from the classroom or training room they were people of very different personality. My own belief is that to manage a group you need to be an effective leader. This is not the charismatic Great Man of fantasy, but a more down to earth and modest character. Whatever our personal characteristics, for certain we need to be experts in reading and managing groups, accepting that we are bound to have a major impact on the way the group behaves and develops.

This is the paradox: we need to be expert at it and to be expert means learning and improving, yet when done supremely well it is a style which cannot be faked because we are being ourselves. Some sage and experienced adult educationists will say that they believe in behaving as if one is transparent with a class, because one is always more transparent than one realizes. These are wise words for any teacher, but they are particularly appropriate for those who teach adults.

Further reading

There are hundreds of books on human groups. This is just a small selection.

Bales, R.F. (1965) The equilibrium problem in small groups, in A.E. Hare, E.F. Borgatta and R.F. Bales (eds) *Small Groups: Studies in Social Interaction*. New York: Knopf.

Belbin, R.M. (1993) *Team Roles at Work*. Oxford: Butterworth Heinemann.

Brown, R. (1999) *Group Processes*, 2nd edition. Oxford: Blackwell.

Luft, J. (1984) *Group Processes: An Introduction to Group Dynamics*. Mountain View, CA: Mayfield.

Rogers, J. (1999) *Facilitating Groups*. London: Management Futures.

Schon, D. (1983) *The Reflective Practitioner*. London: Temple Smith.

Hay, J. (1996) *Transactional Analysis for Trainers*. Hertford: Sherwood Publishing.

Notes

1 The best account of the Stanford experiment is the official website: www.prisonexp.org which claims that closed institutions like prisons are as bad for the oppressors as for the oppressed in terms of self-esteem and moral courage.

2 Harvey, J. (1988) *The Abilene Paradox and Other Meditations on Management*. Lexington, MA: Lexington Books.

3 Blass, T. (2004) *The Man Who Shocked the World: The Life of Stanley Milgram*. New York: Basic Books.

4 To read more about Lewin's life and work, the best short account can be found at www.infed.org/thinkers/et-lewin.htm

5 For a clear account of this and a reflective study on its implications, read *Mobilizing the Organization* by John Bray, George Litwin and Kathleen Lusk Brooke (Prentice-Hall International, 1996).

6 Bethel-Fox, C. and O'Conor, F. (2000) *The Primary and Secondary School Classroom Climate Questionnaires*, London: Hay Group.
7 See Further Reading, page 105.
8 Tannenbaum, R. and Schmidt, W.H. (1958) How to choose a leadership pattern, *Harvard Business Review* 38(2): 95–101.
9 Tuckman, Bruce W. (1965) Developmental sequence in small groups, *Psychological Bulletin*, 63: 384–99. The article was reprinted in *Group Facilitation: A Research and Applications Journal*, Number 3, Spring 2001 and is available as a Word document: http://dennislearningcenter.osu.edu/references/GROUP%20DEV%20ARTICLE.doc
10 Schutz, W. (1958). *FIRO: A Three-Dimensional Theory of Interpersonal Behaviour*. New York: Holt, Rhinehart & Winston.
11 See Further Reading, page 105.
12 Berne, E. (1964) *Games People Play*. New York: Random House.

5 Facilitating

The biggest single movement in education of all sorts over the last 130 years – since the beginning of universal access to education in the UK – has been the transition from teacher-focus to learner-focus. Look at those photographs of vast Victorian classes of young children sitting in obedient rows and compare them with the joyful buzz of activity in even the most conservatively run primary school classroom of today to see how astonishing the difference is. We have moved from teaching to learning, from teacher as source of the only knowledge that matters to teacher as conductor and facilitator. The importance of the learner as thinker and problem-solver with the responsibility to manage and be at the centre of his or her own learning has become paramount. To lead most kinds of discussion, to run a role play, to conduct a teleclass, to design and run a simulation, to lead an action learning set or to work inside a curriculum using problem-based learning, you absolutely have to be an expert facilitator.

You may find it helpful to read this chapter in conjunction with the previous chapter. This has a more theoretically slanted explanation of how to understand what typically happens in groups.

Is facilitation what this group needs?

Facilitation is a vital tool for anyone who is helping adults learn. Literally it means the process of *making something easy*.

There are two factors that you need to consider in deciding whether what you need is facilitation. One is the content of the learning, the other is the nature of the learning climate that you want to create (page 85). As far as the content goes, facilitation will have at least some place when the formal aims include:

Self-insight – the foundation of most of the psychological disciplines and of any subject where there is a behavioural focus.
Understanding relationships, whether in the actual lives of the learners, or in any number of subjects in which relationships feature, essentially the Humanities – for instance, literature, history, politics, business studies.
Creativity.
Problem-solving of any kind.
Team work and collaboration.

Where climate is concerned, all of these suggest that facilitation will be needed:

- *No one has all the power.* This is fundamentally true of most situations where adults are learning. Your group can abandon its learning at any point: they are not your prisoners. Even if they do not physically walk out, they may object in dozens of ways.
- *There are no right/wrong answers.* There are few subjects where it is legitimate to insist on one opinion. Take any subject you like: the origins of the universe, whether last night's sitcom was any good, the quality of a particular newspaper, whether the latest war is justified, how to cure a cold, if or how developing countries ought to be helped, whether women are better drivers than men . . . Whatever the subject, it is likely that there will be as many opinions as there are people.
- *It is important for people to own their opinions.* This is part of what makes for learning. It is about the struggle to gather the facts, to weigh them up, to seek out your own emotional bias and prejudices, to come to conclusions to which you feel commitment, not compliance.
- *Self-management* is an integral part of the learning – as it is for instance in action learning or problem-based learning.

Facilitation is not the same as several related activities which may look superficially similar:

- *Chairing a meeting,* which has an end point that usually results in agreeing a decision. The Chair reserves a degree of power in order to control the meeting.
- *Chairing a debate,* where the confrontational format is designed to emphasize differences in order to explore an issue.
- *Group therapy,* where the point is cure. The aim is to do it through group exploration on the assumption that members of the group are dysfunctional. Members of learning groups may feel dysfunctional in other aspects of their lives at some point – who doesn't? But when your aim is learning pure and simple you must make the assumption that you are working with healthy, resourceful people. Group therapy leaders use facilitation skills, but the end purpose is different.
- *Guided discussion,* where the tutor's aim is to transfer knowledge by gently leading the group to a conclusion he or she thinks is the correct answer. This may indeed be legitimate but it is not facilitation. Where it happens, the tutor may be confusing fact with opinion and may also be misjudging where it is appropriate to insist on fact

and where it is better to encourage a range of opinions. When this happens, it may accurately be described as fake facilitation.

Fake facilitation

It is easy to assume that facilitation is what is happening in the group discussions you lead. But you need to be clear about the difference between the real and the fake. Fake is seductive and here is why. We can too easily assume the mantle of authority that the profession has acquired from teaching children. Furthermore, many of us are unaware of how much influence we have with our groups and of how easily this influence can be exerted affectionately as well as brusquely. It is often as easy for the teacher of adults to do this as it is for the schoolteacher, given the diffidence of adult learners, some of whom may be anxious not to declare themselves too soon:

> I wondered if this class was, to be honest, a bit too much of a beginner-y event for me, in the sense that I suspected I did already know more than most of the other people there, but I didn't want to show off, so I kept quiet.

> I knew I'd blush if I spoke, so I never spoke.

> Discussion seemed to be a competition between three or four people in the group with the tutor enthusiastically joining in, so I thought I'd just let them get on with it.

Classroom or training room discussions, closely analysed, will often reveal how frequently tutors capitalize on their traditional authority and on the reticence of the participants. This may be useful and necessary at the start of the engagement but can become destructive if it continues. Many discussions in adult, further or higher education and training are far from being as free or equal as they need to be because tutors, often unconsciously, guide, manipulate and dominate proceedings. For instance, you may feel obliged to follow every comment from a student with a longer one of your own. Group members will hardly ever talk to other group members under this system. The communication may be brisk and lively, but it will be in several sets of two-way traffic, participant to tutor, tutor to participant. An analysis of this sort of discussion usually reveals that the tutor talks almost all the time. (For some early research proof of this, see page 222.)

It is hard discipline as a tutor to keep your mouth shut, to listen, and to show signs of listening instead of talking. Most of us are good at talking and especially enjoy talking about our subjects. Not talking can be exquisite agony, as any experienced tutor will know.

Some tutors may encourage student contributions, but may set up what has accurately been diagnosed as a 'guessing-game'. The game is played so that the student can hardly ever win, as in this brief transcript from a class comparing two poems by Wordsworth. The atmosphere of the group was entirely friendly and informal.

Tutor: Well now, you've read the second poem again, I hope. (*Murmurs of agreement*) One thing that struck me, one thing I'm wondering, did you see any striking difference between this poem and the last one we read?

Student 1: It's longer! (*Laughter and pause*)

Tutor: Well . . . yes!

Student 2: It is that this poem is somehow more . . . well, not so personal, it seems to have less of Wordsworth himself in it?

Tutor: Yes. But I was thinking of something else.

Student 3: The language is not so rich? Fewer metaphors?

Tutor: Yes, a good point. That's certainly true. We'll look at that later. Anyone got any more ideas?

Student 1: I don't like it! (*Laughter*)

Tutor: Any more bright ideas? (*Pause*) Well, what I was thinking was that this poem is much more in the ballad vein, isn't it? It's reminiscent of the old simple Scottish ballads – can anyone tell us what a ballad is?

In this situation the tutor has said in effect to the group, 'Now guess what I've got in mind?' The trouble is that there may be dozens of legitimate points of comparison between two poems, any one of which the tutor may have in mind. The class plays along for a while, then says or signifies by silence the equivalent of 'I give up', after which the tutor announces the 'answer'. Not only does this sort of technique suggest to a class that there is only one acceptable and right major point of comparison, it also suggests that responses to a poem have to be tackled in a particular order (the suggestion about metaphor was pushed aside for 'later'), and that it is the response the tutor has in mind which is the most important one. Such facilitation technique ignores the possibility that students themselves can and should make fresh and direct contributions of a quality which would surprise facilitators who think theirs are the only interpretations which count.

Guessing-games develop out of confusion between facilitation and 'question and answer'. There are subjects – mathematics, for instance – where it might be legitimate for a tutor to say something like, 'Can anyone tell me what the square root of forty-four is?' because there is only one possible answer. It is surprising how few such subjects are, and at what a low factual and academic level they have to function for it to be possible to deal with them in so summary a fashion.

Tutors may press their own views in other, more subtle ways. They may reward someone who offers a view agreeing with their own by nodding vigorously or by saying, 'Yes, a good point', or by following it up with some forceful elaboration of their own. They may frown doubtfully at a student giving an opposite opinion, or simply by the coolness of their nod on receiving the comment imply that only courtesy prevents them saying that such a comment was ridiculous, or inappropriate. They may initiate the discussion and prod it along with leading questions, as in this sociology class (again the atmosphere of this particular class was noticeably relaxed and uninhibited):

> *Tutor:* Don't you think society is still rather hard on never-married women who are also parents? We see this moral panic stuff over and over again, don't we?
>
> *Student 1:* Well no, I think that's a bit *passé* now when you have so many famous women who've chosen it as a way of life.
>
> *Tutor:* Even so, I think we all disapprove of someone breaking the moral code.
>
> *Student 2:* Yes, and the children suffer because they never have a male role model.
>
> *Student 3:* Well I'm a single mother and I resent the idea that my children are suffering.
>
> *Student 4:* You can't apply this to individuals; it's the general social effect we're talking about here and I agree there's still the idea that the good old nuclear family is best. Single parents probably get discriminated against in all sorts of ways. My sister had a baby at 16 and my parents behaved as if the world had come to an end. They put really strong pressure on her to have an abortion because, in spite of everything, they still felt it was something 'people like us' didn't do.
>
> *Tutor:* Yes, that's right. Why do you think that is? Is it that we all feel threatened by someone who doesn't conform? (*Nods of agreement*)

The phrasing of the tutor's initial question has given the group a clue either to his own view, or to what he interprets as the common view of a familiar social problem. It may be that the tutor can offer the group evidence on how 'society' views single, never-married mothers – surveys, novels, articles – but he notably does not do this. He quickly tries to encourage the group to confess to prejudice themselves, and seizes on a personal anecdote told by one student as the occasion to drive home his point by virtually accusing the student who told it of prejudice herself. In such discussion the tutor gives it a gloss of freedom, but in fact he is seeking confirmation of his own view and moral standpoint (and in the extract quoted, eventually wins it superficially) almost as firmly as the tutor in the guessing-game.

The information and sources that tutors use for discussion may easily be chosen to support their own views. The group here is usually at the mercy of the tutor unless its members are lucky enough or enterprising enough to discover the bias for themselves:

> Between school and university I took a year's voluntary job, but to keep my hand in I thought I'd go to an extra-mural class in my own subject – history. It appealed to me because it was advertised as a course using original documents of the period, with lots of opportunities for discussion. It was very interesting and the lecturer was superb – a real enthusiast. I only discovered how incredibly partisan his view of the period was when in my third year at university I realized how his enthusiasm for one school of thought had totally affected the documents he gave us and the evidence we used for our discussions. He was quite unaware of what he had done, I'm sure.

Real facilitation inevitably exposes the ambiguities and complexities of a topic. Many tutors, searching for a way to find a framework for their students that will hold widely diverging views, will also attempt to impose a 'conclusion' on the discussion which can easily be a false representation of what has been said:

> It puzzled me at first, but I never recognized his summaries as accounts of what we had all said. After a bit I realized that the summary represented (a) his own opinion, (b) what he wished we had said. I think we must have disappointed him by not being such a bright class as he'd hoped. We certainly weren't up to his standards.

The educationist R.W.K. Paterson made the point eloquently in a paper written in the early 1970s:

> One inevitably wonders how many ... counterfeit discussions are staged in adult classes by tutors whose confidence in their own preferred views disables them from taking the views of their students with the utmost seriousness required of all the participants in authentic educational dialogue. I am referring less to the assertive and dogmatic tutor than to the kind of tutor who unobtrusively and skilfully synthesizes the various discussion contributions of his students, by judicious selection and emphasis, into a neatly structured

> and rounded proposition or body of propositions, which are then represented as the 'conclusions' of the 'class discussion' although they have in fact been evolved by the tutor, who has ingeniously utilized the discussion, always more or less under his discreet control, as an educational device for arraying precisely this body of propositions, deemed by him to be of some importance to his students at this stage of their classwork. The teaching skill exercised by such a tutor may be of a very high order, and the results gained may be of great educational value. To the extent that his students believe themselves to be participating in a genuinely open-ended dialogue, however, they are being misled; and to the extent that he believes himself to be 'conducting a discussion', he is misleading himself.[1]

– and the real thing

Real facilitation is as different from any of the tutor activity described above as a fake Rolex is from the genuine article. Since writing the first edition of this book I have trained many hundreds of people in facilitation skills. Some of these learners have begun by assuming that because facilitation literally means *to make something easy*, the activity itself is easy. In fact it is one of those activities that looks easy when done superbly well. It can be relatively unusual for a good facilitator to be thanked in any more than the token way that politeness demands. This is probably because, when done well, it appears effortless to the point of seeming invisible. It is the art that conceals art.

Process not content

As a facilitator you are the neutral servant of the group, not its knowledge expert. Facilitation is about separating the process from the content. The distinction is sometimes described by using the apt analogy of an iceberg. The content is the task or the subject. It is what everyone can see and acknowledge. Content is safe because it is visible and appears manageable. The process is what lies underneath the water and cannot be seen, but lies in waiting to wreck the unwary. Process is about the human relationships of the group: its unspoken and possibly ever-shifting hierarchy of influence, its emotions, many of which will be denied or hidden, its blockages and barriers to learning. Process is more frightening because it cannot be so readily controlled, therefore it can appear easier to ignore or overlook it. You can only become an expert in the emotions of the group if you have the authority that comes from genuine ease with yourself, that is you have the kind of self-confidence that comes from knowing and accepting yourself very well, including your own hot buttons. You can stand apart from your own agenda because you know that your role is to manage the process rather than the content of the learning. In fact you are more likely to be an expert on the process of the group than an expert on the content of the discussion.

Seeing the process patterns

Over the years I have been running discussions, teaching and facilitating events of all sorts and I have noticed many common patterns. You need to be alert to these and other common phenomena because if you are not alert to them, you can't do anything about them. So watch out for:

- men making assertions where women ask questions;
- men talking more than women, unless it is a women-dominated group;
- men taking charge of any reporting back from small groups, even where they are a small minority in the group;
- ping-pong dialogues developing between facilitator and one or two participants;
- the person sitting directly in your eye-line speaking more than others;
- the people sitting directly to your right and left speaking least;
- the people who speak least saying less and less as the event goes on and vice versa;
- people colonizing one seat with their coats and briefcases and returning to that seat constantly so that it becomes 'theirs';
- people sitting next to those with whom they feel they have most in common. So, for instance, all the younger women may sit together, or all the people from the same department;
- all the phases of group development that I discuss in Chapter 4.

Where they continue for any length of time, such patterns can be destructive and could lead to dysfunction. They are dangerous because they exclude. Where you notice them happening, break them up by drawing attention to them. This can seem alarming to many groups because most of us are unused to the underlying dynamics being exposed. By exposing them you are doing for facilitation what therapists call *holding*. This means creating a safe place where, unlike a more usual kind of discussion, it is not threatening to speak with truth but also with concern for the feelings of your fellow-participants.

The simplest way to do this is to review the group's process regularly. This means asking people how they feel about the discussion and also asking them to name the patterns themselves. Useful questions here are:

- Who has spoken most?
- Who has spoken least?
- How well did we listen to each other?
- How well did we deal with conflict?
- How well did we manage our time?
- How far have we met our objectives?
- What has not been said that perhaps should have been said?
- What have you learnt from the way the discussion has gone?
- What mark out of ten would you give the discussion for enjoyment?
- What mark out of ten would you give it for usefulness?
- What feedback do you have for me as facilitator? (A particularly important question as it shows that since you do not curl up and die after hearing feedback, the same is possible for the participants.)
- What would help make this a better discussion next time?

You may also want to consider simple changes which break up patterns – for instance by making a point of sitting in a different seat yourself after every break and by being super-aware of your own patterns of interaction. An example would be that if you find yourself tempted to join in a ping-pong dialogue, you would notice and manage it.

Real facilitation therefore comes from a subtle and relatively rare combination of confidence and humility. It does not depend on having formal authority. You want people's respect but you don't need people to agree. You will have what the writer and humanistic psychologist John Heron[2] in his book, *The Facilitators' Handbook*, calls *distress-free authority*, the kind which is relaxed enough not to be fazed by people who oppose some dearly held view of your own. Real facilitation is about taking at least initial responsibility for the learning climate and about being able to create a place where group members can share diverse knowledge and experience and for that diversity to be valued. As a true facilitator you will immediately spot and challenge the premature convergence of thinking and will protect a minority opinion. If the discussion seems to be closing down too soon, you will be able to open it up again. You will also spot and name blockages; you are unafraid of conflict and emotion – in yourself or others. You don't need to be liked by all members of the group all of the time. You will understand that you don't need the group to reach a consensus unless there is some authentic need for there to be one.

Contracting with your group

Would-be facilitators can get the role confused and so can groups. I find it essential to clarify my role, either at the outset of a whole piece of learning or for the part of the session where I am moving from expert in my subject (the traditional role of *teacher*) to facilitator of the process. Explain the role as you see it. Then suggest that it will help to agree a contract about how you are going to work, around three areas:

1 Mechanics

How are we to handle the mechanics of our meetings? This will include topics such as:

- whether or not mobiles should be switched off;
- Whether first names should be used, or titles and surnames;
- punctuality;
- timings of breaks;
- how any messages from colleagues or family will be delivered;
- alerting you and the group to planned absences.

Potential problems can sometimes be headed off through what you send to learners in advance (see also pages 47 and 256). In some organizations (and the bigger they are, the more likely this is to be true) there is a maddeningly casual attitude towards whether or not people actually turn up on the day of the course and also towards late arrivals and early departures. I remember one such event for the NHS where we had limited numbers to 25 people and had a waiting list, such was the demand. Yet on the day, we were lucky if 18 appeared, with typically no apology or explanation from the no-shows. Alert to this now, we will emphasize the importance of actually attending if you are offered a place, explaining the inconvenience it causes fellow participants and the tutors because the design will have been geared to the expected number of people, and pointing out that although participants are not personally paying for the course, it is very far from free. I run a regular course on facilitation for one of my NHS clients and she sends out stern emails once people have applied for and obtained a place, telling them that if they drop out it is *their* responsibility to find a substitute. This has resulted in a number of somewhat startled but eager last-minute attendees. There is also a penalty option – the non-appearing participant's organization will be required to refund the notional fee for attending the course. The same client also emphasizes that there is no slack in the programme and that the course will start at nine sharp and end promptly at five with full attendance expected throughout the two days.

The apparently bland topic of *mechanics* will give you plenty of material to begin shaping the climate in the course itself. For instance, most groups will say that they appreciate punctuality, but do they still expect you to sheepdog them from the coffee room back into the session? If so, are you prepared to do it? If not, explain that you will be back in the room promptly at the agreed time and will start the session again, regardless of how many people are actually in the room. How will you and the group handle latecomers? Can you personally promise that you will always arrive and finish promptly? Mobile phones are an annoying intrusion but there may be times when someone is expecting an important phone call and needs to leave theirs on. Enabling people to talk about their needs in this way is often the beginning of establishing an atmosphere where honest disclosure is welcomed:

> One member of the group did ask permission to leave her phone on and calmly explained that she was waiting for a hospital consultant to call to give her histology results. She had had a preliminary operation for breast cancer and this call would determine whether or not she needed another. Her phone did ring and she dashed out of the room. Her sober face on returning said it all but the support and quiet acceptance she got in that group was just so important in quickly creating the safe climate that benefited everyone.

> Late arrivals are a plague in London and any of us can get caught up in traffic or stuck on the Tube, but some people use it as a mask for poor planning. I ask my groups to make a buddy arrangement with a partner where they exchange mobile numbers and phone their buddy if it's clear that they are going to be unavoidably detained first thing in the morning. Having to take responsibility in this way immediately cut down the late arrivals in my programme from about 10% in any one week to virtually nothing.

It is obviously essential for you to stick to whatever rules are agreed. Not practising what you preach is the surest way to lose the trust of your group.

2 What does the group want from you?

From mechanics, move to an explanation of the facilitator role, telling the group how you see it. Within that framework, ask the group what they want from you. Most groups understand principles such as participation, respect and openness and will suggest ground rules of this sort. Rather than just meekly accepting words like 'honesty', write them on the flip chart but then ask the group how they would define the behaviour that went with this word. This may reveal widely varying interpretations which it will be useful to discuss. Depending on the nature of the subject, they may also suggest that confidentiality is important. It is asking a lot of any new group that they sign up to this. You may hear the phrase *Chatham House Rules* used, a reference to the political think tank discussions held at the Royal Institute of International Affairs where absolute openness amongst participants is encouraged and expected in return for an absolute promise that confidentiality will not betrayed – and by and large it is not. Although expulsion from membership is the sanction at the actual Chatham House, the Chatham House Rule is morally rather than legally binding, hence its force.

The group may also want you to make some sort of brief guidance on whatever its subject matter is. If it is appropriate, then agree, while explaining where it may not be appropriate and indicating where you expect the group to manage the knowledge input. Where you have doubts that any such rules are realistic, or where, even more importantly, you disagree with their wisdom, then you must say so and discuss them with the group.

To do it properly this process will take time, but usually it is time well invested. When you and the group are meeting over some weeks or months you probably cannot afford *not* to invest this time. Write the rules up on the flip chart as they emerge from the discussion and consider asking for a volunteer to key them in later for emailing to every member. Having such a record and taking it seriously enables you to use such ground rules as a benchmark whenever the group reaches some kind of crisis point:

> I was running a course on counselling which ran over three terms, one day a week. It was essential to the course design that we started each day promptly and with a pairs exercise. There was one person who was consistently late, causing a degree of upheaval whenever she came in. The group was able to confront her openly and courteously, using our initial contract. It turned out that she had childcare problems, but the discussion then hinged on why she had been unable to mention this at the time we were negotiating the morning arrangements. Unless I had made the big deal I did of agreeing our contract and ground rules, there was no way this group member could have done it so easily and, as it turned out, so productively. After that, I noticed that whenever our ground rules seemed to be in danger of breach, some other member of the group would challenge in the same way. Our contract became a living document, valued by every member.

3 Tell the group what you want from them and ask for their comments

Unless you have a sophisticated group well used to facilitation, your thinking on this topic is likely to be ahead of theirs. With experience you will have your own list, but these are some ground rules that I find invaluable:

- *One person at a time: one issue, one thought, one idea.* It is amazing how many apparently urbane groups can find this hard. A colleague and I worked with a BBC group of 14 people over a period of two years to help them build their team and improve their performance. At the beginning, there was such chaos when it came to discussion that we had to insist on apparently childlike rules. One of these was that anyone wanting to speak would first raise their hand – their suggestion. Yes, these were people in well-paid jobs, none of them younger than 35, but they still needed this elementary help in order to learn the useful discipline of only one person at a time speaking.

- *One agenda: the group's.* At the start, you may also have to work harder than feels comfortable to get people to refrain from:
  - telling anecdotes (in my company/street/family/team we ...);
  - interrupting;
  - not listening;
  - queuing to speak;
  - giving advice.

  Explain that it is especially important to help people recognize how often they may be introducing their own agendas rather than working on an issue brought by someone else. Alerting group members to the likelihood that you will gently but firmly interrupt the flow by saying something like *Whose agenda are we on now?* may help people learn to recognize what they are doing.
- *It is OK to admit to mistakes and uncertainties.* This is vital. You will be using facilitation and discussion because there are no clear right or wrong 'answers'. When this is the case, it is essential for people to be able to own up to what they don't know and feel uncertain about. Explain that they are responsible for their own learning, not you. Say you will lead the way here. If you make a mistake or are uncertain, you will own up.
- *Take responsibility for your own learning. Ask for what you want.* If there is something they don't like, or don't agree with, then you expect them to name it. This does not mean that they will get whatever it is that they want – though it may. Either way, it is better for the feeling to be voiced than to remain underground where it might become toxic, resulting in corridor mutterings that will undermine the climate of honesty for which you will be aiming. It is more difficult to put something right retrospectively.
- *Say 'I' when you mean 'I'.* It is surprising how often people say 'we' or 'people' when what is meant is 'I'. Explain that you will challenge participants who resort to generalizations of this sort. Your group will soon get the hang of it and will realize how much better the discussion is as a result.
- *Address others by name or as* you *rather than as* her or him.
- *Feelings are facts.* It can still astonish me that some participants will declare work, or academic study, a feelings-free zone. Some of my

coaching clients, for instance, have told me at one time or another that they leave their feelings at home and that emotion is inappropriate at work. The implication is that emotion is irrational. This is in itself a piece of false logic. No topic worthy of discussion in a learning environment will be without emotion. All opinions have emotion attached to them. Surfacing this self-evident truth makes it possible for emotion to become part of the discussion.

Ask for what you need in terms of homework and other follow up or preparation. If you need assignments completed by a deadline, say so, say why it matters – not least that it is a sign of participants' commitment to the course – and explain clearly what the consequences of non-compliance are.

Be clear about what you are not going to do as well as what you are going to do. Be prepared to say which of these conditions, if any, is non-negotiable. For me, they are all non-negotiable. They are my terms for running the event and I am prepared to defend them to the hilt because they are based on deeply held values about what matters in any learning group – but you may feel differently.

You may find that this preliminary conversation creates exhilaration because people can see immediately how different it is. It may also create puzzlement or even apprehension. If so, that is fine. A facilitated discussion will be different from virtually all other discussions which you and your participants have in their lives. This is because, unlike all those other discussions, no one has to defend a position, score points or to triumph. No one will be threatened with the withdrawal of love, promotion or attention. No one has to be right at all costs. There is no face to lose. What is happening in the here and now is what matters, not old grudges which have to be nursed until they burst out again. It isn't a debate. Cleverness is not what counts, though wisdom is. It is OK not to know. Learning is what it is all about. That is what makes a facilitated discussion, whose aim is learning, so powerful.

It is also worth thinking about your attitude to your own power and authority and maybe discussing it with the group at this early stage. John Heron[3] has suggested a simple model of understanding different facilitation styles. He calls them:

Hierarchical: the tutor takes responsibility for planning, gives a degree of theoretical input and is in control of the design for learning. The tutor is a charismatic presence in the group while still maintaining positive regard for others.

Co-operative: the tutor and group share responsibility for learning. The tutor asks neutral questions which elicit self-knowledge from the group. New rules may emerge as a result of the group taking more responsibility for the climate.

Autonomous: the tutor delegates design, rule-making and input to the group.

It is not possible to have a neutral style in facilitating. You will be doing one style or another – or some blend of them at any given time. The Hierarchical style is most probably the one you will need to employ at the beginning of any group's life, though there are indeed groups where Autonomous is the one adopted from the start, but the chaos, bewilderment and resentment that this creates will be too much for most facilitators, and indeed most groups. See also my chart on page 87 for more guidance on the pluses and minuses of different ways of managing your own authority within the group.

High-impact interventions

John Heron has also usefully classified a range of six overall interventions that facilitators can make. He calls them *Modes of Facilitation*, defining modes as the different ways in which facilitators can handle decision-making within the group. His dimensions are:

Planning: interventions that are to do with the goals of the group.
Giving meaning: helping the group to make sense of experience.
Confronting: raising the group's awareness of the gap between saying and doing; tackling its resistances.
Feeling: handling emotion.
Structuring: choosing which methods of learning are best suited to the event.
Valuing: creating the kind of climate which gives people recognition.

Facilitation is an art, not a science. Another facilitator could run the discussion in a different way and achieve equally good – or equally disastrous – results. You only have that one opportunity to decide what to do. When training new facilitators I have observed that inexperience means that many intervene too little and have too narrow a palette of interventions. They over-rely on one or two techniques and then get lost when these don't work. Experienced and skilled facilitators have a wide range of interventions, all of which will have their place. Expert facilitators work as much from the heart, trusting their intuition, as from the head. However, to get to this stage, you first have to learn and practise the techniques. These are some of the approaches and interventions that work for me.

Being prescriptive

Prescriptive interventions are the ones where you take control. Many of them will be to do with planning. It may be particularly important to do this at the early stages of the group's life – the Telling phase where the group is uncertain about what is to come, what is expected, whether or not they like the other people, how confident they feel. You are being prescriptive when you

plan the programme;
design its learning objectives;
choose companion facilitators;
decide how any evaluations will be carried out;
make any kind of intervention in the group.

The process of agreeing ground rules, described on page 115 is a prescriptive intervention, even though the content may come as much from the group as from you.

Any theoretical explanations you give as input to the programme are also prescriptive, as are any corrections you make on matters of fact during the discussion.

Supportive interventions that create trust

One of your main tasks as facilitator is creating trust. Participants in a discussion have to feel safe. It has to be all right to say what you think without fear of attack, whether from the tutor or other participants. The most certain way to achieve this is to behave in a way which models trustful behaviour yourself. There is no place in facilitation for sarcasm, put-downs, jokes at other people's expense, showing off your own superior knowledge, gossiping or clumsy interrupting. As a facilitator you have a duty to protect members of the group from this behaviour. If it does surface, challenge it:

> *Postgraduate medical tutor*
> I was facilitating a discussion about the concept of the Expert Patient. It was our second meeting. A row suddenly blew up between two members of the group, both of them GPs. Voices were raised and one accused the other of arrogance. I calmly intervened, reminding them and the group of our initial contract where, among other ground rules, we had agreed the rules of feedback, circulated to all and to which everyone had signed up. I asked the instigator to rephrase his comments so that they were feedback and not accusation. There was a moment of utter frisson in the group but it was a turning point.

Facilitators also show support by protecting minority opinion and making sure that it is heard, as this facilitator did:

> *Politics tutor*
> The students were third years, so you would expect at least some degree of maturity. But because this was a notably left-leaning university, the accepted opinion was always going to be towards socialist ideals. One student somewhat stridently put forward his views about market forces and got immediately leapt on by the other 15 – or so it seemed at first. I reined in the discussion and said, 'Let's hear what Paul has to say here', and invited him to expand on his views, clarifying and summarizing as he went. I reminded the group that our purpose was to look at ideas rationally and that there was always merit in looking at the opposite of the accepted view. A more moderate discussion immediately followed and it was clear that there were others in the group who were not so anti as it had originally seemed.

Supportive interventions are about showing people that they are valued. We all need affirmation, just another word for recognition. Notice what people are saying and comment on it. Learn people's names during the first session (see also page 50) and use them frequently but not over-frequently. This will help others to do the same.

Make comments which show that you remember people's contributions. Encourage others in the group to do the same. Use phrases like:

> That's an interesting idea.
> Going back to the point you made earlier, X, I can see that...
> As X said when we began our session today...
> X has usefully reminded us again that...

These interventions need to be maintained outside the formal sessions as well as inside them, balanced of course with the need to pace yourself and look after your own needs:

> The facilitator was all charm in the training room but the second we left it she shut us out. Her whole face closed down and she wandered off on her own or muttered into her mobile. I began to believe that her apparent interest in us was not authentic because she seemed to be able to switch it on and off at will.

It is vital to maintain respectful behaviour in other ways outside the formal learning environment. Never be tempted to join in gossip by adding your own private views on members of the group. Keep your distance. You can never be best friends with members of the group while you are in the facilitator role. Although the gossipers may seem to be enjoying it at the time, privately they will be thinking, 'I wonder if he/she could be saying this sort of thing about me.' News of your indiscretion will for certain speed its way back to the person you were discussing. This kind of behaviour will destroy the trust that you are working so hard to create in other ways.

Listening with respect

Facilitation is about respect for each and every participant. It means being able to listen without judgement, even when you fundamentally disagree with what the other person is saying. It means listening without feeling the need to criticize, collude, blame or trivialize the other person's concern, and without trying to persuade them that your view is right and theirs is wrong.

When you listen with respect, you give your whole attention to the other person. This is real attention, not fake attention. You are *fully present* for them. This means that your effort goes into trying to understand properly what is in their heads rather than queuing to speak yourself. Beware of getting distracted by wanting to impress or to discharge some of your own anxiety. It will be obvious to an observer when you are listening fully: your body will be open, your expression friendly but not overwhelmingly so, your demeanour calm but alert. This is not something you can *try* to do. It happens naturally when you are listening without judging.

Summarizing

Summarizing is the facilitator's best friend. It shows that you are listening because unless you are listening you cannot do it accurately. It gives you a degree of control in the discussion, something that inexperienced facilitators find challenging. Aim to summarize at least once every ten minutes and possibly more frequently than that. If you do nothing else but this during a discussion, you will be doing a useful job. Listen for the main themes. Note the agreements and disagreements. Remember that your role is not about drawing conclusions. Use the group's language and metaphors rather than your own. Keep interpretation out of it. Summarizing is about keeping track of the ebb and flow of the talk. Useful phrases here are:

- *So to summarize where we are . . .*
- *It feels to me that a summary of the main lines of our discussion would be useful here . . .*
- *So what I've heard X and Y say is . . . and what I've heard A and B say is . . .*
- *. . . so that's what I think I've heard – is that right? Or, That's what I*

> *believe the main themes have been, but have I left out anything important?* (Ending with a question allows the group to correct you if there is something that you have conveyed inaccurately or omitted.)

If you are getting confused yourself, it will be true in nine cases out of ten that the group is too. So say something like:

> Can anyone help me here? I'm getting confused about where we're going with the discussion at this point. I've heard X point and Y point made, but I'm a bit lost about what that's contributing...

Beware of becoming addicted to detailed note-taking. It will literally take your eyes off the group and reduce the amount of observation you can do. School yourself to jot down a few key words as reminders. With practice you will find that you can probably do without even these.

Interrupting

You will often have to interrupt. I have noticed how difficult new facilitators can find this. The reason is that interrupting is considered rude in our society and we all learn as small children that good manners demand polite listening to our elders and betters. If you carry this belief into facilitating a discussion you will make your job much harder. The discussion will flow around you and the less you intervene, the less the group will come to expect leadership from you and the more self-doubting you will feel.

Nine times out of ten the group will be grateful for your interruptions – 'Thank goodness someone's in control!' The secret is to do it with confident self-awareness. You are interrupting because the learning of the group demands it, not because you enjoy the sound of your own voice. You will also be doing it with respect and courtesy.

When to interrupt:

- One member of the group has had a lot of air time.
- A group within the group has had a lot of air time.
- Discussion has got stuck at one point.
- A topic that has already been dealt with satisfactorily is reopened by one person.
- The discussion is generating a high level of emotion but the emotion is not being acknowledged.
- Discussion is going off at an unproductive tangent.

Only you can decide whether any of the above are 'true' or your own distorted version of truth. Trust your intuition but check this out with the group if in doubt. Useful phrases are:

- I'm going to interrupt you here...
- My sense is that we've spent long enough on this ... how does it seem to all of you?
- Can I stop you there, X...

All of this needs to be accompanied by the appropriate body language. In fact, often the body language will be enough to alert the group to your intervention: a lean forward, an intake of breath, a small hand-gesture – and so on. Do this cleanly and with assurance. If you look timid, no one will notice.

Timekeeping

Part of your role, certainly at the beginning of the group's work, will be to keep an eye on the time and to show the group that this is what you are doing. Sit where you can see a clock, or take off your watch and put it on a table within easy glancing distance. Most adults cannot work without some kind of break for more than two hours, maybe less if they are smokers. Keep scanning the group for signs of physical tiredness – for instance, droopy posture, or people looking at their watches. Monitor for signs of mental tiredness such as perfunctory discussion or long silences. Remind the group of how much time has been used, or is left. Here are some useful phrases:

- I notice we've been discussing this aspect of the topic for ten minutes. That seems like quite a lot to me, but how do you feel?
- Have we exhausted this aspect?
- We've got ten minutes before we break. Would you like to carry on with this topic or move on to something else?
- We've had an hour and a half. I've noticed that some people are looking a bit tired. Is it time for a break?

Clarifying

When people are struggling to understand or to put forward a view, they can get – or sound – confused. The signs of this are tortuous sentences, contradictory ideas, jumbly syntax maybe combined with a degree of obvious fluster. Alternatively, the comment may be so brief that it disappears into the flow of the discussion and is at risk of getting lost. Your role is to clarify what the person is saying. You can do this in any number of ways, but useful phrases here are:

- So, I think what you're saying here is...
- So, can I just clarify that? You mean that...
- That sounds interesting but could you just clarify whether you mean x or y ...?

Clarifying and probing questions are essential to effective facilitation. They are necessary because there will always be people who find it hard to make their meaning clear. This could be because they speak too little and are too cryptic in what they say, or because they are so verbose that they and everyone else loses the thread of what they are trying to say. With the cryptic speaker, try saying 'Say more about that ... ?' With the garrulous person try saying 'So what's the bottom line point you're making here X ...?'

Questioning

Skilful questioning is essential for good facilitation. Some questions are more useful than others.

Questions to avoid

Double questions simply confuse people. For example: 'When you say you like working with computers, why is that? Is it any computer or are you more keen on the Mac?' In this example, there are two questions and the respondent will have to concentrate on remembering both halves of the question in order to reply.

Leading questions suggest the answer. For example, 'Have you thought that the internet might be a good way to find this information?' The obvious answer is expected to be 'Yes', thus sparing the respondent the trouble of thinking for him or herself.

'Advice in disguise' questions are well meant, but again, prevent learning and create opposition in the hearer's mind. For example, 'When I faced this problem, I found that it helped me to take it very slowly. Don't you think you'd find the same?'
Avoid any questions that begin:

Is/isn't ... ?	Have/haven't ... ?
Was/wasn't ... ?	Has/hasn't ... ?
Does/doesn't ... ?	Must/mustn't ... ?

There are about 30 of these constructions in English. Questions beginning this way are always advice in disguise. (See also Chapter 8 on coaching.)

Rhetorical questions are an even more obvious technique than leading questions. They suggest that only the most dim person could ever disagree with the thinly disguised proposition in the question. For example, 'Wouldn't you agree that anyone who likes sixties music is a bit sad?'

Powerful questions

The most powerful questions are also the most difficult to ask. It takes practice and skill to avoid falling into any of the traps above. Remember:

- keep it short and simple;
- the ideal facilitator's question is no more than seven or eight words long.

For example:

> So what do you think about that?
> When that happens, what do you do?
> What's your view?

Three even shorter questions which I often use are:

> So . . . ?
> Because . . . ?
> Tell me more . . .?

An even more extreme version of this approach is to remain silent. If you just look encouragingly at the person who is trying to speak, nod and wait, you may find you get surprising results. This technique can often help the under-contributor who struggles to find a place in the flow of talk.

The most useful questions for facilitators invariably begin with some version of the word *what*. A question beginning 'What . . . ?' obliges the respondent to find his or her own words and cannot be answered 'Yes', 'No' or 'Don't know'. Here is an example which compares an *advice in disguise* question with a *what* question on the same topic:

> Would it be an idea to lose weight by joining a Weight Watchers group? (Advice-in-disguise. The questioner has already got his or her own idea about the solution to losing weight.)

Compare this with the far more open:

> What are your ideas about how to lose weight?

Using closed questions effectively

Closed questions have their place. They are useful when you are in a prescriptive role, most probably at the earliest stages of your work with a group.

You ask them because you expect agreement. Typical issues would be when you sense that:

- discussion on a particular topic has been exhausted;
- a topic has been tiresomely reopened when it appeared to have been definitively dealt with some time before;
- the group looks tired;
- it is time for a break;
- one person has been dominating.

Examples of useful closed questions are:

- Shall we move on?
- I think we're going round in circles here; is it OK to stop at this point?
- Everyone is looking a bit droopy. Shall we have a break now?
- I think we need half an hour for a break. Is that OK?

Confronting blockages

Most learning groups get stuck at some point. The typical signs are that the discussion begins to have a round-in-circles character, or to ramble off into what seem like unproductive byways. Signs of distress or boredom begin to appear in individual members: folded arms, chairs pushed away, people scribbling and doodling or playing with their mobiles, avoiding eye contact. Alternatively, the discussion may flow into facile cliché or easy options:

> *Nutrition and food hygiene tutor*
> I was facilitating a group where we had built in an action-planning phase at the end of the session. From being really sprightly and engaged, people suddenly began to look shifty. The few actions that were suggested were ones that demanded little or no effort. I stayed very calm but gently reminded the group that we had set ourselves demanding goals for our project and that if we stuck to the low-level activities suggested, we were not going to meet them. I asked, 'What's the problem with something more demanding?' We then had ten minutes of fruitful discussion about their fears of what the more demanding work would involve and also discussed ways of confronting the fears.

To deal with the blockage you have to notice it. It may be an issue that is so obvious that it takes on the characteristic of what experienced facilitators dub *The Elephant in the Room* – something so big that it has to be edged around, so embarrassing and apparently dangerous that everyone knows about it but no one can talk about it openly. Here your best option is *Name That Elephant* – as this tutor did:

> *Management development course tutor*
> As the course continued, I noticed that whenever I set up a pairs exercise, there was one member, X, that no one seemed to want to work with. He had made constantly disparaging remarks about me – he always knew every theory, had read every book, had already been on a similar course. People were avoiding him in the breaks and clearly muttering about his behaviour whenever they could. As soon as I realized this I knew I had to deal with it. Before starting the next session, I asked the group to consider the topic of our learning climate and asked, 'What's helping?' Followed by 'What's holding us back?' After uncomfortable silences, people began to hint at their views on X. I said, 'Yes, I've noticed, X, that you seem to be spending a lot of time on your own.' I heard the collective breath of the group drawn in. 'How does it feel to you?' X began his usual stuff about how much he knew, only to be interrupted by a member of the group, angrily challenging him and saying that if he couldn't stay courteous to me and to them and to stop boasting, she thought he ought to go. X swept out of the room in a rage and I did not follow him. The group was desperately upset and we then had to agree what we were going to do. Cutting a much longer story short, one person was delegated to talk to him outside while the rest of the group decided on what terms they would have him back. I reminded the group of the rules of feedback we had agreed at the beginning of the course. When he returned, both they and I were able to describe the impact of his behaviour on us and to ask him to moderate it in the interests of everyone's learning. This was clearly painful for X to hear, but slightly to my surprise, he opted to stay inside the group. That was one giant elephant, well confronted. Without the confrontation, this group would have fallen apart, I am sure of it.

As this description makes clear, the role of facilitator does not imply that you have to put up with coarseness, rudeness, or personal attack.

Other approaches may include the direct: 'I think that as a group you seem to be avoiding the issue of . . . '

Or the indirect: 'I'm wondering what's being avoided here?'

The art of confrontation is to remain calm and centred yourself, reminding yourself that you are doing it in the interests of learning. As with any other intervention, ask yourself what its purpose is. The only purpose should be to aid the learning of the group. Remember that you are describing behaviour, not condemning or judging it. If you do it too ruthlessly you will become aggressive and will lose the respect of the group. If you are too indirect, the message will become so softened that people will not hear it.

Other kinds of confrontation

In everyday life a lot of us will run with enthusiasm from confrontation. As a facilitator you will need the courage to do the opposite: to confront whenever you see behaviour which is getting in the way of the group's learning. One of the most common will be when gaps emerge between what the group says it values or wishes and what it does in practice. One of my colleagues was facilitating a group which had as one of its aims the improvement of communication between its members. One member of the group, Y, asked X, another member, a particular question about a simple piece of factual data held by X. In reply, X looked down, fished in his briefcase and said 'I've got it on my BlackBerry. I'll send it to your mobile now'. Instead of letting this extraordinary behaviour pass, thus allowing it to become a juicy piece of corridor gossip to be enjoyed after the meeting, my colleague calmly intervened:

> X, I notice you've been asked a direct question by Y but instead of answering you've said you'll use your Blackberry to send it to her.

Note: my colleague was using the rules of feedback – describing the behaviour and not judging it. He then continued:

> I'm wondering what the impact of this has been on Y.

Note: again he did not condemn the behaviour, merely made a space in the conversation for the other person to speak – in effect giving her permission to say what her real feelings were.

X's mouth dropped open in amazement. Surely everyone was used to him BlackBerrying them all the time, even when they were in the same room?

Y quickly intervened:

> Y, I can't tell you how discourteous it seems to me. It's as if you can't be bothered to speak to me and we're sitting directly opposite each other! I feel hurt and annoyed just as I did when you did the same thing in our meeting last week.

X and Y were then able to have their first truly honest conversation about X's communication preferences without any further intervention from my colleague. Five minutes later, however, my colleague did ask:

> I'm wondering how this links with what you have been saying about improving communication between you all?

Discovering that is it possible to have this kind of conversation without mutual rage and, even better, that it improves rather than damages the relationship is often a turning point in the learning of the group. This is where facilitator behaviour adds incomparable value. Even though the number of words spoken, as here, may be small, their impact is considerable.

Handling tears

The more important the topic to the group, the more you can expect strong emotion from time to time. Inevitably, there will be times when someone gets upset and cries. Some tutors feel that this is the ultimate horror:

> I was running a course on fair selection for human resources staff in an organization. Put bluntly, it was about how to make sure that there were no embarrassing tribunals. About a third of the way through the day, we were dealing with practice selection interviews, and doing it through role play. Suddenly, one of the participants burst into tears. It turned out that her partner was out of work and had been rejected for a job at an interview the day before. She was overwhelmed with worry about the mortgage and it was all too close to home. I just froze – 1 didn't have a clue what to do.

In my experience, it is rare to get much warning of such an occurrence. People can sit on their emotion for a long time and disguise their distress, but then it suddenly bursts out. The keys to coping are:

- stay calm yourself;
- accept that the person's crying is not your 'fault';
- do everything you can to preserve the other person's dignity;
- deal with the immediate distress; don't try to find out the underlying cause at this stage;
- ask the person what they would like to do;
- give them the option of leaving, if that is what they would prefer;
- with *great* discretion offer a hug or a comforting touch.

It is a mistake to assume that people are 'forced' or 'made' to cry. Crying is a choice, even if it is made at an unconscious level, so it is the responsibility of the person who has made that choice. Your responsibility is to react appropriately. It is also a mistake to assume that people will regret the crying or even feel embarrassed about it. The experience may be usefully cathartic, as this account shows:

> I was doing a counselling course because it's a skill I need to have at work. We were halfway through the course – it was a series of one-day events. The subject of bereavement came up, and – I don't know why – during one of the practices where we were always told it was not a role play and had to work with real issues, the subject of the death of my mother came up. She had died ten years before, but I found myself crying uncontrollably. My 'counsellor' was wonderful and so was our tutor. We stopped and the tutor came over and sat down quietly with me, just lightly touching my arm. No one else looked embarrassed, though some told me later that they had been. It was all handled really well and I felt wonderful afterwards – really 'lightened'. In retrospect, I realized that I'd never really grieved for her properly and that event started a useful healing process for me.

Self-disclosure

Used appropriately this can be a powerful intervention. An authentic disclosure of your own feelings can have major impact on the group. As ever, the guiding principle of whether to speak or not must be: 'Will making this statement or asking this question contribute significantly to the group's learning?' If the answer is yes, then it is worth the risk of seeming self-indulgent. Places where it could be appropriate might be:

- Self-disclosure is part of the group's agenda and you need to model the way; you are giving permission for feelings to be honestly described.
- The group is discussing something that has triggered an uncomfortable memory, feeling or response in you and it is likely that they will notice some change in your demeanour. Explaining its origin will short-circuit any tendency for the group to misinterpret what they see.
- You are personally challenged in some way by a member of the group.

One of my colleagues on our coach-training courses describes how we make effective use of self-disclosure:

> We ask people to work on 'real' issues, no role play, so it is obvious to me that we have to do the same thing ourselves when we do demonstrations of particular techniques or approaches. All of us in the faculty have to decide how far we take personal disclosure. I usually feel it is OK to take a risk. I choose topics, some of them very personal, on which I really do want some coaching and in doing so I know I am stepping beyond the normal tutor persona of apparently totally-together person. It's a fine line. If we display too much vulnerability then we are not modelling the maturity of the excellent coach. But if we display none then we are missing opportunities to show the group that we, too, are human and that in coaching, you don't have to be 'bad' to get better. The effects are profound. The honesty, vividness and depth of the material with which participants work is immediately elevated and it is common for all of us to be asked, years later, when we meet participants again, how the 'story' ended – they don't forget.

Managing participation

In a good discussion most members of a group feel willing and able to speak when appropriate. Many of the anxieties of tutors and the grumbles of group members concern the numbers of people participating in any one discussion. Three typical comments illustrate familiar situations:

> A lot of people there had been going to these classes for years. They knew each other and they knew the tutor, so no one else got a look in.

> My *bête noire* was a man who would always try to prove me wrong at great length. He was being forced by his organization to attend, so he always felt he had to show he already knew everything that I was teaching. He tried to dominate every discussion.

> As a tutor, I always thought our discussions were good, but one evening, for interest, I counted up the number who had said something. I was horrified to discover that only 6 out of 16 had said anything.

Even in a group where everybody contributes at some time, there will always be some who talk more than others. This can be a cause for concern if those who talk most are preventing other people from joining in, or are seeming to waste the group's time with rambling anecdotes, with harangues, or simply with information too difficult for the rest of the group to understand. Adult groups often contain one member who is more knowledgeable than the rest. You may find it tempting to engage one prominent individual in discussion – sometimes simply out of pleasure in talking, sometimes because of a cowardly wish to placate someone who might otherwise become bored and restless. The short-term solution is to let him or her get on with it, but if you habitually allow one person to dominate a group you are only storing up trouble for the future. It is unfair to other people, who eventually become irritated and fidgety and may leave rather than sit through more sessions of a dialogue between a tutor and an apparently favoured participant.

It is better instead to encourage people to develop self-criticism about the quality and length of their own contributions. You can set the pace by inviting the group to evaluate each other's contributions: 'Does anyone have a comment on that?' or 'What do other people think?' In a group where this capacity has been encouraged, participants are often able to interrupt a lengthy contribution either with challenges and questions, with comments of their own or, as I saw once in a philosophy class, simply with a good-humoured, 'You've had three minutes by my watch, time to let someone else in now!'

Over-contributors

There is more than one reason for the over-contributor's behaviour. For a start, they may know a lot more than others in the group and be eager to offer it. They may like talking and be unaware of how much potential this has for annoying the rest of the group. They may simply be looking for recognition – prominence rather than dominance. They may be setting themselves up as a rival tutor, overtly challenging your expertise and your right to lead the group. In the course of doing this they may attract followers, leading not just to a rival tutor but rival factions. Or they may be like Charles Dickens's character Mr Dick, the gentle eccentric in *David Copperfield*, who soon brought every discussion back to the beheaded English king, Charles I. The phrase *King Charles's Head* has come to be used for the obsessed person where all roads lead back, with tedious predictability, to the same topic. A basic assumption that behind every apparently irritating behaviour there is some positive intention, if only you could unravel it, is probably a better place to start than to assume that the motive is malign.

Whatever the reason, over-contributing has to be managed and the person who must manage it is you – at least initially – and to manage it you must first spot it. Make it a priority to notice the patterns of contribution.

Some possible tactics, any of which could be right, depending on the circumstances, are:

- Harness their energy by asking them to undertake extra research, give short lectures and special assignments. Note that here your task will be to keep a careful balance between letting them tyrannize a group, on the one hand, and letting them waste their talents, on the other.
- Undertake regular process reviews (page 115) where the question 'Who talks most?' will enable other members of the group to name the talker, increasing the chances of raised self-awareness and thus more frequent self-monitoring. You may want to ask the group how useful they find the talker's contributions. Where the frequent talker is genuinely contributing something valuable, this will enable the group to say so. If they see it as pointless showing off, they may be able to express their annoyance.
- Consider the possibility that they are on the wrong course and suggest that they re-enrol for something that will be more appropriate for their experience.
- Manipulate the seating so that their favourite position (usually immediately opposite you) is taken by someone else.
- Cut through their comments courteously by summarizing and then turning cleanly and deliberately to someone else.
- Some kinds of persistent talker are persisting only because they feel unheard. If this is so, then saying something like, 'X, I notice you've said a or b thing four times this morning. Would you like to take a few moments to tell us why you feel so passionately about this?' A moment of formal recognition like this can do three things simultaneously: it shows the person that their efforts have been noticed, it gives them a hint that they may have been over-contributing and it allows them to have their say properly.
- When you see them taking breath, do what John Heron calls *Traffic Cop* – firmly holding up a palm conveying *Stop!* while you simultaneously turn to someone else by beckoning with your other hand.
- If all of this fails, then you may have to resort to the undesirable tactic of talking to them privately. This is undesirable because all such transactions are better if done openly and not in secret.

Under-contributors

Silent members, or people who speak only rarely in a discussion, can present problems when you do not want to bully people into speaking but want to see everyone make some sort of contribution. As with over-contributors, they must be managed. Not to do so will lead to the group becoming unhealthily preoccupied with the silent person:

> *Tutor, music teaching course*
> We had one student who always sat in the same place – the one nearest the door. After four meetings, she was the only person in the group who had not changed places and the only person who had not spoken in the group discussion. I am experienced enough to know that this is a tell-tale sign of something wrong. A lot of energy was going into avoiding her and frankly into gossiping about her and how they all disliked her, though the dislike seemed to me to be based on extremely flimsy criteria – essentially that she did not join in – but no one knew why.

There is no single reason to explain why people are silent. People who do not speak can be silent as a way of showing disapproval of what the rest of the group are saying; they can be silent out of shyness or diffidence or lack of motivation to learn; silent out of embarrassment; silent because, although they would like to speak, conditions never seem right for them to take the plunge; or simply silent because they prefer to listen to other people rather than to talk themselves.

You must judge each case on its merits. There is no evidence to equate participation in discussion with learning, and if people prefer to be silent it could be an impertinence to try forcing them to speak. The secret is, once again, to observe closely. Who is looking withdrawn? Who is looking unhappy? Who usually has a lot to say but has been unnaturally silent? Who has been fidgeting, possibly as a sign of frustration at not being able to get into the discussion? Attempting to draw out a quiet, self-contained person by asking direct questions may face him or her with an excruciating ordeal and may, in any case, fail to produce a response. I remember a woman in one of my groups who simply stonewalled my attempt to be helpful by shaking her head silently and staring down at the table. Other people may feel you have provided them with just the opening they have been waiting for, but your effort will usually be more successful if directed more widely than at a single individual – 'Some of you have special knowledge of____. Would any of you like to say something on this?' Again, the rest of the group can be encouraged to look to each other for contributions, to get to know who has particular knowledge of or unusual opinions on some issue and can therefore be expected to say something valuable.

When a reserved or less dominant member does make a brief contribution to a discussion, it is often helpful to rein in the discussion at that point to ask for further elaboration – 'It might be interesting if you expanded that point'. Alternatively, you can suggest a general pause in the discussion by saying something like, 'We seem to have covered a lot of ground rather quickly. Can we stop to think for a moment?' You may also want to say, 'I notice that four or five people have had a lot to say on this topic. Can we hear now from the people who haven't spoken yet?' You can combine this with making brief eye contact with the people who have remained silent. Focusing the discussion at one stage like this is often a useful way of allowing slower or more introverted thinkers to catch up and speak if they want to. There may be opportunities to do the same thing at the beginning and end of a discussion. I have seen some tutors encourage silent people to speak at these points by saying, 'We left a lot unsaid at our last session. Is there anyone who would like the last word?' Such invitations have, of course, to be followed by a generous pause, otherwise they might just as well not be made.

Sleepers

An extreme version of non-participation is the group member who yawns frequently and openly, closes his or her eyes or actually falls asleep. Perhaps your immediate assumption when this happens is that boredom has literally driven the person to sleep. This is always a possibility, but other explanations are more likely: the effects of medication, a new baby whose demands are disturbing parental sleep, a heavy lunch, a hangover or even the serious sleep-disturbance condition narcolepsy where the sufferer falls involuntarily asleep for seconds or minutes at a time.

Don't ignore the sleeper, not least because no one else will be able to. The potential for all-round embarrassment is enormous. Create an immediate break, sending the rest of the group off for a leg-stretch, tea or coffee. Take the person aside, say what you observed and ask, respectfully of course, what the explanation is and use your discretion from there. Part of your duty to create a climate of trust is to encourage people to tell you at the outset if there is anything you need to know about their circumstances which will be mutually helpful. Having made such a request of one group, all of them senior clinicians in the NHS on one of my training courses, one of the group bravely said that he had a non-life threatening but serious illness and was taking a particular medication. He told us that this might well send him to sleep at various points during the day. Having ascertained that he really did want to remain on the course, all its members, several of them, like him, distinguished doctors, agreed a protocol for managing his drowsiness. This forestalled any embarrassment and worked well when the predicted naps did indeed happen.

Problems of over-dominant and too silent members can often be solved by splitting the group into smaller groups for some part of the class time:

> *Literature tutor*
> We start off as one group – about 15 of us – going over the week's written work, looking at a new poem or chapter. After coffee we divide into however many groups can be divided by three or four.

> Each group has a question written on a piece of paper. All the questions are closely related but different, and based on the topic we discussed before coffee. This takes 20 minutes, strictly timed. We then report back, compare questions, and have what is usually a most useful general discussion to finish off. With this system everybody who wants to can speak, and everyone is obliged to give really close attention to the text.
>
> *Media studies tutor*
> There are 25 students, two tutors. We watch the video extracts together, discuss it for ten minutes, then split. People who never speak in the large group normally say quite a lot in the smaller one.

It is not unusual for the first five minutes of the discussion to be the slowest and the most difficult to manage, and the part of the process that you may dread most. The best ways of encouraging discussion seem to be to ask people to prepare for it by thinking, reading and writing, to reassure them that silence does not matter, to make it clear that you really have withdrawn from your role of expert by saying, 'Would anyone like to comment?' or some such phrase, and no more. Most importantly, you must provide the group with an initial stimulus as emotionally gripping, or as intellectually intriguing and as complex, as possible. This could be a lecture, a dramatic reading, a film, a case study or simulation or anything else which demands an immediate response. Film and video are perhaps particularly useful in loosening tongues, as many people are used to discussing them informally without the strain that may be associated with academic discussion.

Remember, too, how much the shape of the room and the type of furniture (see page 101) contribute to atmosphere and eye-lines. If your aim is a discussion which involves everyone, it is more or less essential to seat the group in comfortable chairs ranged in a circle, as that is the only way people can see or address each other easily. Where you have a group sitting lecture-style in straight lines, most people will only have one good view, and that is of you, so naturally they will be far more likely to address their remarks to you than to each other. The temptation to cap every student comment with one of your own will be almost irresistible.

Ultimately, the patterns of participation in the group will tell you what is going on inside it. In your career as a facilitator you will eventually meet every possible form of challenge and resistance, whether it is from over-contributors or under-contributors or from people who arrive late and leave early, whisper at the back, fail to deliver on their promises, start factions – and so on.

Only you can decide what to do. The ultimate sanction is to ask the person to leave, or maybe to lay down your terms for their staying. I faced this myself with a participant on one of our training programmes, when I realized that there was one person whose presence in the group was having a number of negative effects, not least because of his adamant refusal to participate in any of the activities. In this case I chose to ask him to stay behind at the end of the second day of the five-day course for a private discussion – a rare tactic since it is virtually always better to have such discussions openly. As soon as we were on our own, he said, 'I suppose you're going to chuck me out'. Since this was someone whom I had already observed to have positioned himself as one of life's victims, it was important to avoid the trap of appearing to be yet another of the people who was persecuting him. After an hour of discussion, we had established that he did want to remain on the programme. However, I had also made it clear to him that continuing non-participation in all the exercises was not an option and that he was welcome to stay, on condition that he changed some of the behaviour that my co-tutor and I were finding disruptive and difficult. In this case, he did stay and his behaviour did change, though only just enough to be acceptable, but I was perfectly prepared to ask him to leave. Sometimes it is better to sacrifice one person than to destroy the group.

An undersung tool: the value of flip charts

Compared with the intricacies of understanding an apparently troublesome group member, it may seem a little naïve and rudimentary to write about how to use flip charts. Flip charts may also seem laughably low-tech compared with electronic aids. But when you take the time to learn how to use them properly, flip charts are a powerful way of increasing the impact of facilitation.

Seeing your words written on a page is another way of giving people acknowledgement and showing them that they have been heard. Where there are two or more sides to a debate, it is another technique for demonstrating this visually and encouraging open-mindedness. A simple bullet-pointed list on a flip chart can clarify the main issues in a way that will reinforce a verbal summary. Covering a whole wall with graphics and charts may also encourage greater creativity.

Inexperienced facilitators commonly make these mistakes in relation to flip charts:

- under-using them;
- putting them in places where some of the group cannot read them;
- writing too small;
- writing in green, brown or yellow pens (invisible to the group);
- crowding too many words on to one page;

addressing the flip chart instead of the group;
writing slowly;
writing everything in capital letters.

Also, if you are unused to writing on flip charts, a mysterious spelling block can sometimes grip you: a word that you know perfectly well can suddenly seem baffling.

To get round these problems, first check that the group can see the flip chart clearly and adjust it if someone complains that the angle is wrong for them. Write in big, lower-case cursive letters, well spaced, and keep facing the group as far as possible, maybe constantly turning around as you are writing. Ask in advance for a generous supply of red and black pens. Use people's own words. If in doubt about spelling, ask for advice from the group. Use bullet points rather than numbering as numbering may seem to imply an inappropriate order of importance. Check that the walls can take blutak or tape and, if you are writing on taped flip pages, ensure that the pens will not bleed through the paper on to the wall. Canny facilitators invest in their own kit of favourite pens as experience suggests that venue organizers who have never in their lives used a flip chart simply do not understand how horrible their half-dead, spindly, green and brown pens are for the visiting facilitator.

If confidentiality is an issue, as it might be for instance in a learning set, check that flip charts cannot be read through a window by outsiders casually roaming the corridor and remove all the flip charts at the end of the session, possibly offering any individual sheets to the people whose material they capture.

Finally, consider carefully before asking a member of the group to undertake the task of scribing. Unless people can do quick and fluent flip chart writing, the pace of discussion will slow while the group waits for the tyro scribe to catch up with them. Also, the pen is, like the conch in *Lord of the Flies*, a symbol of authority. If you decide to hand it over, do so knowingly.

Your role

Your role in an authentic discussion is, then, a taxing one. You must first of all make sure that the participants understand and share a common view of what discussion is by inviting them at the outset to discuss the discussion process, and by making it clear that your own role will be that of impartial facilitator rather than active teacher, of careful listener rather than frequent speaker. You must be ready to clarify issues so that groups understand what they are discussing, and why. You must be ready to relate the issues of one discussion to issues raised and explored on previous occasions. You must see that the group eschews personal attacks and violent sarcasm, as well as dull restatement of old prejudices. You must encourage and protect minority views. You should make sure that people learn to distinguish between fact and opinion, and be ready to feed in the resources which could supply facts and opinions giving an opposite, even an unpopular view. You must set the linguistic tone by using language that everyone can understand. You must make sure that opportunities are kept open so that people who want to speak can speak. You must encourage the art of listening as well as talking.

If you can do all this, and at the same time train your group to take over these functions too, you are offering your group a chance to learn in a unique way, by measuring minds and experiences with other people on equal terms. You will do all of this through your own authenticity, by tapping into who you truly are and showing others that person. When you use any of the interventions I describe in this chapter you will not seem perfunctory or mechanical. You will be able to sense where the energy is in the group and will be able to work with the grain of it in a fluent and unforced way.

The philosophical and democratic case for discussion, as well as by implication its educational justification, has never been made so powerfully as by John Stuart Mill in his essay *On Liberty*, first published in 1869, a case which can still serve as a model to any teacher, trainer or tutor of adults today:

> There must be discussion, to show how experience is to be interpreted. Wrong opinions and practices gradually yield to fact and argument; but facts and arguments, to produce any effect on the mind, must be brought before it. Very few facts are able to tell their own story, without comments to bring out their meaning. The whole strength and value, then, of human judgement, depending on the one property, that it can be set right when it is wrong, is that reliance can be placed on it only when the means of setting it right are kept constantly at hand. In the case of any person whose judgement is really deserving of confidence, how has it become so? Because he has kept his mind open to criticism of his opinions and conduct. Because it has been his practice to listen to all that could be said against him; to profit by as much of it as was just, and expound to himself, and upon occasion to others, the fallacy of what was fallacious. Because he has felt that the only way in which a human being can make some approach to knowing the whole of a subject, is by hearing what can be said about it by persons of every variety of opinion, and studying all modes in which it can be looked at by every character of mind. No wise man ever acquired his wisdom in any mode but this; nor is it in the nature of human intellect to become wise in any other manner.

The next three chapters look at related but contrasting approaches to learning: action learning, problem-based learning and coaching. All work from the assumption that it is right to make adults responsible for their own learning. All reverse the traditional approaches to knowledge where the teacher is assumed to be the prime authority; all are built on the assumption that learning to learn is the fundamental aim of any educational process and all depend on excellence in facilitation if they are to work.

Further reading

Egan, G. (1973) *Face to Face. The Small Group Experience and Interpersonal Growth.* Monterey, CA: Brooks Cole.

Heron, J. (1989) *The Facilitator's Handbook.* London: Kogan Page. This book is essential reading if you want a thorough and subtle theoretical grounding in the skills of facilitation.

Rogers, J. (1999) *Facilitating Groups*. London: Management Futures.

Schwarz, R. (2002) *The Skilled Facilitator.* San Francisco, CA: Jossey-Bass.

Yalom, I.D. (1995) *The Theory and Practice of Group Psychotherapy*, 4th edition. New York: Basic Books.

Notes

1 Patterson, R.W.K. (1970) The concept of discussion, *Studies in Adult Education*, 2 (1).
2 See Further Reading, above.
3 Ibid, above.

6 Action learning

A manager has just returned from the meeting of his 'Learning Set' and is struggling to explain to a colleague what 'Action Learning' is. He can see from her sceptical expression that she thinks this Action Learning/Learning Set stuff is just another soft excuse for a day away from the office.

> *'We discuss our difficulties and challenges'*, he begins.
> *'You mean you sit around all day listening to each other's problems? What – like a therapy group, competing for who has the most tragic problems you mean?'*
> *'No, no'*, our manager explains, *'It's tough, it's disciplined, it's definitely not therapy. It's hard to explain unless you've done it, but it's one of the most significant pieces of learning I've ever been engaged in – and I've done a lot!'*

As this story shows, one of the common difficulties of action learning is explaining it to people who have never experienced it. In similar vein, one of my colleagues was attempting to explain to her brother (a doctor) what she did when she facilitated a learning set. His disbelieving expression was immediately followed by an incredulous – 'You mean they pay you money to do that?'

In fact, once you get past these understandable prejudices, action learning is one of the most powerful tools at the disposal of anyone committed to adult learning, and despite what my colleague's brother believed, it works courtesy of expert facilitation. The principal pioneer of the method was a thoughtful genius called Reg Revans.[1] His theories were shaped in part by the experience of his father. Revans Senior was one of the investigators of the Titanic disaster. He saw this calamitous and avoidable event as an example of the difference between *cleverness* and *wisdom*.

Wisdom, as Revans describes it, is the need to be doubtful about your own qualifications, to be aware of the limits of your knowledge and to know what you don't know. This is what action learning explores: taking risks, never assuming you have the right or only answer, focusing on what you don't know rather than rehashing what you do know.

Revans started his career in the Cavendish Laboratories in Cambridge in the 1920s and worked with Ernest Rutherford, the Nobel Laureate who discovered the structure of the atom. What made the Cavendish unique was its openness to collaborative enquiry. The scientists who worked there were dealing with enormously complex problems steeped in the contradictions and conflicts of the known physics of the time. People from diverse fields shared their findings, and more particularly their doubts and questions, challenging each other's theories and research. This was what made their astounding discoveries possible. It is this approach which makes action learning different from what Revans calls 'Programmed Learning' – the existing knowledge which is taught in schools, colleges and universities. So how is it applied for adult learners?

Action learning happens through learning sets. A set is a group of up to eight people in roughly comparable situations either in the same or different organizations. They meet for anything from two hours to a whole day once every few weeks, initially with a professional set facilitator for a period of six months to a year. Each set member bids for time and presents the group with a live problem. There is a difference in action learning between a *puzzle*, which has a predictable, known solution and a *problem*, which has so far eluded solution. In fact, a good meaty problem for an action learning set will be one in which every potential solution has a negative possible impact on at least one of the main players involved in the problem and where every obvious solution has already been considered.

Once the problem-owner has presented his or her issue, the set gets to work, asking disciplined and skilful questions. Most set members will need training in learning how to ask this kind of question. These are the questions which are not advice, not autobiography ('Well, when this happened to me, I ...'), nor judgement. They will be a blend of tough, hard-truths, with challenge and unequivocal support. Having listened quietly to other people's comments and questions, the problem-holder then explores the issues again, virtually always getting new perspectives and, most importantly, new insights into themselves. Commonly, each person will have a project of some kind on which they will be working during the period over which the set meets. Revans himself has also said that for the individual set member, the core question is 'What makes an honest man, and how do I become one?' He also summed the action learning process up as 'the upward communication of doubt'.

This is a quick overview. Let's go back a few steps.

The underpinning philosophy of action learning

Many of you will have attended courses and found them interesting enough at the time. But how much did your actual behaviour change as a result? The answer may be *very little*. The ideas may have seemed intriguing but soon enough so-called real life comes to claim you and the intensity of the experience immediately fades. Or, if your aim is to apply your learning in a day-to-day situation, you may find that the culture of the people around you, whether in an organization or in a family, slowly but surely erodes your good intentions because what you plan to do is at odds with how those people generally behave. Or possibly the skills seem much harder to apply than they appeared to be in the safe environment of the course, or there are few opportunities to practise and, without reinforcement, the learning fades. Alternatively, your courage may fail – it just seems too hard. Overall, one of the reasons that so much course-based learning does not stick, particularly where behaviour is the issue, is that we are working with pre-packaged solutions and ideas. These may be perfectly good solutions worked out by excellent people, but they may not work for you. This is the area that Revans calls 'Programmed Learning', not implying that is wrong (quite the contrary – it is essential), but that it has limits. Action learning addresses the place where what we don't know is as important as what we do because what we don't know is what is holding us back.

This is why action learning is different. It starts at the point where other kinds of learning may leave off: with implementation. In an action learning set, the learner is working on his or her own issues – the ones that really matter. Action learning, like coaching (to which it is a close cousin), is quintessentially about change, that is the *action* of the title. The problem you will bring to your fellow set members as a learner is the one where you are stuck and where being stuck really matters because something critically important is at stake. You know you have to change but you don't know what to do or how to do it. In action learning you will be expected to work through the implementation processes: diagnosing, getting data, planning, managing resistance, adapting and carrying it all through to the end point.

Much conventional learning conspires to conceal all of this. When we teach on a course, and I am as guilty as anyone else of this, it is easy somehow to convey that we are offering a magic formula and that all anyone has to do for success is to apply it. Revans, with typical tongue-in-cheek verve, described this as being 'an expert in past knowledge'. If you as the learner don't get the solution you want, then maybe you should be trying just that little bit harder. The same is true in working life, especially in many professions – for instance, management – where failure is punished so harshly. When this is so, it can become harder and harder for an individual to own up to ignorance or uncertainty. I see the same thing in my very senior coaching clients where they frequently report the inexpressible relief of permission to be vulnerable in the coaching room – often literally the only place where this is possible.

You can see this at its most extreme in politicians, where, as several of the more honest senior members of the cadre have remarked (after leaving government), to admit to uncertainty is to guarantee political death. The former Secretary of State for the Home Office, David Blunkett, for instance, has described lying awake at night during his time in office worrying about what to do, believing it impossible to confess to doubt and feeling obliged to conceal what he called his *dreadful collywobbles*. I noticed that this admission was predictably followed by a great deal of journalistic sneering about his alleged weakness in owning up to the stress. Posing as supremely confident at all times leads to something that, again, many of my coaching clients, most of them extremely able people, will wryly own up to: Impostor Syndrome – the belief that, some day, someone will find them out.

Along with this is the assumption in action learning that only you – the problem-owner – can really know your own issue and all the myriad complexities that surround it and only you can carry through the changes. This is why, as with coaching, advice is pointless and merely undermines the advice-receiver. You are the expert in your own issue. You do not need to defer to the faux expertise of others. Action learning assumes that your own experience is the best possible teacher, as long as – and this is an important condition – you know how to review it. Similarly, action learning is built on the principle that the opportunity for genuine reflection is a rare luxury. Mostly we hurtle from one commitment to the next with little chance to slow down and consider what is really going on for us. We may rarely consider:

> Why did I do that? What was the response I got when I did? What else might I have done? What does this say about me? How self-aware am I? What were the consequences of my actions? What might have happened if I had done something different? What did I learn from what I did?

Finally, given all of the above, the input of others is essential. Left to ourselves, we will flounder in the same old morass. Working with others on the basis of absolute equals and in an expertly structured learning environment, it is possible to put forward the problem, to express uncertainties, to expose assumptions, to be supported and to be challenged in equal measure. Hence the importance of the set.

Differences between action learning and other interventions

Action learning is different. Here are some of the ways in which it differs from other activities that may superficially look similar:

Training	Action learning does not normally have any taught elements, though the aim of learning is the same. The focus is on a real project which will actually be carried out. The topic is suggested by the individual member

whereas in training, the curriculum is controlled by the trainer/tutor.

Counselling, therapy and support groups Careful listening to individuals who have problems may be common to both, but the aim of action learning is to translate thought into change through a project. Participants are assumed to be mentally resilient people. A therapy group is essentially about insight and also into curing something that is psychologically wrong – not the emphasis in action learning. A therapy group will also have an expert in psycho-therapeutic processes as its leader – not the role of the set adviser. A learning set is also more than just a support group, as challenge is a vital part of what happens.

Facilitated discussion A set adviser certainly needs to be able to facilitate discussion but this is a means to a particular end: action and change. The discipline of working steadily around the group on the basis of one person at a time as the focus also makes it unlike other kinds of discussion.

An organizational meeting Action learning set members work as equals. Their only aim is the learning of individuals. There is no formal chairing or decision-making and vote-taking.

A seminar or tutorial There are no prepared papers or academic presentations in an action learning set and discussion will flow in a more spontaneous and unstructured way than would be normal in a seminar or tutorial where the stated aim is the exchange of ideas around a particular piece of academic knowledge. The set facilitator is not a subject expert.

A team meeting A learning set is not a team. Unlike a team, the set does not have specific roles and responsibilities. There is no interdependence as there has to be with a team. The set will usually meet only for the purposes of learning, and from a wide variety of organizations or departments, though it may sometimes share a common project, in which case it may also have to function as a team.

Quality circles Action learning is normally undertaken voluntarily and focuses more on individual than on organizational learning.

The benefits of action learning

Action learning has innumerable benefits as a flexible tool for adults. All are subtle, and none tend to be immediately obvious to the novice set member.

Understanding that you are responsible for you

It is easy to fall into the trap of assuming that you are somehow the victim of someone or something else. I commonly see this in how some of my coaching clients initially present their issues. They will talk as if they are the prisoner of their organizations or bosses ('The organization won't let me do something;' 'I can't do this or that thing') and in other ways that betray their assumption that they are to some extent powerless. Action learning challenges this assumption. Set members are trained to ask questions such as 'Which bit of this problem do you own?' Or, 'What's your own responsibility for how this situation has come about?' Far from it being offensive to be so challenged, in practice it is exhilarating, just as, most of the time, it is in coaching. It is immensely invigorating to understand that you do have power and that by taking control of your own life you can change it.

Gains in emotional intelligence

Emotional intelligence, or EQ, means the ability to manage your own and other people's emotions skilfully. It has become an important indicator of career achievement in many fields, where, for instance, the early success that is associated with a high IQ may peter out because, in spite of their high scores on conventional measures of intelligence such as verbal reasoning, the people concerned have little idea of their impact on others and lack the social skills necessary to influence or manage them. The skills necessary for a learning set to work are extremely similar to the skills of emotional intelligence as defined by Daniel Goleman[2] and others: self-knowledge, self-management, understanding and creating rapport with others. For instance, to operate successfully in a learning set, you have to know and then practise the difference between real listening and pretend listening. You have to be able to set your own ego to one side, to ask penetrating questions which are for the benefit of the other person rather than asking questions to demonstrate your own cleverness. These are all essential skills in virtually any job or life-role.

A learning set confronts its members with frank feedback given in a supportive environment. This may be the one place in which people can get feedback which is free from the need to score a point at someone else's expense, to prove superiority, or to mask personal weaknesses through projecting them on to someone else. By making yourself vulnerable enough to admit to uncertainty, by being able to ask for what you want from other set members, by being able to accept help, you open the door to such feedback. Self-awareness is a gift. When you have it you understand better how to manage yourself because you know your own hot buttons and how to avoid triggering them. You know what your impact is on others and you begin to understand what makes them tick, too, so you are more likely to get what you want.

Learning about groups and teams

An experienced facilitator will also draw attention to the process of the group (see page 114) as well as its task. Understanding that such processes are at work in all human interactions has been a revelation to many set members. Their levels of psychological awareness have usually deepened considerably as a result of attending the set.

The set gives valuable practical experience in learning how to work as a group. This is because all formal hierarchy is stripped away. No one can assume that they have a right to dominate merely on grounds of positional authority. Power will still be an issue in sets, but it will be dealt with differently. For instance, I once facilitated a set where one of only two men in the group was calmly taken to task about his constant use of the word *girls* to describe the mature women in his work team. The women in the set were able to explain clearly and without stridency how this and other language was unwittingly betraying sexist assumptions that might well have got him into deep trouble at some point in his future career.

The discipline of learning to listen and ask questions rather than to make speeches and assertions or quarrelsome bids for power is a profound one indeed. Similarly, people will often report increased capacity to live with uncertainty. Ability to manage ambiguity in oneself and others has often seemed to me like a *sine qua non* for robust mental health.

Leaps in learning

By working on the margins of the known and grappling with the uncertainty of the complex unknown, the chances are that participants will make major leaps in understanding and skill. This is because in truth they are learning how to learn as well as learning to deal with whatever problems they have come to the set to solve. Sometimes what is learnt may be a simple transactional process – maybe a different way to handle one particularly difficult meeting. The chances are, however, that people will mostly make transformational changes – for instance, not just to handle that one difficult meeting but to know how to handle any difficult meeting because what they will have been working on with fellow set members is a whole person approach – underlying attitudes, hopes, fears, rational and irrational, as well as the practicalities of how you actually behave.

As the great Carl Rogers, the founding father of person-centred therapy, commented in another context[3]

> Anything that can be taught to another person is relatively inconsequential and has little or no significant influence on behaviour.

Real problems get solved

The problems may be personal, academic or organizational or some mix of all of them. The point is that action learning provides a way to get something significant done by delivering change. Set members also describe greatly enhanced ability to deal with organizational complexity because by working on a specific project where the set can provide a constant base of reference and new ideas, the set member begins to understand how systems work. Since most action learning involves projects, members also learn a great deal about the realities of managing change, understanding that the actual practice is different from the neat parameters of the theory. Where the focus of the work is an actual project, it would be normal for people to say that their project management skills have also been significantly enhanced. There is nothing like knowing that you are going to be called to account for progress on your project by your fellow set members to bring you face to face with the necessary project management skills.

This is most probably because one of the major benefits of action learning is the hugely increased self-confidence that almost all set members report. How does this come about? My guess is that it has to be because set members have learnt how to suspend judgement and at the same time to ask the truly powerful questions which take their colleagues to new levels of understanding and to be on the receiving end of the same processes themselves. To be accepted and to be respectfully challenged means that there is far less need to conceal who you really are.

Practicalities

A set is usually organized by the commissioning institution, virtually always by someone who has experienced the methodology and knows its power. This person will approach and enrol the participants, book the venue and the facilitator. There is no one main type of set. It may consist of people with similar jobs in different organizations, people with similar jobs in the same organization, students in higher education whose subjects are similar or different. Composition of the set will depend on the reasons for commissioning the work in the first place.

The ideal number for a set is six, but I have known sets work well with as few as four members and as many as eight. Six is ideal because there are enough people to give variety of views and backgrounds but the group is small enough for each person to expect a decent amount of air time. The set may meet for a half or whole day, though some operate for as little as two hours at a time. Typically there will be a three- to six-week gap between meetings and between five and eight meetings altogether. I was once a member of a set which kept going for two years, but this was in the teeth of evidence that dwindling attendance meant that its life was effectively over some time before that. It was only our liking for each other's company that kept it going for so long beyond its natural life span.

The first meeting is usually spent introducing the concept as there are virtually always several members who have not met action learning before. After a brief background to the history and rationale of the method, the best way to explain it is to have a mini-round of problem-solving which will give members a capsule notion of what to expect. Usually it is also vital for you as the facilitator to introduce people to the skills of action learning: listening, questioning, reframing, summarizing, challenging, giving feedback. You will find advice on all of these topics throughout this book. Many facilitators also ask people to give a brief autobiography at this session, maybe using the technique of drawing a lifeline on the flip chart with highs and lows indicated. Another possibility is to ask members to introduce themselves using a prompt like this, encouraging people to decide how much they are willing to share with others at this early stage. A good way of encourage the appropriate degree of disclosure is for you as set facilitator to kick off the process:

My name	
My contact details	
Current job	
Highlights/lowlights of life experience	
Highlights/lowlights of career experience	
Personal circumstances	
Leisure interests	
What I believe I do well	

What I believe I do less well	
What you need to know about working with me	
My reason for being part of this set	
Assuming this set is highly successful, what I will have achieved is...	
People, living or dead, fictional or real whom I admire – and why	

This session will also explain what will make for a typical project on which each member will work.

What is a 'project'?

As the name implies, this approach to learning is all about action. The action happens outside the set – the set is merely the vehicle for pushing it along. So for action to happen, there has to be a focus for it. Ideally this will be a project which continues throughout the life of the set. When action learning fails it is often because participants have not had this focus and the set becomes just another pleasant discussion.

In preparing set members for their choice of project, offer them these criteria:

- The issue must matter: resolving it will have the power to transform something important.
- It should have potential to develop the individual – for instance to grow their confidence.
- It should be achievable: for instance it should be possible to accomplish it within the time frame of the set's life and it should be within that person's power to implement.
- It has to be chosen by the set member. A project chosen by someone else – for instance a line manager – will not have the same sense of ownership and urgency.

However, in some ways the word *project* may be misleading. Think of it as a convenient label for gathering up everything that the set member wants to achieve. For instance, the overall project for our trainee coaches is to achieve the Diploma in Coaching and also to become excellent coaches. But in each of the three half-day learning set meetings, individuals will bring ongoing issues from their recent work with clients – for instance how the coach handled a tricky situation with a client who cried her way through the entire session. So examples of projects might be: how to move from manager to leader; how to introduce a culture of empowerment in an organization; deciding where to go next in career and how to get there; tackling a culture of absenteeism in an organization; growing a small business; creating and running a team.

During the life of the set, it is normal for each person's project to change and evolve. The presenting issue often turns out to be merely the surface. Finding out what lies beneath and its inevitable connections to our own assumptions and behaviour is what makes the method so powerful.

The set facilitator's role

Everything I have written in Chapter 5 applies to facilitating a learning set. As with any other group process, discussion of ground rules is imperative. For instance, maintaining confidentiality is critical to the success of the methodology and negotiating active assent to what this means in practice will reassure people that they can be more than superficially honest with each other. It will also be vital to agree expectations around attendance, and how the group will deal with people who default. Voluntary attendance is an important principle in action learning but where the assumption is built into a course, this may not always seem possible. One of my own early experiences as a set facilitator was undermined by the insistence of my client that he expected everyone he nominated to be present. I pricked the giant bubble of resentment that this created by telling the set that if anyone found after two meetings that they really were not getting anything out of the process, then they were free to leave.

There is the same necessity to live the values of excellent facilitation by modelling questioning and listening skills yourself and overall to manage the process, not the content. In particular, your role is to ensure that each person has a fair share of the time and to forestall any temptation to let discussion drift into nice chat. Assume a thirty-minute slot for each person and agree an order in which people will present their issue.

Start the set with a strictly managed round of headline catch-ups from each person. Essentially this is an ice-breaker (page 50) and you might want to use some kind of simple structure such as *Prouds and Sorries*

Since we last met, I'm proud...
Since we last met I'm sorry...

– to give it shape.

There are innumerable ways that each member's time-slot can be structured. I was trained in action learning methodology by my friend and colleague Dr Judith Riley, and have found that her approach – my version of it is described here – works well.

- Ask the member whose turn it is to spend no more than five minutes outlining the issue using these headings:
  - What the issue is
  - What led up to it
  - Why it is such an important issue for me now
  - Who else is involved
  - What I have already tried
  - What would make for an ideal solution for me.
- Now ask the problem-holder to sit out where he or she can see and hear the rest of the discussion but take no part in it. The discussion will include questions that have occurred to people while they have been listening or ideas that the problem-holder could find it useful to consider. This part of the process may take ten minutes.
- Use the flip chart to write down all the main points that the group makes – don't edit; use their language.
- Invite the problem-holder back into the group and ask for his or her immediate responses. At first people will find it eerie to be in the room and to hear people discussing them, but with experience will become accustomed to it.
- Ask the problem-holder to use the flip chart pen to star any of the group's ideas that he or she has found especially interesting or would like to have clarified. Allow another ten minutes for this.
- Ask the problem-holder to facilitate the last five minutes of the time slot with an emphasis on what action he or she might take as a result of the discussion.
- It is important to keep the group strictly to the agreed time slots. I have also found it better to stick to each member of the group having the same amount of time, otherwise it is possible for one person, extra-needy in his or her own eyes but not necessarily the most actually needy person in the group, to dominate. Resentment may not be expressed at the time, but it will probably be there and if left unchecked will destroy the set because it has, in effect, become a support group – not the purpose of action learning.
- Spend the last twenty minutes of the whole-group's time on feedback. Again, you might like to introduce some kind of structure to this process, asking each person to contribute a few minutes by completing these sentences:
  - What has worked for me today has been...

- What worked less well for me was...
- The contributions I specially valued were...
- What I can do next time to ensure that our time is well spent is...

At each subsequent meeting of the set, part of each person's time slot will also include being held to account about the progress he or she has made between meetings. In itself this is a powerful incentive to action and change. Set members become skilled at scenting diversions, implausible excuses and all the other ways in which human beings can procrastinate. Members of a well-functioning set will become experts in respectful challenge when they see this happening.

After four meetings, the set may be able to work without you. This will happen because you have trained them to take over your role. See it as the best compliment that could be paid to you to have them say, 'Actually we don't need you any more – we can do it ourselves.'

What can go wrong?

Action learning, like any other approach, is not right for everyone or every circumstance. Here are some of the things that can damage it:

- It does need mature people willing to open themselves up to the risk of seeming less knowledgeable and less sophisticated than the front they usually present to the world and not everyone will have this level of maturity.
- The composition of the set can be wrong. My own first experience of action learning was nearly floored by the insistence of my commissioning client on putting six people in similar roles in the same organization together, without understanding their own belief that they were in violent competition for the same resources and therefore could not possibly be expected to trust each other.
- You do need to be an expert facilitator and to hold your nerve when faced with demands for lectures and the conventional comforts of more traditional kinds of participant role.
- Naïve participants may not understand the benefit to be gained from learning to listen to others – they enjoy their own part of the limelight but see the rest of the day as a waste of their valuable time.
- People may also not see the benefit of learning to ask questions: impatience to give advice and find pat 'solutions' for the other person can get in the way. Early training and constant feedback from the facilitator is the way around this problem.
- As a facilitator you will also need toughness in managing the process

of the set, otherwise it can become all talk and no action, or all action and no learning.

Applications

Action learning has come a long way from its early days. From being seen mainly as a way of solving organizational problems, it has emerged as a powerful methodology in its own right with a wide range of applications in higher and further education, in prisons, in community development, in management development and in personal learning of all sorts. Here are some examples:

- A group of clinicians all with responsibility for public health in different organizations but in the same region. Aim: to share best practice and undertake one significant project which would improve public health.
- Undergraduates and postgraduate students on work placements meet to share experience. The focus is how to link the theoretical work of their courses with the confusing complexity of the workplace through undertaking one continuous project.
- Groups of parents wanting to improve their parenting skills where the 'projects' varied from so-called toddler taming to negotiating with teenagers.
- Small-business owners in developing countries supporting each other and sharing expertise in the common project of growing their businesses.
- BBC editors where the purpose of the set was to develop managerial skills.
- A set from different functions in the same organization whose task was that each was undertaking a project with the aim of improving customer service.
- A group of trainee coaches meeting as a follow-up to a course. The aim here is to embed the learning of the course and to help fellow participants with the problems that they are meeting with their practice clients.
- Doctoral students where the project for each was the completion of their thesis.
- First-year undergraduates where the focus was on study skills, including research.
- Managers who had each been made redundant. The focus here was on career-review and job-search and the project was for each to find a new job.
- A group of chief executives from a wide range of sectors, all leading

medium-sized companies. The aim was to offer support in common challenges but also for the participants to explore what would need to happen to make their organizations even more successful.
- A set whose members are owner–leaders of small entrepreneurial companies, sponsored by a local Business Exchange meeting to work as consultants to one another. The 'project' for each is: how can I grow my company so that it is many times more profitable? Between meetings, the group visits one member of the set in his or her workplace.

Variations

As an approach, action learning has come of age to the extent that many people are using the techniques without the label. Others are giving the name action learning to processes that are in fact one of the other variants discussed above. Many people in practice also blend a 'pure' learning set approach with other kinds of learning. For instance, where action learning is part of an academic course, as it is in our own coach-training events, participants are required to read named books and articles as part of the preparation for the meeting. It is also common for sets to commission some taught input which is woven in to classic learning set techniques. Attendance at the set may not always be totally voluntary. The overall theme for the meetings may be chosen by the organization rather than by the participants. These and other variants are common. I do not think this matters too much. Action learning has become a flexible tool, often introduced without fuss, blended in seamlessly to other kinds of learning. If the methodology and ideas are new to you, the best way of finding out about it is join a set yourself. First-hand experience is the best teacher, as ever.

Further reading

These books all give further practical help as well as guidance on the underpinning theory.

McGill, I. and Beaty, L. (2001) *Action Learning: A Guide for Professional, Management and Educational Development*, 2nd edition. London: Kogan Page.

Revans, R. W. (1998) *ABC of Action Learning*. London: Lemos and Crane.

Weinstein, K. (1999) Action Learning: A Practical Guide, 2nd edition. London: Kogan Page.

Notes

1 See Further Reading page 158.
2 Goleman, D. (1995) *Emotional Intelligence: Why It Can Matter More Than IQ*. New York: Bantam Books.
3 Rogers, C. (1969) *Freedom to Learn*. Columbus, OH: Merrill.

7 Problem-based learning

Problem-based learning is one of the few genuine innovations over the last few decades in approaches to teaching and learning. Starting in medical education, it has now spread to many other areas of learning and has been used successfully with all age groups.

What do you need to do to turn a raw 18-year-old into an excellent doctor? Forty or so years ago, the answer would have been couched in terms of the medical science that students were expected to understand. The curriculum was invariably delivered in discrete subject areas – anatomy, physiology, pharmacology and so on – in tiered lecture theatres or in laboratories and dissection rooms. Education was about the acquisition of knowledge. Students were not really required to think, only to absorb a mass of data in order to reproduce it through a written examination. A moment's reflection will remind you that it was not only medical education that had these characteristics. The same could have been said of almost every type of professional education and of much schooling as well. It is fascinating that the medical profession, so often criticized for its conservatism, has in fact been in the van of innovation where training and education are concerned. In today's medical schools, students are more likely to have at least some and sometimes the greater part of their education delivered through the approach known as 'Problem-based learning'. Where this is the case, the stand-alone lecture has been replaced by a curriculum with complex clinical problems at its heart. As with so much else that has changed in education and training in the last forty years, the core of the transition has been from teaching to learning.

What is problem-based learning?

A group of four or five learners is presented with a real-life, complex and messy problem contained in a few paragraphs of text. Like all such problems, the available information is limited. It may contain inherent contradictions and puzzles. The task of the learners, with the help of an expert facilitator, is to identify what assumptions they are making about the problem, what the missing information is, where it can be found and how to understand it. They spend an hour on this discussion before agreeing who is going to pursue which tasks and when they will meet again to share their information. The following week they present their findings to their facilitator/tutor who then introduces a further iteration which gives yet more depth to the same problem and the process is repeated for another week, after which a new problem is introduced.

Assessment methods vary hugely in problem-based learning. Sometimes work is assessed through traditional essays and examinations. Learners may also be required to keep learning logs (see also page 272) and reflective diaries. These will be assessed for self-insight and psychological understanding rather than for factual knowledge. Group projects may be peer-assessed as an important part of the learning on the assumption that knowing what the assessment criteria are and how to apply them is a valuable skill in itself. Commonly, there are also evaluations by tutor and fellow learners on each individual's contribution to the group. These may or may not contribute to final assessments for degrees or other qualifications.

An example

When you are new to the concept, it can be hard to get your head around what is involved. So here is an example of the kind of case[1] that might be presented to first-year medical students as part of a problem-based curriculum.

> *Cara*
> Cara, aged eight months, has been brought in to A&E by ambulance after her mother reported an episode of apnoea, accompanying a fever, and also described her as 'having had a fit'. This is her third admission in six months. In the ambulance, the paramedics reported that Cara became unresponsive with definite tonic-clonic movement of all four limbs. This phase lasted about 90 seconds.
>
> Cara is now quiet but responsive and, apart from some crying on examination, seems to be in no distress. Her limb movement is normal. Her rectal temperature is 40.1 centigrade, pulse rate is 110/ beats/minute, BP 95/65 mmHg and a respiratory rate of 24 resp/min.
>
> Cara's mother, Justina, is distraught and angry. She demands that you deal immediately with Cara, and claims that the child's illness has been brought on by the MMR vaccine that she was given three days previously. She says she remembers an article in the *Daily Mail* claiming that the vaccine is damaging and that there is a medical conspiracy to cover it up. She says that she believes her child will become autistic and that the current illness is a direct result of the vaccine. She threatens to sue the hospital unless you can sort Cara out immediately.
>
> Cara was born in the same hospital after 36 weeks of pregnancy weighing only 2.2 kg and her records show that the birth was a

> forceps delivery after a 36-hour labour. At two days old, Cara was jaundiced with significantly elevated serum bilirubin levels and was consequently exposed to artificial light in a protected isolette for two days. The jaundice resolved without further treatment.
>
> Justina is aged 22, a full-time mother, lives with Cara's father and has a son aged 6 and a daughter aged 4 from an earlier relationship.

The students will have an hour to agree which issues they should research in order to make a sound diagnosis and decide next steps. They will agree which areas everyone should research – because they are so fundamental – and which can be divided up between them. They will have a week before they present what they have discovered to their facilitator–tutor. Initial discussion of the problem will take thoughtful students into identifying a number of areas, including: childhood illnesses and how they manifest themselves; convulsions and their causes; immunology; the impact of media on public health issues and how doctors should handle them; infectious disease in childhood; family dynamics; teenage pregnancy; post-natal paediatric care; sociological and epidemiological dimensions of public policy; legal liability; communication skills – how to deal with a distressed parent; primary care and its interaction with emergency medicine. Contrast this with how the same material might have been taught in the past: probably separate lectures on immunology, paediatrics, general practice, public health and so on. The chances are, too, that the crucially important sociological dimensions and also the essential psychological and communication skills would not have been taught at all.

Like many apparent innovations in education, problem-based learning has claims to being an ancient technique. It has some similarities to Socrates's dialogues and to Aristotle's directive to challenge what he called *appearances* (beliefs, assumptions) by looking for contradictions. It also has some resemblance to Hegelian thesis–antithesis–synthesis dialectic and to the accounts given of how some aspects of the work of gifted teachers such as the twentieth-century educationists Maria Montessori and John Dewey were applied in practice. The project method in primary schools, established for over thirty-five years, is another close relative of problem-based learning. Case study has been a feature of management education for fifty years and the movement towards so-called *discovery learning* of the 1960s has many similar features.

The term is also increasingly used to mean widely varying approaches, something which may upset its more evangelical proponents. It is useful to think of it as a spectrum, going from the simplest to the most complex:

> *Level 1:* The type of arithmetical or other simple problem we all became familiar with at school: if three people take x hours to do y task, how long will it take five people? Here a problem is given a simplified real-life

cladding. The process is basic calculation or applying logic to a conventionally delivered piece of theory – and there is only one right answer.

Level 2: A more complex problem with a few loose ends. The answer has to be sought from relatively limited resources, also available in the classroom – for instance through listed internet sources. Again, there are probably right/wrong answers based on obtaining the correct facts through relatively limited research.

Level 3: A sophisticated case study is prepared by the tutors. Although sometimes fictionalized, it will most probably be based on a real situation. It may run to dozens of pages and contain a good deal of interesting complexity. This is the tradition developed in business schools where a case could take several days of study, with the financial results over several years of the company, its publicity campaigns, its stock market performance plus many of its internal documents all included in the material presented to learners. The task, working either in groups or individually, will be to produce hypotheses to identify underlying causes of the crisis revealed in the case and to suggest solutions. In these senses all of this is similar to problem-based learning. However, there is a critical difference: the copious data has already been synthesized by the case-writer.

Where the case is based on a real organization, the tutor may also claim to know 'what really happened'. I put this in inverted commas, since *what really happened* will always depend on who you speak to and how you interpret what you hear. I well remember attending an organizational development course in New York where one of a legion of consultants who credited himself with 'turning around British Airways' presented a detailed case to back up this claim. He was roundly challenged by several senior BA employees who happened to be in the audience and who told him how wrong he was. Who was 'right'? Everyone and no one. In a complex organization like BA, the only truth is that multiple perspectives are the name of the game.

So, although enjoyable for participants and valuable in developing judgement, data analysis and diagnosis, the case method is limited by its intrinsic design. There will be some assumed *right answers*, probably more loosely defined than in the simple arithmetical example of Level 1, but predetermined nonetheless. Looked at through the lens of problem-based learning, most of the more challenging work has already been done by the person who developed the case study. Even where documents are the actual documents, these will have been chosen while others have been rejected. In effect, whether they recognize it or not, the authors have produced the equivalent of a TV drama-documentary and thus it is open to all the challenges that any example of this genre poses:

How true is this? What can we deduce about the assumptions of the editor? Whose voice has not been heard? What has been left out? What alternative explanations could there be?

Essentially this is what Maggi Savin-Baden in her book *Problem-based Learning in Higher Education*[2] calls *problem-solving learning*. Her comment is:

> ...the solutions are always linked to specific curricula content, which is seen as vital for students to cover in order for them to be competent and effective practitioners. The solutions are therefore bounded by the content and students are expected to explore little extra material other than that provided in order to discover the solutions.

Level 4: A problem is prepared which unites several streams of a conventional curriculum. The task is to discover which information and ideas will tend to lead to a solution. A great deal of information will be missing: identifying which will be critical is part of the judgement that will be involved and also which skills will be required to manage it effectively. There will be no one right answer: any number of solutions could emerge. Some specialist parts of the curriculum are delivered this way; the rest is delivered through traditional means.

Level 5: As in Level 4 except that most of the curriculum is delivered this way. The problem-based approach will be interspersed with specialist input such as traditional lectures and seminars on discrete subjects, but essentially this is the supporting act, not the starring role. Learners may be encouraged to originate their own research and specifically encouraged to challenge orthodoxies.

The case for problem-based learning

There is a strong case for problem-based learning. In any situation where problem-solving skills are needed, and practising medicine is a prime example, it makes obvious sense that teaching should have problem-solving as its foundation. This was the rationale behind the work of the early innovators in McMaster University in Canada where its pioneers, Barrows and Tamblyn,[3] observed that the actual skills that clinicians need are far more to do with judgement, synthesizing complex data and ability to sort through the ambiguity of complex presenting issues than with memorizing. The case-based approach they developed was a flexible one in which students were not expected to deliver pre-packaged right answers, but to develop the ability to think creatively. This is true of every area of professional life, and the applications of problem-based learning now go well beyond medicine and have become common in all areas of the curriculum and in schools and colleges of all sorts.

As with action learning, problem-based learning depends on people assuming responsibility for their own learning. It depends on the idea that no one can do the learning for you. Problem-based learning makes this assumption utterly clear. In exploring the answers to the questions posed in a case, you learn how to research and analyse data in a way that promotes independent enquiry. Research also shows that learners enjoy the approach: it is involving. Indeed, it is so much fun that some critics have claimed it to be mere *edutainment*: a sop to the supposed need of consumerist modern learners to be entertained at all times just as it is assumed that they cannot bear separation from their i-Pods, DVDs, BlackBerries or mobile phones.

In asking why problem-based learning appeared when and as it did, it is probably not coincidence that it developed in medical education at just the point when it was clear that the amount of known and emerging medical science could not possibly be packaged into a conventional course – there was simply too much of it and it was becoming more specialized all the time. The same is true of all other professions. Curricula cannot expand infinitely to absorb this increase in knowledge, especially when, as in higher education, there is such pressure on resources. A move to teach the *process* of acquiring knowledge – rather than its end product – then becomes inevitable. So the abilities that are specifically needed through problem-based learning are skills such as retrieving information, analysing data, generating hypotheses, appraising ideas critically, seeing connections between disciplines and producing innovative ideas yourself. These are all about learning how to learn. The emergence through the internet of ready access to research and ideas of all sorts has also made it possible to support problem-based learning cheaply and easily without always having to resort to elaborately stocked libraries, though this of course depends on the subject and the level of complexity at which it is being learnt.

Where problem-based learning has been used to teach an entire curriculum, the benefits have sometimes been unexpected. One such has been that it has forced tutors to reconsider core assumptions about standards, content and values. The process has raised questions such as,

> Who decides what counts as knowledge here? How relevant is this particular part of the curriculum now? How consistent are our standards? What are we excluding that maybe we should be including? Why is so much learning about knowledge acquisition rather than being about knowledge-creation?

Another advantage of the approach is that it teaches social skills. For instance, like action learning, it works through small groups and the group can only succeed if everyone delivers on their promises and plays a full part in the work. So by working on a problem with your group you are also likely to learn how to be a team member, negotiate, debate, confront poor performance, persuade or to give a presentation. Collaboration is an important feature of life in most professional roles and problem-based learning gives a fast-track route to learning how to do it. Along with this goes the development of emotional intelligence, where, as with action learning, the chances are that working through a learner-centred approach will increase self- and other-awareness. These are all life skills which also have cash value in working life.

In any institution in which teachers are also learners and researchers – and of course we all should be on this journey ourselves continually – problem-based learning has a particular satisfaction because learner and teacher are working in absolutely parallel processes. At its best, problem-based learning is enjoyable for the staff who run it. It creates motivated, energized learners, matched by motivated, energized staff.

Variants

A endless number of further variants has appeared as the problem-based approach has become better known. Such variants include the following:

- Learners are each asked at the outset of a day to identify a problem based on a real dilemma that they have encountered in their jobs. One problem is chosen and is then researched and discussed by others in small groups as the closing session of the same day. This variant actually sounds like a hybrid of action learning and problem-based learning.
- Learners are divided into matched pair groups, taking it in turns to act as consultants/clients working on the same problem. When in the client role, the group assesses how far the consultant group has reached the stated objectives of the project.
- A philosophical or ethical question is set by the tutor. Learners have to identify which skills they already possess in order to begin work on the issue and then set about finding the widest possible range of opinions in order to deepen their understanding of what the basic issues are.
- The presenting problem focuses on skills. This variant works well for short events. Learners are asked to consider what skills they will need in order to solve the problem, then to consider what attitudes and assumptions lie behind these assertions, what challenges there might

be to such attitudes and who might have written key texts on the relevant subjects. Follow-up work, with the guidance of the tutor, might be to agree a reading list to be discussed at the next meeting.
- The problem is focused on a particular subject area – for instance, in a social work curriculum, it could be the law, but the learners are asked questions which require them to broaden out to sociological, medical or psychological research.
- The problem is a practical project, for instance in a media studies group to make a short film, or in an engineering course to create a particular product. In both cases, the learners will have to meet a set of tightly defined specifications. They will work intensively over a week-long period to identify what will lead to the success criteria being met and then work on the 'product' with a well-resourced workshop or design studio at their disposal.
- The problem is presented with a strong resemblance to a traditional essay question – the sort that begins with words like *Justify* ... *Explain* ... *Identify* ... This form of problem-based learning can seem highly structured, with learners being directed towards a tightly defined list of internet-based and other resources.

The tutor role

As with action learning, your role is to facilitate, not to teach. The skills are the ones I describe in Chapters 4 and 5: excellent questioning, knowing how to manage the process of the group, being able to promote individual learning and to be able to anticipate problems before they become messes. The secret is to provide enough guidance on the processes of learning without stepping in to try to do the learning for the group. Early on in the process, your role, as in action learning, will be to train the group in the process itself. This will include explaining what problem-based learning is, anticipating the frustration that some learners will experience at your apparent refusal to behave in the traditional teacher role, emphasizing the communication skills that will make the process work well, encouraging mutual respect, leading the process of contracting over behaviours such as punctuality, regular attendance and completing assignments on time.

It is an active role. Your responsibility is to direct the learning process, prompting deeper enquiry. So in this role you will be performing a number of high-level functions. Here are some of them, with examples of the kinds of questions that you might ask or statements that you could make:

Focusing discussion: Today we're looking at X and the purpose is to do Y.

Checking on comprehension: How well do you understand this technical term? How clear are you all on the issues so far?
Encouraging connections: What connection do you see between this theme and that one?
Challenging prejudice: What is the evidence for that assertion?
Encouraging dissent: What other ways could there be of thinking about this?
Making feelings legitimate: What is it about this issue that is provoking such strong feelings? What does the research have to say about the emotional dimension here?
Opening up thinking: Where are the information gaps here? Where else could you look?
Correcting factual errors where you see them emerge.
Seeking underlying causes rather than focusing on superficial symptoms: This is how it looks on the surface, but what could lie underneath?
Exposing the decision-making process: How are we deciding what matters and what doesn't here?
Showing learners useful techniques for mapping and synthesizing ideas.
Acting as an expert resource to the group – in effect consulting to it – where you have specialist expertise that they might find useful.
Offering robust feedback (see Chapter 3) to individuals and to the group.

Finally, one of the most important behaviours for a tutor is to model appropriate learner behaviour yourself. One of the main purposes of problem-based learning is to counter the tendency to bluff your way through life. Problem-based learning encourages the opposite – owning up to ignorance. This is why a skilled tutor will be perfectly prepared to say, *I have to admit that I don't know the answer here – it's out of my own area of expertise.*

Designing the problems

As with any piece of learning it all starts with objectives (page 243). Working backwards from assessment and evaluation, what objectives does this piece of learning have? How will you know that learners have achieved these objectives? What knowledge, attitudes and skills will these learners have acquired en route? What economic, social, political and technological factors are involved? It often helps to tape together several sheets of flip chart paper and to make yourself a visual map of these various learning domains (*concept maps*) and to work on this task with colleagues representing the multi-disciplinary areas that your eventual problem will involve. The resulting spidery sprawl will show you the interconnections on which your learners will also have to work. Given what you know about the context, for instance what your typical learners are likely to know already, what might make a nice, messy, maddeningly inconclusive and realistic problem on which your learners can work?

Now the task is to map the likely resources that could or should be on hand. This information search can embrace books, articles, film, newspapers or live data of one kind or another – for instance interviews with skilled practitioners. Your role here is to test the feasibility of your scenario as a focus for problem-based learning. Ideally, you want to make it possible but not too easy for learners to track down what they will need. You will usually have to refine your scenario at this point. Since this is a major investment in your own and other people's time, it will be worth regarding the first run with actual learners as a pilot, reworking the scenario so that you improve its quality for its next outing.

Does it work?

Research into medical education suggests that problem-based learning is at least as effective as traditional methods where acquiring knowledge is concerned and also produces more rounded doctors with far better diagnostic skills. It also shows that when you look at measures of enjoyment and involvement, whether from faculty or from learners, problem-based learning emerges as clearly superior. But evaluation here is as tricky as it is in every other kind of learning, a topic I deal with more fully in Chapter 12. Problem-based learning presents particular challenges, not least because the term may be used to described processes that in reality are like comparing apples with oranges – both are fruit but with significantly different flavours and botanical characteristics. Also, since the whole philosophy on which it is based is learning how to learn, it seems odd to use traditional methods of evaluation. Better methods might be to look for ways of assessing learners in a 'real' environment against more sophisticated criteria than the mere acquisition of factual information.

What will make problem-based learning work?

Skilled, committed tutors

Many years ago when I was a young, new and green education adviser for the BBC, I was kindly taken to one side by a more experienced colleague who was on the verge of retirement. Knowing that I was interested in innovative classroom methods, she forewarned me not to be disillusioned if I saw only partial success when I went to see such methods in action. 'A weak teacher can hide more easily behind traditional methods', she explained, 'but it takes real talent to make these newer methods work and there's far less of that around than you may think.' These turned out to be true and wise words and they apply as much, possibly more, to problem-based learning as to any other innovative approach to education. If you only believe half-heartedly in this methodology, if you do not have a high level of facilitation skill, if secretly you are yearning to resume the safe role of expert dispenser of knowledge, then you will not be able to make problem-based learning sing. If this is so, then when your performance is evaluated by trained and sceptical observers, it may well read something like this – a far cry from the ideal:

> Data collected from the observations and videotapes were markedly different from the self-reported data obtained from the students and faculty. The observers noted patterns of interaction and involvement, such as some students not participating at all for the full two hours, communication directed mostly toward the tutor and not among the group, one member sleeping during the tutorial, and a group in which the sole female member was relegated to a secretarial role. No cohesion was evident in these groups. Several aspects of productivity were not addressed. Goals were not articulated, methods for achieving goals were unclear, measurement of achievement was non-existent, and no time was spent in planning for future sessions. There was no evidence of reflection on any aspect of group behavior.[4]

Gathering data for this chapter from young friends who had experienced the technique at university also revealed a wide variation in approval ratings ranging from intense endorsement, the very memory provoking animation and smiling, to cool indifference. Where coolness was the overall feeling, it was largely for the kind of reason reported by this former architecture student:

> The problems all seemed a bit too simplistic and it felt like writing a sort of guided group essay. The staff talked about independent learning but there always seemed to be a predetermined answer. Quite often my group would come up with something radical and different and we'd have enjoyed producing it, only to be swatted back by the tutor because it wasn't the answer he had in his course manual. He loved giving us mini-lectures too to show us where we were mistaken. Of course everyone needs guidance and correction when you are plain wrong, but I don't think that was what was going on here. Architecture isn't like that – when you get to year six of a seven-year course, you are very aware that there are no easy or obvious answers.

Managing change with skill

Problem-based learning upends traditional assumptions so like any major change it can only be introduced with careful preparation. This tutor's candid comments illustrate some of the resistance that will inevitably arise:

> My Department Head was really keen on this PBL stuff. Oh how I hated that acronym. I admit that at first it sounded ludicrous to me: how were people ever going to acquire all the knowledge they needed with something that came across as so loose and whacky? How were we ever going to cover the curriculum? I attacked it as a daft idea at several of the meetings where we discussed implementation and I think I probably came across as an old dinosaur. It was clear that I couldn't opt out and keep my job longer-term so I reluctantly went along with it, making noisy comments wherever possible about the decline in standards etc. Gradually I came to see how much more motivated everyone was, including, I have to admit, me! No going back now . . .

This all-too-understandable reaction is probably why problem-based learning has been easier to introduce as a result of major change, for instance in new institutions, either those starting literally from scratch, like the more recent medical schools, or where two or more organizations have been merged. Similarly, unless the approach is underpinned by collaborative management practices which themselves are underpinned by deeply held core values of the same type, the whole enterprise can founder in a morass of bureaucratic turf wars with problem-based learning taking the blame as scapegoat.

Training and briefing

Either way, it is unlikely that problem-based learning can work without a full investment in briefing and training for everyone who will be involved, from tutors, to administrative support staff, to learners themselves. Tutors need copious support and feedback in their early days of working with the approach – it's not always easy to make the transition as the real-life issues engulf you.

Learners need introductory workshops backed up by manuals which reinforce the approach. Younger learners, especially those force-fed in expensive cramming establishments, may at first be horrified and frightened by the responsibility for their own learning which problem-based learning gives them. They may have heard the words 'take responsibility for your own learning' but interpreted them as 'be a good boy or girl and work hard on your own but give teacher the answer you believe he or she wants to hear'.

Consistency

Where the curriculum is a mixed economy, people may find it hard to reconcile the different messages they are getting from other faculty. For instance, nurse training rightly includes time spent on wards as well as time in an academic environment. It can be bewildering for the trainee when the ward works from the old apprenticeship model of do-as-I-say-and-don't-argue, but the university works on the basis of a more autonomous approach. Similarly, learners used to what some have called the *bootlegging compromises* of actual professional life can find it hard to match this with the purism of academic theory. Learning how to reconcile these multiple agendas can be challenging and it may sometimes seem easier to retreat into the safety of the known and the traditional. Sponsors of problem-based learning therefore need to be able to keep their nerve and to expect a slowish start-up while this process beds in.

Time and other resources

In its earliest days, problem-based learning was thought by some to be a way of economizing on the scarce resource of staff time. It is not. The reality is that you merely use staff time in a different way. In fact, in many ways it could consume more staff time. An obvious case in point would be that if instead of working with several hundred students and one speaker, you are working in groups of five, each with their own tutor, then you need more tutors. There must also be generous access to research resources. Without this, it will fail.

Further reading

Wilkerson, L. and Gijselaers, W.H. (1996) Bringing problem-based learning to higher education: theory and practice, in *New Directions for Teaching and Learning*, No. 68. San Francisco, CA: Jossey-Bass.

This is a fast-moving field and many subject areas now have their own associations and websites, specializing in different age groups and academic levels. The best resources for further reading, constantly updated, come from the universities such as Delaware, McMaster and Stanford as well as the Dutch universities which have pioneered developments in this fascinating area of learning and teaching. The Delaware site is a good place to start: www.udel.edu/pbl/

All the books already given as references in this chapter are also useful introductions to the subject.

Notes

1. I have adapted this material from the excellent website of Queen's University in Canada which has an online handbook for both tutors and students to prepare them for problem-based learning: www.meds.queensu.ca/medicine/pbl/PBLHndbk2002.pdf
2. Savin-Baden, M. (2001) *Problem-based learning in Higher Education: Untold Stories*. Buckingham: Open University Press.
3. Barrows, H.S. and Tamblyn, R.M. (1980) *Problem-based learning: An Approach to Medical Education.* New York: Springer.
4. Tipping, J., Freeman, R.F. and Rachlis, A.R. (1995) Using faculty and student perceptions of group dynamics to develop recommendations for PBL training, *Academic Medicine* 70(11):1050–2.

8 Coaching

When the pupil is ready, the teacher will appear.

(Chinese proverb)

What's your image of a *coach?* Is it someone frustratedly chewing gum in the dugout and barking orders at their players? Is it a schoolteacher earning a little extra cash by working with bored children to get them through their GCSEs? Both of these are common uses of the word, but increasingly it's being used in a different way. Glancing at a weekend supplement in a popular newspaper recently, I noticed that a whole crop of TV makeover experts were being described as *coaches*, whether their subject was how to be a parent to tantrum-prone teenagers, lose weight, declutter your house or make a fortune from property development. These people are experts in their subject – or would like us to think that they are – and their approach is essentially about benign or brutal ways of telling people what to do whether it is through a Table of Shame (*Your diet is disgraceful*) or how to use the *naughty step* to tame a toddler. Mostly, where TV is concerned, the emphasis is on brutality – in fact, when I was approached recently about appearing in such a series, the researcher emphasized that *tough* was really what she was looking for. As the audience, we are meant to enjoy the squirming pleasure of seeing someone else's humiliation before they submit to the (often correct) advice of the expert about how to put their relationships, appearance or house to rights. This is not the approach I describe in this chapter, though it may have its place. When I coach, my aim is to encourage my clients' self-confidence and belief in themselves. They are people who want to get to the next level of effectiveness – as decided by them, not by me.

Coaching is another approach to learning and, like all the other methods I discuss in this book, the basic assumption is that someone wants to change some significant aspect of their lives. It is about closing the gap between potential and performance. Coaching is a fast, effective, tailored way of doing this. In this chapter I am going to assume that the coaching will happen one to one. It is perfectly possible to use the same techniques to coach a team, but that is a subject beyond the remit of this book.

When you are in the business of adult learning you will have many opportunities to coach. For instance, when someone on your course gets stuck at the same place time after time:

> I was teaching garden design and one of my students kept coming to me for suggestions about planting schemes. I began to realize that I was doing all the work and her learning about planting was nil. I went on a course myself about using coaching techniques and realized that this could be the answer. Next time she approached me with her request, I said 'Right, let's do some different thinking here. What are *your* ideas about what this garden needs?' At first I just got a blank look, but slowly her own ideas began to come out and we ended up with a much more self-assured garden designer! By not coaching, I was actually undermining her confidence, though of course my intention had been the exact opposite.

You may want to incorporate a coaching approach into all of your teaching. In my own work with groups, this is increasingly what I am doing. However, I also now spend at least two thirds of my professional time working one to one with people in organizations as their coach. I meet them for two hours at a time over a period of a few months. Six sessions is about the average. They are usually too senior to go on courses and may already have done all the courses their organization offers. Furthermore, they are always reluctant to spend days at a time away from the office. They see coaching as a way to get targeted and confidential help in the areas where they want to make fast improvements in their performance. You may be able to incorporate this kind of activity into your work, or you may simply be looking at opportunities to do briefer and more informal coaching as a seamless part of the other teaching or training that you do. The principles are the same, whatever the setting.

Coaching has a literally infinite number of possible applications, but some ways you might use it include helping people to:

- recover their interest and motivation after a crisis of some kind;
- make decisions about whether to follow one path or another;
- learn how to learn;
- resolve a problem;
- undertake reviews of their careers;
- make decisions about life direction;
- understand themselves and the important people in their lives (work or home or both) so that their relationships are more enjoyable and productive;
- acquire skills;
- develop their creativity.

What is coaching?

This is the definition I use in my book *Coaching Skills: A Handbook*:[1]

> The coach works with clients to achieve speedy, increased and sustainable effectiveness in their lives and careers through focused learning. The coach's sole aim is to work with the client to achieve all of the client's potential – as defined by the client.

This definition is underpinned by six key principles:

1. Learners are resourceful: they do not need to be fixed or patronized.
2. Your role as a coach is to get learners to the point where they are able to tap into this resourcefulness. It's not to *tell*, to give advice or to find the solution for them.
3. Coaching addresses the whole person – so potentially everything about those learners, what is going on in the rest of their life, feelings as well as the logic of the learning task, can be included in the coaching agenda.
4. It's the learner's agenda: so the learners define how they want you to help them and on what.
5. For purposes of the coaching, learner and coach are equals: to coach in the way I describe in this chapter you have to abandon feelings of hierarchy, superiority – or inferiority for that matter – in areas such as age, background, intellect or status.
6. Coaching is about change and action. If learners do not wish to change then you cannot coach them.

In this sense coaching is intimately connected to the approaches I have already described in the chapters on learning and on facilitation. Additionally, as with problem-based learning and action learning, coaching is built on identical assumptions: that the role is to facilitate learning. Because the word coach is used so freely to describe a wide range of processes, some of them different from what I describe here, it is worth making similarities and distinctions clear. For instance, the traditional sports coach always knew best. The coach observed the player and then offered advice based on the observation: 'Take your swing further back behind your left shoulder'; 'Hold your racquet like this'; 'Begin your run to the goal sooner'; 'Keep your eye on the ball ...'. The high levels of dependency this kind of relationship creates are well documented in sporting literature. Athletes come to doubt their own judgement, distort their efforts to fit the preconceptions of the coach and in effect hand control of their game to the coach. When the coach praises and grunts 'Well done', what the coach means is, 'Yes, good, you are following my commands'. The inevitable resentment this creates means that in the long term, the flaws in the relationship become obvious. The athlete may realize that he or she needs a different coach, perhaps more the sort I describe in this chapter, or may believe that he or she simply needs the same but more so – another technical expert whose advice will be more reliable – and so the same cycle starts all over again.

Essentially, in the approach to coaching I set out here you are explicitly handing control of the change process to the learner. You accept the person unreservedly and do not judge their frailties and hesitations at the same time as you are prepared to challenge their self-limiting assumptions. You have questions, not answers. You are raising their awareness of everything that is going on in their situation, emphasizing that the choice of what to do is theirs. Your work with them is to define their goals and the actions that will make those goals real through a subtle blend of high challenge and high support.

Differences and similarities between coaching and other disciplines

Coaching shares a solid foundation of skills with many of its sister-disciplines. You may be wondering whether 'coaching' is just another word for counselling or psychotherapy. Coaching has few of the associations of shame and secrecy which have haunted therapy, and it is possible that it sometimes attracts people who could benefit from therapy. However, although there are overlaps, I don't believe that coaching and therapy–counselling are different words for the same process, but let's look first at what they have in common. All start from the assumption that it is desirable to have what the great American writer and thinker in this area, Carl Rogers,[2] described as 'unconditional positive regard' for the client. There is no place for judging, sarcasm or sneering in coaching. If you don't or can't have respect for your client, then don't coach him or her. You cannot be a good coach without excellent listening skills, or without a generous quantity of personal presence and the ability to ask excellent questions. All of these are needed equally when you work as a therapist, counsellor, mentor or trainer. There are certainly grey areas. For instance, there are coaches who act as therapists and counsellors in all but name and therapists who in effect coach. There are trainers who take a coaching approach to their courses. But in general, the differences are important. My emphasis as a coach is on the future, on goals for learning and on action. When I encounter a client who has some seriously unresolved issues from the past, I know my boundaries and refer them to one of several good psychotherapists, though this happens a great deal more rarely than you might think.

Coaches do not pose as experts except on coaching. There are no 'schools' of coaching as there are in psychotherapy, though it is possible that some may emerge as the profession matures and grows.

Coaching as it is now practised in the twenty-first century owes almost all its techniques and approaches to the decades-long experience, thinking and skill of counselling and psychotherapy which has preceded it. There are hundreds of rival schools of psychotherapy, for instance Rational Emotive, Person-Centred, Humanistic, Gestalt, but all share to some extent a belief that the client has some psychological dysfunction in their lives and therefore needs a cure (the literal meaning of the word therapy). My friend and colleague, Julia Vaughan Smith, makes the point in her book *Therapist into Coach*[3] that the role of the therapist is to work with a client to the point where he or she is resourceful enough, or, as she puts it, has sufficient ego, to benefit from coaching. Counselling and therapy work in psychological depth with the client, looking at deep-seated issues which may be holding the person back. There may also be an emphasis, less likely in coaching, on insight – into understanding why certain patterns of unhelpful behaviour recur. It is not true to suppose that modern therapists customarily work for years with their clients – therapy is time-limited just as coaching is and nor is it always true that therapy is backward-looking. Many forms of therapy are as future-directed as coaching, indeed might just as well be coaching under another name. However, in general, coaching moves more quickly than therapy and in most cases is a great deal more goal-focused.

The context is also influential in coaching. So, in a typical therapy session, the presenting context is largely the inner life and close personal relationships of the client. In executive coaching, the dominant market for coaching in the UK, the initial context is work, which is why the fees are paid by the organization. This brings with it a different dynamic because the organization takes a keen interest in whether it is getting a return on its investment. However, nothing is quite as straightforward as it can seem and some sceptical observers have suggested that so-called life-coaching where the client is paying for him or herself is really just CBT (cognitive behavioural therapy) for the Worried Well who can afford the apparent indulgence of a coach.

Coaching may also seem to resemble training. Indeed, as some coaching is practised, it is more like one-to-one training than anything else. The difference between the approach I describe here and training is that in coaching you have no curriculum and your subject expertise is irrelevant except in so far as it may give you some license and credibility to work with the client. However, training as it is often carried out has a more generic and less individually focused flavour. It may also be more difficult to deal in depth with the interpersonal skills that coaching is so well placed to handle.

Maybe your interest in this area is because you have been asked to be a *mentor*. The word 'mentor' comes from the Greek legend where the learning of a young son was entrusted to the care of Mentor, an older, wiser man. Many organizations now run mentoring schemes where the accumulated wisdom of an older person is made available to someone younger. This can take two forms: *Sponsorship Mentoring,* where the mentor is in effect the mentee's patron and will overtly aim to further his or her career, or *Development Mentoring* where the mentor may have no power or wish to propel the mentee's career, but does understand the issues and environment of the mentee because he or she comes from something similar. Classically, mentoring has involved the transfer of knowledge from mentor (person who knows) to mentee (person who doesn't). Normally, in development mentoring, the mentor will not be in a line management relationship with the mentee. Where the mentor uses a coaching approach, this can be a wonderfully powerful stimulus to learning. When a mentor coaches, he or she is far more powerful than when in the traditional mentoring role of just passing on advice. Like coaching, mentoring has spread its wings and is now used well beyond its original workplace setting to encompass schemes for persistent offenders, people who are addicted to alcohol or drugs, novice entrepreneurs and older schoolchildren who mentor younger schoolmates – and many more.

The being and doing selves

In coaching we are looking at both the Being Self and the Doing Self. The Being Self is the core person: who we really are, how we feel about ourselves, our deepest commitments, beliefs and values, how our earlier lives have made us what we are, our relationships. The Doing Self is about the skills we bring to our professional, academic or leisure tasks, our work roles – our visible, public face. It is the Doing Self that you will usually see first in coaching:

> I need this or that skill. Will you help me?
>
> I've got a new job and I'm finding it difficult. I can't understand this concept: will you explain it?

But the Doing Self may not find the answers to the problems until the Being Self is also engaged. Sometimes, the Doing Self is being compromised because the Being Self has been allowed to wither.

People will benefit from coaching when there is pressure for change in either arena. For instance, there may be pressure in the Being arena: relationship problems, ageing, redundancy, health. Or there may be pressure in the Doing arena: a boss who demands better performance, a change of job which needs different skills, and so on. Often there is a mysterious lack of progress in the Doing arena, in spite of teaching, mentoring and advice. The reason may be that the Being Self has not been engaged. When you coach, you give yourself and your client permission to work with both.

Where might you use coaching?

Coaching is an ideal intervention when any of these conditions are present:

- There is a great deal at stake for the individual – if the issue is neglected there could be serious consequences.
- The learner has already tried all the obvious self-help tactics such as asking a friend for advice.
- You know that the learner has the ability and aptitude that they need but somehow they seem to have lost motivation.
- There is a dilemma that the learner seems unable to resolve alone.
- The learner is tending to make the same mistake repeatedly and seems to lack understanding of why this is happening.
- The learner seems to lack some of the self-awareness that would explain a frustrating block.
- There are relationship problems in the learner's life and these are barriers to his or her learning progress.
- The learner needs to increase the range and depth of his or her interpersonal skills.
- A course has stimulated the learner's interest and now he or she needs to develop a deeper understanding or skill on a one-to-one basis.
- You hear the learner make a generalized assumption that he or she can't do something which experience and instinct tells you that this learner could do perfectly well.

In all these cases, coaching would be my first choice of intervention. Here are some examples of how other tutors have used it:

> *Case study 1: Recovering interest and motivation after a crisis of some kind*
> Marita is a first-year university student, living away from home for the first time. As the eldest in a family of five, with three young step-siblings, Marita was used to responsibility but also used to steady structure and to the unquestioning support of family life. The painful ending of a first serious love affair in her first term was followed by a bout of glandular fever and all this has left her tired and self-questioning. She begins to get behind with assignments and is struggling with her formerly favourite subject, Anglo-Saxon, finding

its grammar and vocabulary far more difficult in the second term than the ease she found at the beginner level of the first term. She is tempted to give it up, believing that she will fail the end of year exam but is also mortified by the prospect of failing after an unsullied record of success in every other exam she has sat in the past. Her normal first line of defence would have been discussion with her mother, Jill, but Marita, acutely aware that Jill is still recovering from the birth of the last baby, doesn't want to add to Jill's stress.

Marita's Anglo-Saxon tutor has learnt some coaching techniques. She sets aside half an hour for a coaching session and asks Marita to stay behind after a tutorial. By building on the trust that has already been created through the tutorial process and using skilful, non-judgemental questioning she soon elicits the above, staying calm, accepting and still during the inevitable tears. *What does Marita really want?* Marita finds that easy to identify – to recover her spark, to get to grips with the language again. *What's standing in the way?* – always a good coaching question. The answer is her belief that she is not clever enough – a typical self-limiting assumption. *What evidence is there for that belief?* Truly the evidence is flimsy! *So what would help get to the goal?* Revisiting the techniques that made the first term easy! *And what were those?* Answer: approaching it steadily, believing that she can do it, making a realistic plan, step by step like a jigsaw, knowing that all the pieces really do fit together – as well as getting to bed early for the next two weeks and saying *no* to distractions. Marita and her tutor agree a simple programme of revision and agree to discuss progress on it after the next tutorial. Finally, Marita's tutor challenges the assumption that Jill will not want to know anything about Marita's difficulties. *Imagine the roles were reversed. What would you want?*

Outcome: after three such sessions, Marita has recovered a great deal of her bounce and is wondering why she ever found Anglo-Saxon difficult. This is because she supplied all the remedies herself: her tutor offered no advice, no remedial teaching on Anglo-Saxon, only skilful questions, unquestioning support and straightforward, friendly challenge.

Case study 2: Dilemmas

Pablo is 30 and at a crossroads with his career. He is a talented musician but his interests are diverse. He plays keyboard with friends who run an amateur rock band, he plays the organ and conducts a church choir, he can teach youngsters the piano, he loves composition. The trouble is that none of this earns a decent living.

Pablo works as a clerk in the Civil Service to make ends meet. But by doing this he leaves himself too little time to practise or to work on his own music. His contemporaries, who unlike him have degrees, are zooming ahead in their careers while Pablo is stuck in work he finds dull and poorly paid. His partner is impatient with what she calls his *wittering and dithering* – she has a steady and well-paid job. He confides all this to his teacher during his work for the Grade 8 piano examination. She talks him through a simple technique for making decisions on such vexing dilemmas. Together they use one post-it note for each of the activities that Pablo enjoys, then Pablo arranges them on a large flat surface in order of preference. Using a different set of post-its, Pablo now makes a list of criteria for making the decision and arranges them in order of importance. A third post-it list sets out the typical road to success for a serious career in contemporary classical music. Exposing his thought processes like this makes Pablo realise that there is no one route which can bring him everything he needs and that one of his problems has been fear of failing, hence his lack of commitment to any one path.

Outcome: Pablo realizes that his one true love is composition and he believes he has the talent but lacks the deep knowledge of composition which could lead to a successful career. He will save vigorously for a year, then apply for a university place as a mature student to expand his knowledge and skill in composition, taking out a student loan eked out with bar work, and also persuading his partner to subsidize him with food and rent bills.

Note: Pablo's teacher has not offered him any advice during this exchange, in spite of her strong temptation to offer him solutions based on what seemed like a similar dilemma earlier in her own career which she resolved satisfactorily by deciding to teach music. Thanks to training as a coach, she has resisted this, as well as consciously drawing Pablo's personal life into the equation because she is aware that no career dilemma can be looked at purely in the context of work.

Case study 3: Learning how to learn

Kay is in her late sixties and has been a member of her T'ai Chi Beginners class for some years. A new instructor, also a trained coach, takes over the class and is intrigued. Why has Kay not already moved on to a more advanced class as several of her friends have done? And why does she continue to make the same mistakes, week after week? If Kay's instructor were to take a conventional teaching approach, he would probably take Kay to one side, explain where she was getting it wrong and show her the correct moves and postures. Instead, he asks her to arrive early the following week and he takes a coaching approach, asking her how she rates her own progress. Kay looks miserable and sheepish. 'I believe I'm hopeless, then I panic', she says, 'and when I panic I wobble and then I look at what the others are doing and try to copy the move, because I forget how it goes, then I'm all behind and get flustered'. The instructor knows that it is this inner critic that is destroying Kay's ability to learn. 'OK', he says. 'For this week, forget all that business of *trying* to learn the form. I want you instead to concentrate on what you are noticing while you're doing it. Tell me what you notice when it's working – ignore the times when it's not. Come and tell me what you've discovered by the end of the class!'

Outcome: Kay has been skilfully distracted from the dispiriting process of *trying,* with its implication that failure is inevitable. Her attention has been turned to looking instead at awareness of successful learning and what helps it to happen. With as little as five minutes of post-class coaching over a period of weeks, Kay joins the more advanced class the following term.

Case study 4: Increasing self-awareness

Michael is a middle manager whose employer has sent him on a leadership training course. Up until this point in his career Michael has been in a specialist role where he has had to manage a small team of other specialists. He is finding the leap from this to leading a much bigger team of other managers extremely taxing. They challenge him, demand a great deal of his time – he thinks unreasonably – and seem sceptical about the value he adds. He is simultaneously looking forward to the course because it will reveal the mysteries of leadership to him and dreading it because he fears that it might tell him that he is unsuited to the role. Michael is 43 but has never really had any straightforward feedback on how he comes across.

One of Michael's tutors for the course, Alan, is charged with running a coaching session for him on the first day. This is a mere 90 minutes but it is critical to the success of the course for Michael. In this session, the tutor will debrief Michael on his 360-degree feedback – a questionnaire that he has completed himself and that also contains confidential information on how his leadership behaviour is perceived by 11 of the people in Michael's immediate team and also by his boss. Self-awareness is the *sine qua non* of effectiveness as a leader. Without it, it is unlikely that any leader will be successful. But Alan knows how vulnerable Michael will be feeling. He gives Michael the report to read quietly. If Alan were to handle this session in teacher-mode, he would do a lot of the talking, explaining and interpreting. Instead, he is aware how vital it is to stay in coach-mode, asking open questions such as 'How does this strike you overall?' 'Which of the messages here need clarifying for you?' 'Which bits of this report would you like us to concentrate on?' There are two equal and opposite dangers in this kind of coaching session. One is to soothe a dismayed client, telling them that it doesn't matter, colluding with their shock by telling them that other people have got it wrong and over-emphasizing the positives. The other is to go overboard on the negatives.

Alan does neither. He is warmly supportive but also tenacious in making sure that Michael understands the messages of the report, including the affirming and positive feedback it contains, and also asks the questions which help Michael to put it into perspective. He asks Michael to assess the discrepancies between how Michael sees himself and how others see him. He ends the session by agreeing an informal contract with Michael to observe him closely during the next few days of the course. In this way he will gather further feedback and will be able to offer even more value to Michael for the second coaching session that will happen on the final day of the course.

Outcome: Michael begins to see himself as others see him. He realizes that he is neither a hopeless case nor an absolute natural as a leader and that he has a lot to learn. In later career when he is a well-regarded Director of Finance for another organization, he will attribute a great deal of his success to the ninety minutes he spent with Alan on that course.

Giving advice

The heart of this approach to coaching is that you do not give advice. Instead, you work on the principle that the choices we make for ourselves are the ones that we act on. The role is about working with a learner to ensure that such choices are made robustly. But it's easy to confuse coaching with advice-giving. Here are two typical situations:

A trainee nurse asks you, a seasoned nurse-tutor, about a problem with a patient. She knows that you have years of experience and says to you, 'What would you do?'

An extremely overweight member of your fitness class asks you for advice about losing weight, commenting admiringly on your own slim figure.

What does a coach do? The easy answers are:

- Tell the trainee nurse how you would solve the problem – after all, she has actually asked you for your experience hasn't she?
- Tell the member of your fitness class exactly what she should do to shed her excess pounds. It's flattering to be asked and it will only take a few minutes.

But let's look a little more closely at what would be likely to happen in reality. With the trainee nurse, she gets her answer and the problem appears to be solved. But in the longer term, several less desirable things could also happen. First, she has not done any thinking of her own on the subject. Second, you are reinforced in her mind as the person with the answers, and her own ability to develop has been curtailed.

With the overweight class member, as well as all of the above, it is most unlikely that she has not already heard all of the advice you can offer. Virtually all of the millions of words written and spoken on the subject amount to four simple words: *eat less, exercise more*. The interesting question is why she has been unable to follow this advice and you are unlikely to get into this territory through simply telling her what she already knows.

So as opportunities for learning, it is probably safe to say that neither of these interventions is likely to be successful. You may feel better, but the underlying issues have not been touched.

Responses to advice

Advice does not work as a coaching tactic for these reasons:

- It introduces the temptation to pose as being wiser than the learner whereas this may not be true, and thus brings an undesirable dynamic into the relationship.
- It undermines the essence of the coaching relationship as a partnership.
- The learner feels guilty or gets annoyed and concentrates on repelling the advice. This leads inevitably to the *Why don't you . . .? Yes, but . . .* game:
  Why don't you get more exercise? It would really help you to reduce the stress.

> Yes, I agree it would be a good idea but I haven't really got time at the moment.
> *OK, why don't you cut down the hours you work?*
> Yes, I'd like to, but my boss won't be satisfied with less than the amount of time I'm giving now...
> *Well you could just tell him to get lost, couldn't you?*
> I suppose so but now isn't really the time.
> And so on and so on.

- It discourages people from thinking for themselves. If they take your advice, then it is your ideas that they are following.
- It does nothing to develop people's resilience and resourcefulness.
- If they take your advice and it goes wrong, then it becomes your 'fault'.
- It is unlikely that you will be telling the other person anything that they have not already thought of for themselves. For instance, advice on health and lifestyle issues is all widely available. The reasons that people do not have prudent lifestyles have little or nothing to do with non-availability of information.

The urge to give advice usually comes from a good place – we want to be helpful. I see this again and again when I am training beginner coaches. They can find the other person's struggle unbearable. From the outside it can seem so obvious what the client should do. If the conversation begins to take a circular feel with the client apparently helplessly answering 'I don't know' to the coach's questions, the urge to tell, to offer suggestions, to say 'If I were you I'd ...' can become overwhelming. By the way, when a client starts replying 'I don't know' to your questions, the reason is that you are probably on the wrong agenda and asking the wrong questions.

Other traps

There are other traps in giving advice. The first is our tendency to read our own biography into what other people are describing:

> *Q:* Give me some advice on how I ought to get started on my essays. I'm procrastinating all the time!
>
> *A:* Oh yes, I remember when I was first trying to write a decent essay I...

The problem here is that there is no way you can ever know what it is like to be the other person. You will never know all there is to know about the situation, its history, its cast of characters or the motivation of your learner, nor should you. What worked for you will most probably not work for them because so much in their situation will be unlike yours, however similar it looks on the surface.

Advice-in-disguise

It is also possible to do pseudo-coaching where what you are really doing is giving advice in disguise (see also page 127). So watch out for phrases like:

Table 8.1

Do you think it would be worth. . . ?	Have you thought of . . .?
Is this really your boss's issue?	Another student of mine tried . . .
Should you consult your partner on this?	Would it be worth doing . . .?
How about . . .?	Could you think about . . .?

Advice and information

There may be many situations where you may have expert knowledge that it is useful to pass on to the client, but a variant of the same principles will apply. Think of this as useful information which you want the client to have. The client still makes the decisions about whether or not to use it.

Offer your information (this may for instance be in handout form) as *one possible way* of looking at the problem. Talk it through and stress that these are basic approaches, which will not always work for everyone in all situations. Ask the learner:

> How does this strike you?
> What seems useful and what seems not useful?
> Which parts of this, if any, could you apply?
> How could you apply them?
> What will need to happen to make this real?

This approach works even in sports coaching, the one arena where you might think that expert input was truly necessary. In practice, many of us in coaching would claim that a good sports coach does not need in-depth knowledge of the sport. This radical claim can be backed up in a number of ways. For instance, the Israeli Olympic champion Mark Spitz was coached by someone who could not swim. For more on the modern approach to sports coaching, see also page 67.

Silencing the inner critic

A group setting such as a training course makes it less likely that you can work in the territory of the inner critic. By this I mean the limiting beliefs and assumptions that we all have. As children we may hear our parents make assertions such as, 'People like us don't do x or y thing' or, 'Who'd be interested in you?' Or, 'Your sister's the one with the brains' or, 'Don't make a fool of yourself' or, 'Pride comes before a fall'. Mostly, parents mean well – these runes are meant to protect us from disappointment or, sometimes, to spur us on – for instance the parent who gives the impression that nothing a child does could ever be good enough. As children we are too impressionable and immature to sieve these statements and we internalize them as generalized truths. As adults they hold us back. They may be buried so deep that we have never really looked them in the eye and seen them for the extremely partial truths that may be buried somewhere inside them.

When you hear learners say, 'I can't, I shouldn't, I musn't ...' take for granted that you are in this territory until proved otherwise. As a coach you need to notice, then surface and challenge the client's assumptions because this will virtually always be an important part of what is holding them back. Coaching, unlike most training and group-based teaching, gives you the opportunity to look beyond the rational territory of the Doing Self (page 179) to the murkier territory of the being self in which the inner critic thrives.

Agenda: the client's, not the coach's

As a tutor you will normally have a curriculum which will dictate a great deal of what happens during your course. You may be obliged to work to academic criteria imposed by an examinations board. When this is the case, you are working to an externally imposed agenda, however creatively you flex and interpret it yourself. One of the biggest differences between training or teaching and coaching is that the agenda is created entirely by the client. This is because only the clients can truly own whatever it is they want to change, and if there is nothing that they want to change, then you cannot coach. But then you cannot expect to teach either. The difference in coaching is that the choice of agenda is entirely down to the individual.

The coach's role

So what is it appropriate for the coach to do? This is what I believe it comes down to:

- To provide a climate of high support and high challenge.
- To show clients that your only purpose is their learning – you have no agenda of your own.
- To establish the client's agenda.
- To agree the goals for learning based on this agenda.
- To ask the questions which uncover and quieten the inner critic.
- To remain unattached to whether or not the client achieves his or her goals while also eagerly wanting the client to do well. 'Attachment' could mean that the coach cares more about being a 'clever' coach than truly helping the client.
- To work with clients on taking the action which will increase their chances of reaching their goals.
- To identify what learning has happened during the whole process.

It is not the coach's role to provide answers, to try to do the learning for the client or to pose as the client's superior in any way.

Authentic listening

Authentic listening is the most fundamental coaching skill of all. Real listening is very hard work, so perhaps it's not surprising that it is very rare to have the experience of being listened to without judgement and with total attention. Many of us pride ourselves on being 'good listeners'. To admit to being a bad listener is rare.

Listening is about communicating acceptance. When we don't listen properly, we communicate non-acceptance. Table 8.2 gives some examples.

Table 8.2 Communicating non-acceptance

Comment	*Effect conveyed to the other person*
I'm sure you needn't worry about that.	Trivializes the other person's worry.
Time will heal – you'll come to terms with it eventually.	You have resorted to cliché because you can't be bothered to think of anything else to say.
Other people cope with far worse things – buck up!	Diminishes the other person.
Don't you think you should...?	Preaching – implies that you know best.
Can we move on here to the really important issues?	Impatience – your concerns are more important.
I think you're right, the real problem is with someone else.	Colluding – covers up the problem.

Listening is the primary tool of a coach. To do it well you have to be 'fully present' for the client. This means:

- keeping your own issues well out of the way – for instance, setting aside your own preoccupations with relationships, health, work;
- making sure that you have suspended judgement: consciously switch it off before you start the piece of coaching;
- keeping the itch to give advice well under control;
- preparing for the client with a few moments of quiet before you meet;
- monitoring your own listening while the client is talking.

Feelings

As a sweeping and certainly unfair generalization, training and teaching probably work more comfortably in the arena of rationality and logic. Coaching can and should work with equal fluency with both objective logic and feelings. No problem worthy of your attention with a client lacks a feelings aspect and no decision on the action which will transform the client's problem into a success will be without feelings either. It may be obvious to both you and the client what the client should do logically. But what is preventing the client being able to act on the logic? Usually the answer is that their feelings are preventing it. To make the desired action likely, it is important to surface and explore the feelings. When you hear a client name a feeling such as guilt, panic, dread, exhilaration, joy . . . always explore it. Ask, 'That sounds interesting – can you say more about that?' When the client has replied, say, 'What is the link between this feeling of (whatever it is) and this issue?' Or, 'How is this feeling getting in the way for you?' 'What would you say to yourself about how to manage this feeling more effectively?'

The coaching session is private and one to one. Remember that nothing the client says to you is going to shock you into a judgement. Make it possible for clients to look calmly all around their issues, emotions as well as all their well-worn logical arguments. The results will surprise them – and possibly you as well.

A format for a coaching session

Let's imagine that you are going to do some coaching. This may be a five-minute one-to-one as part of a general session of teaching, or it may be the full-blown two-hour sessions that I now typically have with executive clients.

This is a format that I find useful. Adapt it to suit your own situation and purposes.

Catching up on last time

Where you and the client have agreed 'homework' between sessions, it is vital to find out what has happened. Useful questions to ask here are:

- What's happened since we last met?
- How did you get on with the work we agreed you would do?
- What have you learnt?

The last is a particularly useful question. Often clients have not done their homework for all sorts of good or apparently silly reasons. There will be learning in it, whatever has happened.

Goals for this session

Coaching is about change. If there is no will to change then there can't be any coaching. It is useful to pinpoint specific goals for the coaching. Useful questions here are:

- What would you like to have achieved, specifically, by the time we finish this session?
- What would achieving that goal do for you?
- Of those goals, what's their order of priority for you?

Looking at the facts

The point of this phase is for the client, not you, to understand what the known facts of the situation are. This is what the writer Edward de Bono calls 'White Hat' thinking in his book *Six Thinking Hats*.[4] White Hat thinking is about facts, reality and certainty. It often gets muddled up with 'Red Hat' thinking – excitement, prejudice, fear and other kinds of attachment to ideas for emotional reasons. Red Hat thinking is also valuable because feelings are important, but it is helpful to separate them out. Useful questions here are:

- What's preventing the ideal from happening?
- Who's involved here?
- What are the facts?
- Who owns this problem?

Generating options

Brainstorming, a process similar to what de Bono dubs the optimism of 'Yellow Hat' thinking, can be a useful skill here, especially for clients who seem stuck or helpless or when there are so many possibilities that it is difficult to choose between them. Introduce it by asking permission and explaining the 'rules' – many clients think they know what brainstorming is but show that they don't by mentioning an idea and then immediately evaluating it. The essence of brainstorming is that any idea, however silly, is encouraged at the first stage.

Brainstorming Stage 1

Any idea however ridiculous or outrageous is permitted. As a coach, your role is to offer funny, absurd, sensible and practical ideas along with your client. Don't swamp the client – it should be an even-handed process.

- All ideas are jotted down (agree which one of you will do this).
- No evaluation of ideas is permitted at the first stage – e.g. no raised eyebrows, indrawn breath and so on.

This stage goes on until all ideas are exhausted.

Brainstorming Stage 2

Agree the criteria for evaluating the ideas – e.g. how will you judge whether any of these ideas are useful or not? Look for several criteria – e.g. cost, practicality, speed and so on.

Brainstorming Stage 3

The ideas are evaluated – by the client, not by you.

Brainstorming Stage 4

The ideas are turned into action. You ask, 'So which of these ideas appeals most? How will you turn this into action?'

Moving forward

Coaching is essentially about three questions: *What? So what?* and *What next?* The key to this stage is the 'So what' and 'What next?' part of the coaching process. Without this skill, a coaching session can seem rambling and unfocused – just a nice chat with a pleasantly non-judgemental person.

Throughout the coaching session, you need to keep up the pace so that 'What next?' is constantly in view. It is a matter of judgement and experience to decide when it is appropriate to move to this phase.

Victims

Some clients get stuck in victim mode. Victims can prevent themselves learning from coaching because they are looking for ways to change others rather than themselves. They may have a terror of taking responsibility for themselves or even a fear of success. (See also page 99 on life positions). Victims come to coaching with the wish to change others, not themselves. Symptoms of victim thinking are sentences that begin:

> If only they'd . . .
> I wish he or she would . . .
> If only other people would . . .
> I can't do this because they won't let me . . .
> I can't . . .

You can challenge this kind of thinking by replying with a question. Table 8.3 gives some examples.

Table 8.3 Replying with questions

Client says	*Coach replies*
If only they'd change their way of thinking . . .	How can you change *your* way of thinking?
I wish he or she would . . .	How can you alter the way *you* respond to him or her?
If only other people would . . .	What choices do you have when other people don't do what you want?
I can't do this because they won't let me . . .	In what ways are you giving other people the power to make these choices for you?
I can't . . .	Do you really mean, 'I won't'?

The key questions

The key questions for moving the client forward are:

- What do you really want?
- What will happen if you do nothing? (Usually the answer is that doing nothing will ensure failure – precisely what the client usually wishes to avoid.)
- What's your responsibility for change here?
- So what do you need to do to make the change?
- Who do you need to involve?
- What will support you?

- What can you do here?
- How, exactly, will you makes these changes?
- By when?

Another excellent question is:

- What do you need to do to make sure that you don't succeed here?

The unexpectedness and cheek of this question usually makes clients laugh, but there is also rich learning in it too.

Accountability

Accountability in coaching is about what the client agrees that he or she will do to make the goals that you have agreed between you real. If your background is in traditional teaching you may need to take care that accountability in the coaching sense does not come to seem like school homework where there are sanctions for non-compliance. In coaching there are no sanctions because your assumption is that clients are responsible for themselves. Clients will suggest the 'homework' tasks themselves in all probability and will also suggest how they would like you to hold them to account:

> Ailsa has been told by her boss that the papers she produces for their Board are full of mistakes such as sloppy punctuation and spelling. She is now working with a writing coach. This coach has asked her to self-assess a particular draft of her work against a named chapter of Lynne Truss's amusing and best-selling rant, *Eats, Shoots & Leaves: The Zero Tolerance Approach to Punctuation.*
> *Coach:* How would you like me to hold you to account on this?
> *Ailsa:* I think I ought to email my corrected version to you by next Thursday so that you can do a Truss on it, in case there's anything I've missed!
> *Coach:* Done!

If 'homework' is not done then there will be learning in what has happened to prevent it. Your attitude as a coach is, 'Well, that's interesting. Tell me what happened there'. Often the apparent failure of clients to deliver on their homework task will suggest what their core blocks and barriers are – in other words we are often in the territory of beliefs rather than in any apparently rational problems such as lack of time or money. It is immaterial to you whether the client has done his or her homework or not. Your interest is in the learning.

The accountability part of the process usually happens at or near the end of the session. The coach asks the client:

'So what are you going to do to make these changes happen?'

In hearing the client's reply, you press for SMART criteria:

- Specific: what exactly is the goal? The more specific and the less vague, the better.
- Measurable: how will you measure your success?
- Achievable: is it realistic and possible?
- Resourced: have you got the time and the money or other resources to do it?
- Timed: by when will you have done it?

Many learners will be very familiar with the SMART acronym because it is used so frequently in setting objectives in performance management systems.

You will also find it useful to ask whether whatever the client is suggesting is consistent with his or her core values. Look for up to three actions for each session, depending on the length of the session and the subject and make a note of them, even if you make very few other notes.

It is normal for people to explore how you will respond on accountability because many of them will have the idea that it is just like delivering a piece of homework, especially if they have not carried out what was agreed. Explore this in the initial session and also when the learner falters. Ask, 'How would you like me to work with you here? Does it help if we keep strictly to what you have suggested or should I be tough with you?' This way you put the responsibility right back where it belongs – with the client.

Coaching is an apparently simple activity that is a demanding and high-level skill in practice. Training, practice, supervision and feedback are all essential in developing coaching skills. It is easy to delude yourself that you already have everything that you need to be an excellent coach. Apart from any relevant subject or contextual knowledge, it needs empathy, maturity, discipline, self-awareness, self-management, psychological insight, courage, focus and a high degree of questioning and listening skill. When it works, people can learn at breathtaking speed and in a way that leaves them feeling good about themselves. Anything seems possible. Coaching seems to me like a core skill for anyone interested in seeing adults develop. As a profession it is growing at an astonishing rate and seems to have much to offer as a mainstream way of helping adults learn.

Further reading

A chapter like this can only be an introduction. At the moment, coaching has little accepted underpinning theory. Bruce Peltier's book on executive coaching (see below) is currently the nearest we have to a comprehensive look at the origins and effectiveness of different approaches to coaching. Most of what has been published has been developed by experienced practitioners, as in these suggestions:

Flaherty, J. (1999) *Coaching: Evoking Excellence in Others*. Oxford: Butterworth-Heinemann.

Gallwey, T. (2000) *The Inner Game of Work*. London: Orion Publishing Group.

Peltier, B. (2001) *The Psychology of Executive Coaching: Theory and Application*. New York: Brunner-Routledge.

Rogers, C.R. and Freiberg, H.J. (1983) *Freedom to Learn*, 3rd edition. New York: Merrill.

Rogers, J. (2004) *Coaching Skills: A Handbook*. Maidenhead: Open University Press/McGraw-Hill Education.

Whitworth, L., Kimsey-House, H. and Sandhal, P. (1998) *Co-active Coaching*. Palo Alto, CA: Davies Black Publishing.

Notes

1 See Further Reading.
2 Rogers, C.R. (1961) *On Becoming a Person*. Boston, MA: Houghton-Mifflin.
3 Vaughan Smith, J. (2007) *Therapist into Coach*. Maidenhead: Open University Press/McGraw-Hill.
4 De Bono, E. (2000) *Six Thinking Hats*. London: Penguin.

9 Role play and simulation

Guests wandering through the hotel could be forgiven for their amazement. There, furiously engaged, are three small groups of senior managers making and flying paper planes. Standing over them is someone with a stopwatch, a ruler and a stern expression. The feverish activity continues until the hotel lobby is covered with discarded planes. One group looks distinctly cross – they are obviously not doing so well. One group looks pleased with itself, the other moderately so. What is going on? The explanation is *management development*, but it will not be immediately apparent to a casual observer. If this is a public sector organization should someone write a furious letter to *The Times* denouncing the whole thing as a scandalous waste of money?

Well, no. These managers are engaged in a powerful simulation called *The Climate Lab*, and are discovering at first hand what it takes to lead a team through engaging in a competitive exercise. The participants are finding out in the most vivid and direct way possible what makes for effective team leadership. What the casual observer will not see is the two-hour long debrief where the theoretical construct is explained and people's experience is looked at in a calmer light than the feverish excitement of the simulation itself.

In the totally different environment of a reconfigured church, something apparently different is going on. Here, volunteers for a self-help charity are receiving training in how to deal with distressed and incoherent telephone callers. In the former vestry, the trainer miraculously turns herself into a variety of 'callers' while the trainee volunteer helper tries to deal with the 'call', watched by the five other members of the group. After the call is over, the group will debrief on what happened and will unpick the learning. If the trainee has not done particularly well, the trainer may rerun the activity so that the participant can learn from the feedback he or she has received. This is classic *role play*.

In a coaching room, coach and client are wrestling with how to prepare the client for a job interview. The client is anxious and has convinced herself that she is *crap at interviews*. The coach has already pointed out that the basis on which the client has made this judgment is flimsy, to say the least – the somewhat crudely given feedback from two 'failed' interviews, compared with a previously impeccable track record of success. The client and coach have agreed that the goal for the session is for the client to leave fully prepared for her interview the following day. The best way to do this, both are agreed, is to do a practice interview with copious feedback from the coach. This is also *role play*.

Meanwhile, in what appears to be a very different course and setting, a group of newly qualified doctors are practising their emergency life-saving techniques – cardio-pulmonary resuscitation (CPR). You cannot practise CPR properly on a living person. So these doctors are learning through a clever dummy called 'Annie ' which will tell them through a printout and with great accuracy how effective their mouth-to-mouth breathing has been and whether they have been compressing the chest in the right place and with the right degree of pressure. This is *simulation*.

More conventionally, a group of young managers is learning how to make robust selection decisions. Each has a pack of materials – application forms, a set of criteria for a job and a folio of other documents. They have to decide which candidates they would shortlist on the basis of what they have in front of them. Elsewhere in the same training centre, another group is looking at a reprinted article from the *Harvard Business Review* which sets out a fictional account of one manager's difficulties. The group will discuss the case and will put forward suggestions about what they would do if they had been in the same situation. This approach is *case study*.

In all these situations, the tutor/coach has found a solution through the various techniques to the problem of how to involve adult learners in the acquisition of a skill or of an apparently intractable and complex mass of knowledge. The more conventional method in every case would have been to deliver a little talk or to suggest reading a book. The 'rules' of effective leadership could be explained along with the various theories behind them. The essentials of how to counsel distressed people could be explained by describing them, as could some simple guidelines on how to shortlist candidates for a job. The young doctors could pick up any first-aid book for a clear account of how to give CPR. The job candidate could have been given a book (print, video or audio) on how to succeed at job interviews. However, none of these approaches on their own would be likely to be as effective as the alternatives I have described here. Simulation and role play are not universal panaceas, but they are exceptionally powerful techniques. I use them constantly in my own training and coaching.

When to choose these techniques

I use simple criteria:

- Does the learning need to include something pacey, involving and fun?
- Is there a principle here that has to be experienced to be fully understood?
- Where there is a skill involved:

- is the skill complex?
- is it unlikely that people will have a realistic view of how skilful they actually are?
- can the skill be improved with feedback?
- is it difficult to practise the skill easily or safely in the 'real world'?

Where you answer all of these questions with 'yes', then there is a case for using the techniques described in this chapter.

There is nothing especially difficult or even novel about using simulation and role play. Simulation as a way of learning has a long history because it is so obviously useful, but in modern times it was pioneered by the British and US armies during World War II and has continued to be an important part of military training. Abandoned villages have been reconstructed as realistic-looking streets, in effect stage sets, to train soldiers who will face real snipers in war zones. Two 'armies' have faced each other on the Wiltshire downs as rehearsal for the actuality of dealing with guerrillas in difficult terrain. Role play has become increasingly common in management development courses. Many classic board games are also simulations in their way – for instance, Monopoly and chess. If you want a convincing explanation of how capitalism works, then Monopoly is as good a way as any of experiencing it.

These approaches are ways of learning general principles through being involved in a particular situation, usually one which could occur in real life, but with some of the real-life time-intervals and distracting detail smoothed out for purposes of laying bare the essentials.

Case studies can be prepared through folders of documents, collections of descriptive material, tapes, video or a mixture of all these, and would be presented to a group simply as the basis of discussion. Role playing takes the process a stage further, when members of the group act out and improvise roles and situations using the information they obtained from the case-study material – or, in the case of coaching, draw on material the client already knows. A full-scale simulation is normally carried out continuously and intensively over several hours using fairly elaborate printed or recorded material, with fresh problems and complications introduced from time to time by the tutor. A simulation may be described, perhaps misleadingly, as a *game* at the point where it turns into a competition between individuals or groups with points awarded for completing a task, usually under time pressure.

How is this type of exercise organized and carried out? Some role playing is so simple that it hardly needs any preparation at all and is absorbed without fuss into work already being done. For instance, in a discussion on running meetings, it would be perfectly natural for a tutor to suggest that instead of simply talking about different kinds of behaviour, the learner might actually try them.

Role play without fanfare: an example

At Management Futures, we run an intensive one-day course called *You the Brand*. We restrict the numbers to four people. Essentially the course is about increasing your personal impact. The people who enrol are in middle-to-senior jobs where their potential for promotion is being limited by over-cautious or timid behaviour – for instance, remaining silent at meetings where they should be speaking up. All the participants have years of experience of attending meetings. When asked, all can describe perfectly well what makes for effective behaviour at meetings. For instance, they will understand how important it is to sit in the right place (the one where you can catch the Chair's eye), to speak early on in the meeting, to sweep the room with eye contact – and so on. The problem is their own reluctance to do it.

Tutor: We could talk about this for ever. Let's do a practice. (Note: the tutor did *not* say, 'Let's role play.')

The room is quickly reassembled as a typical meeting room with a table and chairs around it. The group takes seats, as they would in a real meeting and a topic for discussion is agreed – a bid for more money in a particular budget.

Tutor: So, Chris, show us – what do you typically do when you want to intervene in the discussion?

Chris: I sit forward a little and try to get a word in; I might say, 'I disagree with x or y person and think we ought to do something different', but I always find that people don't listen to me.

Tutor: 'Always'? There must be some exceptions! When it works, what are you doing?

Chris: Probably I speak a bit louder and make more obvious body movements

Tutor: So show us what that looks and sounds like.

Chris: OK – a bit like this (leans forward with more dramatic gesture) and probably I'll also say a little more.

Tutor: Yes, *a little more* probably means triple or quadruple the kind of brief statement you made just now – my own hunch is that unless you do this you would be far too easy to ignore. So – you now want people to support your bid. Show us what you need to do to get heard properly.

The next ten minutes is then spent with the group working to give Chris structured practice in keeping up the determination, and with it the pace, more substantial content and the volume of voice that will mean greatly increased impact. Other members of the group might try interrupting, distracting or tough questioning, with the tutor stopping frequently to ask the group to ask for Chris's own view on how it is going and to offer Chris feedback on what is working well or less well. In this way, Chris will actually experience what it is like to do the different behaviour – but within the safety of a training room, not in the much more risky environment of a real meeting where the consequences of failure would be so much greater.

In language teaching, role playing may seem a normal extension of work done practising dialogues and drills, and only becomes more recognizably something novel and different when the tutor sets up a 'scene' with the appropriate props.

For instance, in one French conversation class the tutor bases the first part of the class time on an episode from a DVD where the characters are ordering food in a restaurant. The students sit in their normal places while they are repeating the dialogue and drills, but they then move in groups of four to a table with knives, forks and plates in one corner of the room. The students 'play' the characters in the DVD, but extend the dialogue according to improvisations of their own and in response to the tutor, who sometimes plays waiter, sometimes another diner. After corrections and discussion they then play the same scene again.

Some tutors prefer to involve members of the group in researching the case-study material themselves: preparing speeches for a debate, or preparing a case for negotiation in an industrial agreement is one way of doing this. In this case the tutor simply presents the group with the barest outlines of the situation a week or a few days beforehand. Others favour variations on what is known in management training as an 'in-tray exercise', where the group members are presented with a batch of case-study material – letters, records, memos, press reports – such as might appear in an in-tray, and are required as individuals and under considerable time pressure to reach the kinds of decision they may need to make in real life.

More usually, tutors will involve the whole group in activity, either all together, in small groups, or in small groups which watch each other and then discuss. Sometimes they will deliberately hold back certain crucial pieces of information and will wait for the group to ask for it; sometimes they will supply a group or an individual with background information or documents not available to the others.

Simulation

It is hard to know where role play stops and simulation starts. Simulation may also shade into presenting itself as a 'game' if competition between groups is involved. Essentially, simulation involves creating a mini world with its own rules, roles and processes. Its purpose will usually be to look at how a chain of interlocking systems affect human behaviour.

Example: The Climate Lab

In the description of *The Climate Lab*[1] with which I opened this chapter, this simulation runs throughout one afternoon in a five-day management development course. The task of each of the three groups is to make the maximum number of paper planes to a tight specification. The planes have to be tested by an 'inspector' (one of the tutors) to see if they perform the correct flight pattern. The groups have the same materials, the same instructions and the same task: to make as many planes as they can within the one and a half hour limit. They work in separate rooms. The only variable is leadership but at the outset the groups do not know this – they invariably assume that leadership is identical in style. But in a recreation of Kurt Lewin's experiment of the 1940s (page 82) one group is led in an authoritarian style, one leader is all peace and love, constantly looking for consensus – the laissez-faire style – and one is democratic, encouraging a degree of discussion, encouragement and involvement whilst also emphasizing the importance of the targets. At the end of the one and a half hour period, performance is compared. Invariably the democratically led group has produced by far the most planes, usually outperforming the other two by several hundred per cent. In a spookily accurate recreation of Lewin's original findings, the group with the authoritarian leader will be meek at first but then, as time goes on, resentment grows. Frequently, the group will sabotage its planes ('I hope no one tries to fly in these planes', said one participant grimly to me, 'because I've made sure they will crash by putting in a few extra folds').

As soon as the simulation is over, each group fills in a questionnaire about the climate within the group – the feelings people had about the clarity of their roles, responsibility, standards – and so on. The climate they feel they experienced is compared with the climate they would have liked. The link of climate with performance is made clear. The lesson is spell out: leadership affects climate, climate affects motivation and motivation affects performance.

There then follows a two-hour debrief where the tutors come clean about the different styles of leadership. Tutors give a short input on the underlying theory, encouraging the group to compare this with the experience of the simulation.

A period of unloading the emotion then has to follow. This is designed to help people separate their personal experience of the simulation from the systems underlying it. The people in the group led by the authoritarian leader are gently given the opportunity to see how their anger and, in some cases, their shame is an intrinsic part of the learning. The group that 'won' has to come down from its perch of assuming that there was some special cleverness that led to their 'victory'. The group led by the laissez-faire leader will find much to ponder in discussing how the lack of leadership led to a preoccupation with its absence and thus a distraction from meeting the performance targets. Another input session explains the concept of climate and the groups' own data is displayed and discussed. Finally, the tutors lead a discussion on the personal and practical implications. How would the people you lead describe your leadership style? How consistent are you? How often do you waver between one style and another? What do you need to do to create the optimum climate?

For people who are leaders at any level in any organization, the learning is profound:

> I found this startling – it made me think immediately about the climate in the group I'm part of at work. It explained so much.
>
> I immediately thought – what kind of climate do I create? The answer wasn't comfortable.
>
> Hearing the actor who had played the part of the authoritarian leader talk about the sheer terror and effort of the role and the feeling of how he was ultimately responsible so had to drive people on – and remembering, though I hadn't noticed it at the time, his chalky, sweating face – it was like looking in a mirror at my own reflection. This experience profoundly changed me – I can't tell you how important it has been to my development as a leader.
>
> It reinforced my belief that the style of leadership I currently do is the right one, and also how difficult it is to do within the general climate of my organization – which is totally the opposite!

Simulation also comes into its own as a way of predicting the consequences of introducing a major systems change. For instance, the introduction of a purchaser–provider system in the NHS of the early 1990s was preceded by a simulation called *Rubber Windmill*. A similar change inside the BBC of the same era was also supported by a day-long simulation. The simulation designers in both cases set up groups which mirrored the new systems and processes. Stripping out distracting detail and compressing time allowed the effects, positive and negative, of the new system to be predicted. The only point of running such simulations is to learn from them. It has sometimes been claimed that although both these simulations showed with utter clarity what the negative consequences of the changes were likely to be, those introducing the changes did not incorporate the learning into the real-life systems.

Simulation is a powerful way of increasing self-awareness. For instance, some management development courses have at their core a day-long simulation where participants are given a batch of company documents to read overnight, allotted roles and then told that they are running the company with a number of tricky decisions to make, all of which are likely to involve conflict. Working in small groups and separate rooms, everything they do is videoed, watched from the darkness of a two-way mirror by the tutors who will be running personal and group debriefs the following day. What emerges is people's typical behaviour in meetings, in decision-making and in negotiation. Unlike the environment at work, everything the participants do is potentially the source of rich and detailed feedback for learning.

Simulation can bring an element of realism and excitement to academic subjects by inviting decisions in a recreated historical, geographical or sociological situation. Thus students of history who might be studying the Battle of Waterloo could be given maps of the battleground, pins to represent groups of soldiers in the different armies, letters, memoranda, biographies, and so on, and could play out for themselves the crucial moves of the battle. In teaching geography to children, some successful games have been developed around events such as the building of the great North American railways, where children have in fact learnt the geography of the country, the map of the routes, and the reasons railways were built when and where they were through the use of a geography game. No doubt simulations could be developed along the same lines for adults.

Simulation can also shade into problem-based learning (Chapter 7). Here is an example, taken from a simulation designed around a three-hour session planned for a group of trainee teachers studying educational policy. The simulation centres on a case study of an 11-year-old whose parents were faced with the tricky problem of wanting their child to go to a different school from the one in which she was offered a place by the education authority. The aims of the simulation were: to inform the students about the complexities of reconciling different 'stakeholders' in the education system; to explore legal rights within it; to explore some of the personal stresses involved in parent–school relationships; and to discuss the criteria on which choice of school might be based. The simulation is run in rounds, with participants taking the key roles involved in the case and making decisions as they went. Each round is followed by discussion where matters of fact and principle can be debated.

The documents included:

1 The child's last primary-school report.
2 A medical report.

3 Two essays written by the child on 'My Ideal School' and 'My Family'.
4 Confidential report on the child from the primary-school head to the chief education officer.
5 Copies of correspondence between parents, heads and the senior officer responsible for education in the local authority.
6 Copies of correspondence between the parents and their local councillor.
7 Long extracts from the two secondary-school prospectuses.
8 Extracts from relevant Education Acts.
9 Extracts from 'Manual of Guidance' for parents.

In a full-scale simulation this telescoped timescale has the further advantage that it makes it possible to see the effect of your decisions and actions in a rapid way that is not normally possible in real life – in other words, there is almost instant feedback.

Advantages

When done well, what are the advantages of this type of learning? First, the element of realism makes it an eminently suitable way for adults to learn. Adults are mostly impatient of teaching which seems remote from the realities of whichever subject we are learning; we want to feel that no time is wasted on vague theory which is going to be of little real relevance and practical value. Thus, if a course for managers is called 'Managing Discipline', the course members may not take at all kindly to lectures on economic or historical theory, however vital the lecturer might feel this information is to understanding current conflicts. Members of such courses are inclined to say that since they conduct their real-life negotiations in an atmosphere of hustling, keen controversy, they expect to see the same atmosphere understood and catered for on the course. It is even better if the same realistic conditions can enter the process of learning itself, only in a way that enables more information to be fed in, in conditions of more certain control than is usual in real life, where inflamed or tender feelings can mean a stubborn refusal to accept new information at all.

A second advantage is that these are entirely active methods of learning. In earlier chapters I have tried to show how important activity is to adult learning, and have stressed how often it is ineffective for adults to be told how to do something without the opportunity to try it out for themselves. Indeed, the approaches I discuss in this chapter may offer a unique chance in certain subjects to bridge the gap between theory and practice. This can be one of the most unyielding problems of planning a piece of teaching where, as in management or teacher training, students will frequently complain that the theory they learnt was a hopelessly inadequate preparation for facing real life. Some kind of simulation or role play may be the most effective way that managers can learn how to conduct an interview or chair a meeting. It is also an excellent way of generating a variety of solutions to problems – for instance, complex interpersonal situations where there is rarely one 'right' answer.

A further advantage of simulation and role play is that because they are realistic, active methods, they have many of the features of learning in real life, with the powerful difference that in real life mistakes can be expensive, disagreeable and mortifying. In a simulation or role play mistakes can be made without retribution. The atmosphere of calm analysis and good-humoured support from tutor and other students makes it possible to see why mistakes have been made and to learn to avoid them in future. In this way a student, who in a business game makes a gross error which in real life would have cost her job, can step back and analyse what moves led her (or the character she was playing) to act as she did. An added convenience is that because of its telescoped timescale, simulation can present learners with situations they are unlikely to encounter every day, and might indeed wish to avoid, but which nevertheless they ought to be prepared to meet. Thus role play and simulation in a public-speaking class might introduce a particularly odious heckler character; a management course for senior nurses might include a difficult situation both with clinical and managerial colleagues.

A foundation assumption behind the use of role play and simulation is that sooner or later people will behave in the ways they normally do – the same patterns will emerge. By stripping away the irrelevancies, the essence of the behaviour is exposed.

Because these methods usually arouse powerful emotions in those who take part, they can be potent and valuable methods for any tutor whose subject involves the development of sensitivity and tolerance. Crude attitude-change is not generally held to be a desirable educational aim in education, but increasing understanding in a way that may lead to attitude-change certainly is. In subjects such as politics, sociology, industrial relations, diversity, religion or literature, many issues can only be approached through a genuine understanding not just of one other point of view, but of the possibility that a whole range of viewpoints may be equally valid. Thus managers, often reluctantly persuaded at first to prepare a set of union as well as management cases for a piece of role playing, may come to understand the strengths and weaknesses, the varying opinions at different levels of seniority, of both management and union in a way that would be impossible from a more passive, intellectualized analysis. Where 'role reversal' is used (after the first run-through, the participants play each other's roles), this effect is particularly noticeable.

Another benefit of this kind of role playing is that its real value can be in the social skills it teaches. Role play confronts any of us with the possible gaps between what we claim for our skills and knowledge and how they actually appear to others. That is why it can feel risky and why, therefore, participants can resist doing it.

This is particularly important in one-to-one coaching. Clients often know what they want to achieve and what they are up against. What is often much more difficult for them to understand is *how* they do what they do and the *impact* of these actions on others. An example would be the client who wants help in how she presents herself at a job interview. She knows that she wants the job. She knows how she rates her own experience. What she typically lacks is any idea of how her method of answering questions is helping or getting in the way of achieving her ambitions.

Coach: So let's do a rehearsal around the typical questions you can expect for this job. Is that OK? (Note: this is a closed question which expects the answer, yes.)

Client: Yes, OK, though I'm already feeling nervous.

Coach: Nervousness can give you that extra bit of edge as long as it doesn't get out of hand. This is just the rehearsal, not the real thing. What I suggest we do is that I'll ask you a typical question and you give your answer, then we'll stop and debrief. OK? So let's start with the one question that is always asked in any job interview: Why do you want this job?

(Client gives rambling answer, starting with why the job will be good for her career, going on to the attractions of working for the organization and ending with a mention that she has just been made redundant from her current post and so is worried about finding something else quickly.)

Coach: So can I offer you some feedback here? I certainly got the idea that you were enthusiastic and keen to have the job. But all of your first minute and a half was about why the job was good for you. I began to lose the thread because you went on talking for another two minutes and I still hadn't heard you say what you were keen to bring to me as the potential employer. I'm wondering if maybe this is why you said the feedback you'd had from the last interview was that you seemed a bit unfocused?

In this example, no real acting is involved on the client's part other than the low key pretence that the coach is the interviewer. The client is playing herself. The agenda is hers and the scenario is generated by her: she has provided all the documentation because it is what she has been sent in preparation for the interview. None the less, she will for certain be doing more or less exactly the same as she has done in her previous job interviews. As the session goes on, the coach can continue to give the intensely helpful micro-feedback that no one else is at all likely to have offered before:

> When you leaned forward, the effect it had on me was...
>
> In your answer to that question I didn't hear any proof that you had actually handled a similar situation – it was just a description of your attitudes and what an employer wants to hear is evidence of track record.
>
> You raised your voice a little at that point and I'm wondering if...
>
> You seemed to lose enthusiasm when I heard you describe...

Coach and client can rehearse and repeat new behaviours for as long as it takes to embed them in the client's repertoire.

What is often important in the kinds of learning served by these methods is not so much absorbing the content of any particular mass of information as learning to understand how one's own behaviour appears to other people. Role play in a group setting can bring further richness, learning to work with others on solving a problem, to accept other people's solutions, their contributions and their right to disagree. Where *how* something is said is more important than *what* is said, role play may, indeed, be one of the most powerful ways of learning.

Role playing and simulation can also be designed specifically to teach people how to acquire, evaluate and use information. In this sense it is closely allied to Problem-based Learning. For example, a group who had enrolled for a course in urban planning undertook a simulation which was worked in pairs over two intensive four-hour sessions separated by a week. To work out several possible solutions to a single problem in traffic control and urban redevelopment, participants were obliged to look up, absorb and use some or all of: Town and Country Planning Acts; several classic studies in urban sociology; local history; academic analyses and appreciations of Georgian architecture; and some elementary principles of civil engineering. During the course of the simulation their tutor presented them with additional complications in the form of resolutions passed by a local pressure group, or announcements of new findings on sites of historical value. Here, the group was involved in a highly sophisticated and elaborate project involving research skills, information retrieval and problem-solving, as well as learning to weigh social priorities and to argue and present a case in a final report. The participants' own opinion of the exercise was that they had learnt more in the two simulation sessions and in the following two hours devoted to discussion and analysis than they had learnt in all the rest of the course put together.

Involvement

Simulation and role playing generate intense involvement among those taking part. It is almost impossible to remain aloof and uninvolved. Even the most stately learner usually finds it hard to stay outside. Some people start by thinking it is going to be a laugh, something they will go along with to humour their tutor. They then rapidly pass to the stage where they are involved but keep some superficial sense of joking distance or irony. In a class such as the urban planning group where the basic emphasis is on academic skills this often remains the predominant mood. Where the whole group is also involved in role playing, even this mood passes, replaced by an entirely absorbed seriousness for the task in hand.

Simulation and role playing are immensely adaptable for groups of mixed ability. They can offer natural opportunities for working in groups, for occasions where people of different abilities can help each other, and where distinctions between experience and ability can at least be blurred if not extinguished altogether.

Disadvantages

No one method is going to be right for every situation and this is as true of role play and simulation as of any other method. The disadvantages are:

- Many people hate acting and will do anything to avoid it.
- Many people love acting and, given the chance, will overdo the drama.
- There is never time or space to give all the relevant information so an edited version has to be produced but in reality you would need to be able to decide for yourself what was relevant and what was not.
- Perhaps the most common practical difficulty is that tutors are often unable to encourage the group to look beyond the rights and wrongs of a particular case. If the material is sufficiently intriguing, group members will sometimes argue it endlessly, but take it no further than that. If the material is less absorbing, they may tend to discuss it in a desultory way for a short time, but will then dismiss it by implying that because conditions in their job or locality are not exactly like the ones in the case study, there is nothing to be learnt from it. This can be a particularly pressing problem with people who

have a narrow but extremely intensive practical knowledge of their own cases while rejecting the applicability of either general theory or other cases to their own.

- There is never as much information available as there would be in real life. People will often criticize a slackly prepared role play on these grounds by saying that they cannot possibly argue the case without more information. In real life there are, of course, often severe limitations to the amount of information that is available. Some tutors believe that a case study on which a complex role play is based should omit confusing and conflicting detail, though, as with problem-based learning, supporters will stress the necessity of introducing it, to teach the principles of relevance and choice.
- Even when the material is scrupulously prepared and well-matched to real life, participants may believe it has still been over-synthesized. This apparent lack of face validity may mean that they hold back from full engagement and may therefore learn less than they could.
- Similarly, in practice, role play is never quite the real thing, tempers never run quite so high, your emotions are never quite so fully engaged as they are in the real situation, because, however realistic the setting, the problem, or the incidental detail, you never forget that you are in a classroom. Particularly where the tutor has stressed that it is not their own but other people's roles that participants are to play, there is always some sense of distance between action and thought.
- Simulations that last a day or more need complex planning involving many minds. The art is to provide enough detail to be plausible and convincingly multifaceted yet not so much that it becomes totally confusing. The research phase can be lengthy. Documents need to look realistic, whether they are presented on a computer screen or on paper. A rough rule of thumb is that for every hour your simulation will run you probably need to allow for at least two days of preparation, often more, for research, activity design and documentation.
- Running the simulation usually involves a dedicated administrator both at the preparation stage and on the day to manage logistics, a suite of rooms and a lavish number of trained observers. The activity-planning and interrelationships of the groups is challenging – it has to run absolutely punctually, with no slack. In the management development example I quoted on page 199, the company running the simulation has built a special training suite in a hotel, with tailored video facilities. You need to be sure that the total quality and participant experience of the simulation is superb so that the investment will eventually pay off and that the product life-cycle will

be long enough to justify expending such a large amount of time, money and effort.

A real-life example

Here is a personal example of how the pluses and minuses can work out.

I recently completed an initial training for accreditation as a mediator and role play-cum simulation was the foundation method of the five-day course. We took part in at least one and sometimes three simulated mediations every day, interspersed with straightforward teaching and demonstration. The course Faculty, all senior and successful mediators, had plumped for role play because they believed it was essential to give us the flavour of what real-life mediation in all its complexity was like. Mediation is a high-level, high-risk activity. Often it follows months and sometimes years of bitter dispute and failed negotiations in which an intense level of emotion is generated and a great deal of money can be at stake. Read the account of any high-profile divorce case for a flavour of how anger and the urge for revenge at any price can prolong such proceedings and massively increase the legal costs. Mediation is designed to cut through all of that and in fact our tutors claimed that something like 70 per cent of all cases settle within a day. To train people in such an activity in a mere five days is a tall order. To be a mediator you need *knowledge*: of what mediation is and how it is different from other, apparently similar, interventions in conflict resolution. You need the correct *attitudes*, notably the acceptance that the mediator's role is to remain unattached to any particular outcome or party to the dispute. Finally, you also need an immense range of *skills*: rapport, creating trust, incisive questioning, calm self-management – among many others. Pre-course preparation involved reading through a text book, plus reading and then absorbing the details of 11 case study briefs, all of them played out through the course. For some of these cases, I was mediator; for others, I had a specific character-role to play with a private briefing not to be shared with any of the other participants until after the role play was completed.

As I and my fellow-participants went through the event, the shortcomings of role play as a learning technique became clear. First, there were several people who felt that the course was the opportunity to pamper their inner Oscar-nominee. To say that they overacted would be putting it mildly. At one point, where a particularly mischievous role player was 'weeping' with his head on the table in 'despair' I caught the eye of my co-mediator and just managed to avoid disgracing myself by giving way to the sort of uncontrollable laughter which actors call *corpsing* – the word is well-chosen because, once started, this kind of giggling becomes unstoppable and brings the proceedings to a halt. Some participants in other role plays had the opposite problem – their chronic embarrassment produced shockingly wooden behaviour. The risk was of the group becoming preoccupied with the quality of the performance rather than with the quality of the learning. This did not make for verisimilitude.

Our personal brief for each case was, of necessity, limited. This led to wild invention on several occasions, when the brief did not provide information being legitimately requested by one of the other parties. On several occasions this distorted the course of the mediation. More seriously, as we got better at understanding the way the cases were constructed, we began to see that stripping out the apparently distracting detail of real life was inclined to lead us to what felt like unrealistically pat solutions. No one wanted to let colleagues down through under-preparation, so getting ready for each role was maddeningly time-consuming and took scarce energy away from other necessary preparation and review.

Nonetheless, I believe that role play–simluation was actually the right technique to use. Nothing else could have conveyed so much so quickly or given so much material for feedback as role play. The final two days gave everyone the chance for challenging sessions where we acted as mediators and these were assessed for accreditation with immensely helpful and detailed feedback given on the spot. Nothing else could have shown us so clearly the range of typical mediation cases, the various necessary stages of a mediation or illustrated so vividly how the need to save face is often what lies behind apparently intransigent attitudes. The state of our skills was exposed as clearly to us as it was to the Faculty. The decision to employ role play as the main method of learning was clearly taken because the cost, risk and lack of control over outcomes that real life practice can involve were all too high. When this is so, the case for role play is strong.

The issue for me was that the role play could have been much better handled – for instance by using professional actors for at least some of the scenarios and concentrating more effort in smaller doses on the critical skill-building elements of the course.

One of the reasons participants may be suspicious of role playing and simulation is that these are not orderly, predictable methods of learning. There are no prepackaged maxims that can be transferred direct from tutor to learner. On the contrary, learners not only have to elaborate on a given situation by actively interpreting it; they then have to deduce the general rules for themselves. This is why the follow-up discussion is so important. It is also why learning through simulation and role playing seems to take much longer and is so much more diffuse and sprawling than a series of lectures. The gamble you take when adopting it is that although apparently more efficient in tutor time, lectures have a poor record where retention and understanding are involved. Role play and simulation greatly increase the chances that real understanding will increase dramatically. Use of these techniques, however, does make considerable demands on the tutor, not only in the time and skill they will demand in preparation, but also in your ability to train your groups to generalize a clear overall picture from a series of specific examples.

Making the methods work

In spite of all these problems, in the right place these are uniquely valuable techniques. It is probably the only way, for instance, that you could train adequately as a Samaritan, because it is the only technique that could give you supervised practice before you are let loose in the real world, where an untrained Befriender would quickly feel confused and inadequate as well as being potentially quite likely to behave unhelpfully with clients. It is certainly the best way for shop assistants to learn how to deal with customers. A few stints of role-played practice at handling an aggressive customer are worth any amount of written advice in the staff manual. But, like any other technique, role play needs care in execution. Normally, you will need to work through all the following stages:

Objectives

Be clear about which objectives you are hoping to meet through role play. If you are going to use it in coaching, then the objective might be simple: to invite the client to understand how a micro-example of his or her behaviour might seem to others.

When you are planning something more elaborate involving several people, write yourself a tightly defined brief before you begin. For instance, if you are thinking of running a role play on selection interviewing, it will probably not be helpful to think vaguely: 'Well, it will do them good to get a bit of practice? It will be better to write down something like: 'Having completed the role play, the participants should be able to define behaviourally based interviewing; demonstrate competence-based questioning; demonstrate asking for examples through open questions and follow-up probes'.

Choose or design appropriate material

To work with your group, the material must be relevant and credible. If you are writing your own, then you may need to check it out with a suitable expert first: one tiny error (for instance, a wrong job title) could destroy the 'willing suspension of disbelief' of your group as surely as it does to spot a continuity error in a film. It is always better to base a role play on a real situation: this gives you the perfect reply to students who protest that such a scenario could 'never' happen, and is also likely to provide you with the small details and complexities that bring a case to life. But beware of scripting a role play too lengthily or in a way that leaves little room for manoeuvre and elaboration. People may feel constrained by all the detail or simply refuse to take part: 'I'm just not like that person; I wouldn't behave like that'.

As in my mediation course, an elaborate role play–simulation that is going to continue for some hours may involve you in preparing detailed individual briefs for different characters. In ours, everyone had the general introduction to the case, but each character also had a confidential brief handed out on the day – typically this was a page and a half of background on the underlying motivation of the character, how the character felt, details that could compromise him or her if revealed and what they might be prepared to settle for, if offered.

Expect success

If role playing and simulation can only be introduced with a great fanfare and with much special pleading from you, then they are probably unsuited to the course.

Role play may be new to some of your group. A simple role play does not need any great fanfare and the words *role play* need not be used. Where you are going to use something more elaborate, explain the difference between 'role play' and 'acting', and describe the normal progress of a typical role play. It often helps to emphasize that acting ability is not really required – *just be yourself within the limits of the information you have available.* Don't apologize or over-explain. It is usually better just to assume that the group will take part and that the approach will be successful. On the rare occasions where a group member refuses to take part, just accept his or her decision gracefully and calmly. It's no big deal. Don't let yourself feel personally attacked, don't argue, coax or waste time justifying the technique. Just suggest that the person sits out quietly or becomes formally an observer.

Consider using professional actors trained in giving feedback

Of course you have to have a big enough budget to bear the additional cost of hiring professionals. But over the last few years the value of actors in role play and simulation has become clear. By definition, actors have no professional embarrassment about playing people other than themselves. They can add realism and therefore greater challenge. It takes away the stress of others having to role play. The specialist company with whom we work, *Re-Act,* are superb at quickly improvising the behaviour of any number of characters. We use them on a variety of assignments where we and they may adopt either of these approaches:

Working on pre-designed scenarios. Here we will have given them a detailed back story on a character, most of which will not appear in the actual role play but is there to give flavour and depth to the part. The part will be the basis of some kind of highly charged encounter which the course participant is likely to be finding challenging to deal with in real life. Examples from our recent work have included being the 'parent' who has just been told by a doctor (the course participant) that his child is profoundly deaf; being a candidate in a job interview in front of a panel of real-life selectors learning how to improve their interview technique; being a 'poor performer' in a military unit where the senior officer (the course participant) has to overcome hostility or indifference by giving straightforward feedback. The investment in time and effort can be justified when you are running the same event many times over.
Improvising, taking the brief on the spot from the participant. For instance, the session may have as its theme *Managing Personal Conflict.* There will have been some general input from the tutor on different approaches to managing conflict, perhaps drawing on helpful theories, or using personality questionnaires to illustrate how different people have different preferred styles, possibly over-relying on one style at the expense of the others. The group may then split into smaller groups of four or five, each with an actor-tutor assigned to it.

The actor will work one to one with each person with the others watching and offering feedback, since there is almost as much to be learned from seeing others' strengths and weaknesses as there is from being in the spotlight yourself. Each participant describes a person whose behaviour they are finding difficult. The actor asks just a few questions which quickly elicit the nature of the other person – their age, job and background. The participant describes a typical event which did not go well. Again, the participant plays him or herself in rerunning the scenario usually for no longer than five minutes – in fact less is often enough. It would be typical for the participant to say, 'This is exactly what that person does – you must know them!' The principle here, of course, is that it is our own behaviour which triggers the response in the other person and this is what will be faithfully reproduced in the training room. After asking the person how he or she thinks it has gone and how that compares with the real life episode, the actor then gives exquisitely detailed and focused feedback, offering the participant the chance to rerun all or part of the scenario. Time and again we have feedback from participants who tell us that this experience is transforming. Its virtue is that people are working on entirely authentic material: their own.

We encourage them to choose a relationship which matters and which has got stuck in a dysfunctional pattern. Learning to recognize the pattern and then to break it by changing your own behaviour is the key. An apparently small change in behaviour can be the source of dramatic improvement in performance.

If you cannot afford actors, and have no handy source of gifted local amateurs, then consider taking the actor-role yourself, using the improvisation technique I describe above. This is not such a bizarre suggestion as it may sound. Most of us who teach have a love of performance lurking somewhere in our psyches. When a client's budget will not run to actors, necessity and a belief in the value of the approach has led all of my colleagues at Management Futures to discover that they can do this – not as competently as the professionals, but well enough – sometimes to their surprise.

Give a detailed briefing before you begin

The briefing is part of the learning because here you introduce the ideas the role play is designed to explore. Tell the group what your objectives are, what the rules are about, how much time is allowed, whether or not the players should confer in advance or consult you. This is also the stage to brief group members who are not role playing but observing. They could, for instance, have an observation sheet which they fill in as the role play progresses. If they are to observe an 'annual assessment' between a 'manager' and a 'subordinate', then they could have a sheet which lists different behaviours which they tick or cross. Tell the observers what you expect them to do later – normally to give feedback to the players. Depending on the type of role play, you may like to give different observers different types of task – for instance, one set could observe the 'manager' and one the 'subordinate'.

Preparation time for participants

Where you have designed a long simulation/role play, allow participants time to study it, perhaps by sending it well in advance of the actual event, suggesting how many hours of study it will take to absorb the essentials.

Run the role play

Keep within realistic time limits. Tell people how much time is allocated and stick to it. Brevity has the virtue that several 'players' (say three pairs) can take part. Five minutes of role play will often generate twice as much discussion. Be prepared to step in if the role play wilts, becomes too intense or begins to ramble away from the main issue.

Make detailed notes – or recordings

In all the stress of the moment, it is easy for participants to overlook or forget what they said and did. Have a prepared feedback sheet ready – or just write fast. Video recording gives unarguable evidence and can be a good idea, but you may have to wrestle potentially unreliable technology in order to do it. Remember that playing back will lengthen the debriefing time. A good compromise can be to play back highlights only or let each participant take away their own video record for private reviewing later.

Rerun the role play if necessary

In the typically short role play involved in learning a specific skill, it is good practice to let people have a second or even a third chance to get it right. Never leave someone with that leaden feeling of failure if you can possibly avoid it. Sometimes it is enough just to rerun the critical minute or so of the role play, coaching the learner in the new behaviours as necessary.

Allow for vulnerability

Most role plays are exposing, particularly if people are playing themselves, or if, as in my mediation course, they are being assessed. Be prepared to reassure and to allow for feelings of embarrassment: 'Did I do it well enough?' 'Do I look silly?' 'What do the observers think?' 'Why on earth did I say that . . .?' Cut short any unrealistically critical self-appraisal – this is more likely than serene and unjustified confidence. Give assessment feedback in private wherever possible.

Debriefing

There is no point in these techniques without debriefing. It is the process of debriefing which helps make the learning points. It is good manners to let the learner have the first word. 'How did you think that went?' 'What did you think of the way you handled . . .?' 'How did it compare with the way you deal with this in real life?' Giving the learner this first chance to speak allows them to wind down and step back from the task. It also begins the process of creating perspective on whatever the issue is.

Next, ask the observers for their feedback. You will already have established the same rules for sensitive and helpful feedback as you use yourself (see Chapter 3 for detailed hints on how to do this) but this process must be handled with infinite care, especially when people have been playing themselves and possibly repeating or rehearsing something which puts them at the edge of their abilities. Here it is reasonable to assume that they will therefore be extra-vulnerable to clumsily offered negative feedback.

Now make the transition into a general discussion about underlying themes. These can be prepared in advance. Has the role play thrown up general trends or difficulties which parallel problems in the real world? Has it revealed insights (we hope that it has) into how similar issues may be handled for real? What tends to get in the way of the ideal solution?

Finally, don't forget to thank and praise the participants for their efforts. Many people will have taken part vigorously, but may privately wonder later if they have done it well enough. Forestall this reaction by making it clear that it is entirely thanks to their skill and commitment that such a valuable discussion was possible.

Refine the exercise

Running an elaborate exercise for the first time will usually reveal some flaws in its design. Regard the first run as a pilot; make suitable alterations in the light of useful comments from participants or observations of your own.

Further reading

Role play is essentially a practical technique. From time to time books of ready-made scenarios appear, but I have always found them of limited relevance to my own groups. If you are interested in learning a little more about the practicalities, the first book below will help. The second is a more academic treatment of simulation and gaming theory and methodology. If simulation and gaming interests you, one of the best kinds of preparation is to ask to observe a well-designed exercise and then to quiz its designer on how it was developed.

Van Ments, M. (1999) *The Effective Use of Role Play*, 2nd edition. London: Kogan Page.

Klabbers, J.H.G. (2006) *The Magic Circle: Principles of Gaming and Simulation*. Rotterdam: Sense Publishers.

Notes

1 Developed by John Bray and based on Kurt Lewin's work as developed by Litwin and Stringer, see page 105. Available from Management Futures Ltd: info@managementfutures.co.uk

10 Delivering information: lecturing, demonstrating and blended learning

At some point in virtually all pieces of teaching and learning it is necessary to give people information – the traditional *instructor* and *interpreter* role of the teacher. For the greater part of 2000 years, this was the main way in which education was delivered. The assumption was that the teacher knows more than the pupil so it is down to the teacher to convey this knowledge through talking. Present-day understanding about learning, the profound social changes of the twentieth century and the availability of information technology have all severely challenged such assumptions. Yet there still has to be a place for transmitting information. The questions really are, what place? And how should it be transmitted?

You could say that the whole learning process can be boiled down to four stages:

1. *Tell me:* the initial stage of acquiring knowledge.
2. *Show me:* being shown how to apply the knowledge or how to turn the knowledge into skill.
3. *Let me:* trying it out and practising.
4. *Assess me:* testing how far the knowledge and skill has stuck.

This chapter is about the *Tell Me* stage. I shall look first at the face-to-face methods of lecturing and demonstrating and then, briefly, at Blended Learning.

When *Tell Me* is useful

There are innumerable times when it is appropriate to give learners information.

Briefing. You need to introduce a course, a day, a session. You have to tell people what to expect: for instance the ritual of explaining fire safety procedure; the structure and objectives of the course; the conventions that need to be observed during it; the nature of an activity or exercise.

Essential facts. By and large these will be uncomplicated and uncontroversial but essential facts that learners need to have. Examples could be: the demands of an examination board; trends in a company's sales figures; company policy on whatever the subject of the course is; regulatory frameworks; the physiology of the human kidney; a concise summary of some great thinker's ideas; the mechanics of how an everyday object works; the chemistry of bread-making.

Conceptual overviews. You may have a unique synthesis of relevant concepts and ideas which is not available anywhere else. Lecturing can be an excellent way of supplying the framework of a subject into which students can slot more learning as they acquire it through other methods. It is a way of giving all the learners the same experience and the same input at the same time. Formal input, where the tutor is the one doing the talking, also allows for checking how far people have understood and also for exploring what they make of the ideas.

Lecturing may be able to highlight the essentials in a way that just reading cannot. It may also be that there is no available literature that can package the information in exactly the way you need to meet the needs of your group. This may be particularly true in subjects where practice leads theory by a long way or topics where research has yet to be synthesized neatly enough for newcomers to the subject to understand. For instance, in the coach-training courses run by my company, it is important for learners to have proper perspective on how coaching has developed over the last thirty years and what differing opinions are emerging about how to do it effectively. We consider that the only way to do this at the moment is verbally because the subject is fast-moving.

Consistency is important. It will be imperative here for key populations of learners to have the same information. In large-scale training interventions it can be commercially vital for the identical message to reach hundreds of thousands of people within weeks. Where you are working to an examination syllabus, there will be givens on which compromise is not possible or there may be particular principles on which it is important to stay firm.

Enthusing. There is a role for motivating and enthusing groups when an expert in the subject conveys his or her own delight in the topic.

Establishing your authority. You may sometimes face a sceptical or perhaps even a hostile group. An example would be any event where people have been enrolled reluctantly or where they feel doubt about whether the course is going to benefit them, maybe because they believe they already have the relevant knowledge or expertise. Here there can be a case for a show-stopping display of your own competence.

Lecturing

I am using *lecturing* as a portmanteau word to describe any occasion, even a very informal one, where a tutor or teacher is delivering information to a group of learners. Lecturing is the simplest and most familiar method of meeting the need to impart information. When done well it can fulfil all of the functions I list above. Of itself, however, this does not fully explain its continuing popularity.

One reason is that there can be tremendous pressure from learners for a method they already know – and everyone knows the lecture method, after all, because we have all been on the receiving end of it as children. Second, nothing is asked of learners other than the appearance of polite attention. This may particularly suit a group of nervous new learners, apprehensive about the demands more obviously active methods may make on them. In groups where attendance is compulsory, lectures and demonstrations notoriously allow learners to undermine the process by inventing other ways to fill the time such as texting, whispering with neighbours, or, as I have often seen at conferences, openly doing the crossword. More respectably, many adult groups like a method where the teacher puts on a show of proficiency because this is an assurance, at least at first, that they are being taught by an expert.

Sheer inexperience and lack of training also drives many teachers of adults to assume that talking all the time is the same as 'teaching'. For the same reason, that crucial distinction between teaching and learning has never become clear in their minds.

Using lecturing as the main method of learning can also be profitable for the provider, so where money-making is the driver, it can lead to this choice of method. A regular part of the junk mail in most offices would be a leaflet offering the £99 seminar which promises easy, quick solutions to common problems – managing conflict, being more assertive, dealing with stress – and so on. One such organization aims at people in HR or coaching and one of its self-described *workshops* attracted me. The essential message of this event was thoughtful and based on sound research. The back-up materials were thorough. However, *workshop* it was not. The only person doing real work was the lecturer as virtually all of the six hours of the day were spent in a shabby, tiered lecture theatre listening to this one poor man talking. To me he increasingly seemed to have the air of someone who was on auto-pilot because he had done the same set piece so many times before. There were about 120 people present so as a commercial proposition it was highly successful. As a learning event it was certainly a flop for me – my attention drifted away continuously and the event offered me no more than I could have obtained from buying the £20 book on which the day was based. I don't think I was alone in this as I noticed that about a quarter of the audience did not return after the buy-it-yourself lunch and by the end of the day roughly half of the original total had vanished.

Similarly, lecturing and demonstrating sometimes appeal to organizers in higher, adult and further education on the grounds that they are 'economical' ways of using a tutor's time: they do not involve elaborate technical or administrative support. However, no teaching method can be described as economical if it fails to meet the prime objective of helping people learn.

The temptation to talk too much

One classic piece of research[1] in the 1950s confirmed how little we may know objectively of our own dominance. Alvin Zander made a study of four teachers of adults who claimed to be committed to student participation, and found that on average they lectured for 27 per cent of the time, matched each student's contribution with one of their own, and made nine out of ten of all the procedural decisions. Other research has tended to show how teachers may have no idea how much attention they are paying to particular students. In one study of a class of 26, the teacher was found to be giving more than a quarter of his attention to the well-adjusted pupils who presumably did not need it. Even after he had realized this, he found it extremely difficult to distribute his attention more fairly.[2] Many teachers will recognize it as a familiar temptation to go on encouraging those who need little encouragement, and to avoid the difficult and perhaps painful or embarrassing job of helping those who may be silent, moody or unstable.

There is a simple solution to talking too much: stop. The difficulty is that the tutors who are prone to doing it are usually totally unaware that there is a problem. There is a rough and ready test for finding out if this could be your problem. Ask yourself two questions:

- Do you always follow a comment from a learner with one of your own?
- Are there people in your group who rarely if ever speak?

If the answer to both these questions is 'yes', then it will be worth taking stock of the situation – perhaps by asking a trusted colleague to observe you and your group in action.

Showing off

Here is a more subtle variant of talking too much, a hangover from the university tradition of great Oxbridge teachers who draw hundreds of students to their lectures. The number of people capable of carrying off such a feat is actually remarkably small: in the 1950s and 1960s there was the English literature guru, F.R. Leavis; in our own time there is the philosopher and mathematician, Stephen Hawking, and there is only a handful of others.

None the less, the tradition spilled over into adult education in the earlier years of the twentieth century at a time when the working class was thought to be in need of rescue through the activities of the Workers' Educational Association and university extra-mural departments. The tradition still survives today, particularly in parts of adult education and higher education where students can be apparently quite happy to sit back and let the teacher get on with it. Richard Hoggart, himself an outstanding teacher of adults, had some wry words of warning which stress both the attractiveness and the dangers of this trap:

> The urge towards a generalized charismatic relationship, that way of showing off one's own personality which ends in the rhetoric of a lay preacher, is the strongest of all temptations. You have to learn to suspect those evenings when you feel a throb come into your voice, your eye seems bright and eager, and the students look up at you with a touch of wondering admiration. Two types of teacher – in any kind of education, but adult education is a specially dangerous area in these ways – should be particularly suspected: the charismatic, an imaginative pied piper of Hamelin; and the systems builder, an intellectual pied piper of Hamelin, who offers a complete guide and system to experience. Men who are a combination of both – some types of Marxist are like that – are the most dubious. Any teacher who begins to acquire fans, disciples, followers, ought to suspect himself until he has examined as honestly as he can the nature of these relationships. He may be getting between the students and their own hold on the subject. We should be glad to be judged by the degree to which our students stand on their own feet, out of our shadows. Which means we have to try to make sure they retain their freedom to be critical of us. Or, if that sounds too grand, ironic about us and towards us.[3]

If you are a teacher talented in the dangerous, hypnotic way Richard Hoggart describes you can easily turn your class into an audience for a personal performance. Often when students praise a teacher for being 'a good lecturer', what they mean is that he or she is a stimulating performer, by turns clown, tragedian, preacher, rhetorician, who rouses emotions at the time but leaves nothing for students to do themselves. Craft tutors can suffer the same sort of temptation to show off their expertise, only of course the 'performance' will take the form of a demonstration. In such cases a large part of the group's time will be taken up by a flawless demonstration by the teacher, which learners may often be quite happy to encourage.

In Chapter 1 I have drawn attention to some of the disadvantages of methods like lecturing and demonstrating, but it is worth reiterating them here, too. They are a strain on the already weak short-term memory capacity of adults. They proceed at one pace, which is most unlikely to suit even a majority of the group. For this reason, the more complex the information, the more ill-suited lecturing is to conveying it. Adults learn best through participation and activity, both of which are absent from straight lectures and demonstrations. Many lectures contain information which could be given more easily through reading – for instance, through books and handouts or delivered online before or after the event. Research has also consistently shown that lectures are a poor method of changing attitudes. In one classic experiment in the 1940s, Kurt Lewin compared the effectiveness of discussion and lectures in persuading housewives to try serving whale meat, a wartime necessity. Thirty-two per cent of the discussion group members claimed later they had actually served whale meat, compared with a minute 3 per cent from the group which had received a lecture.

Professor Carol Kauffman of Harvard Medical School has summarized the research on how much people retain from various methods of instruction as follows:[4]

Table 10.1

Method	*Percentage retained*
Lecture	5
Reading	10
Audio-visual	20
Demonstration	30
Discussion	50
Practice	75
Teaching others	90

Feedback is difficult, too. Once launched on what to you is an enjoyable exposition of your subject, it is easy for you to be blind to boredom, restlessness or incomprehension in your class. Adults are, in any case, often diffident about admitting there is a process or idea they have not understood. Conventional teaching techniques like lecturing and demonstration frequently help teacher and learner conspire together to cover up failure:

> I took it into my head to do a lot of the work on our property refurbishment myself and found a class which included plastering. The teacher was a nice guy but had no idea about how to teach. He'd just go sweeping up the wall – 'Whoosh!' lovely. He talked all the time, but we were never told how to go 'whoosh' ourselves. However, he did pause for a few seconds from time to time to say 'Any questions?' There never were any. To answer our questions he'd have needed to go right back to minus square one and he made you feel he was going to get through his syllabus or bust, so we let him get on with it, nodding all the while as if we did understand. It was less trouble to leave the class than to explain to him that he was going about 50 times too fast.

Even the claim that lectures can be motivating may be more pious hope than reality. Most of us have sat through innumerable lectures of one sort or another, but how many are truly memorable in retrospect? Most of us who teach are simply incapable of routinely supplying the acting ability, originality and panache which an inspirational talk requires. The number of people who earn a living as an aptly named *motivational speaker* is small and the highly lucrative nature of the reward probably correlates with the rarity of the skill. The same is true of politics and preaching where identical gifts are needed. Even where the performance is terrific, how much of the content is retained? In the last few years I have attended several conferences where there was a keynote speech by a particular presenter. He is an unusual man: his ethnic background and personal philosophy distinguish him from the herd. He has charisma. While he is speaking people look engaged and there is a lot of laughter. The first time I heard him I enjoyed it. The second time I thought, 'I've heard all this before.' The third time I recognized the same rather poor-quality slides and the same jokes and did not laugh much. In spite of having heard him three times, I could not tell you now what the theme of his speech is though I certainly remember the vividness and warmth of his presence. This is consistent with research showing that people generally remember more about *how* a lecture has been given than they remember about the content.

In spite of all these disadvantages, both lecturing and demonstrating have their place in the range of techniques suitable for adults. Lecturing may be a poor way of stimulating thought or changing attitudes, but research has consistently shown that it is at least as good as (though not better than) most other methods at conveying simple information.

Demonstration also has advantages. Where motor skills are involved, it shows what a skilled performance looks like and provides a trail of visual clues which are much easier for people to remember than words, video or diagrams alone.

Making it work

As with every type of teaching technique, lecturing and demonstrating should never be the sole methods used but you can improve their effectiveness immensely by careful preparation and presentation.

First, it is best to keep them short. Ten to fifteen minutes of uninterrupted *telling* is as much as most adults can absorb. The limit for demonstrations probably ought to be even shorter – five minutes. Many of the disadvantages of these techniques can be overcome, at least in part, by using the 'broken lecture–demonstration' technique where you speak for no more than ten minutes and then plan in some small group activity. Ways to do this could include: quizzes, asking pairs to come up with examples of your themes, building in a skill-practice, asking people to identify the questions that your exposition has raised for them.

Structure

A useful cliché about giving a talk or demonstration is this: *First you tell them what you're going to tell them, then you tell them, then you tell them what you've told them.* Signposting helps people follow your argument and it shows them where you and they are in the flow of what you are saying. Ways to do this include:

- Label the whole piece of input in a way that clearly states what it is about. That way you shape expectations from the start.
- Tell people whether you want to invite questions as you go or whether you would prefer them to save their questions until the end. Let them know how many minutes are allocated for questions if this is the method you prefer.
- Use a number in the title – for instance *Seven Ways To...*
- Reinforce the title by writing it on the flip chart or whiteboard, or electronically with slides.
- Choose a recognizable format such as chronological, or a structure where you present using a points-for/points-against or points in ascending or descending order of importance.
- Tell people how long your talk will be and stick to this limit rigorously. Emphasize your self-discipline by using phrases such as, 'So in this last five minutes I'm going to...'
- Saying at the outset, 'I'm going to talk about the case for x and I'll be dealing with this in three sections...'
- Then when you finish each section, move cleanly on to the next one

by saying something like, 'So that was my first point. Now, to the second . . .'
- Summarize the entire piece with a crisp précis of the whole talk.

The importance of stories

Human beings love narrative. *What happened next?* is what keeps us engaged. Dry facts do not engage people's attention. Always work out how you can tell a story instead of reciting facts or giving opinions. The best lecturer I know is actually a wonderfully skilled storyteller and his material is an expertly strung-together series of case studies. These make his points for him – he never has to labour them.

Learn from journalism: human interest is what keeps people's attention. Even if the points you want to make are factual, think carefully about how to make them come alive through human interest. Storytelling is an art and like any art it can be learnt. All stories in the world – film, novel, play, conform to this format:

Stage 1: Things are going along fine.
Stage 2: There is a crisis.
Stage 3: The hero/heroine has to struggle with his or her own resourcefulness. As the observer, listener or reader we want to know how it will turn out. Will the hero/heroine be successful or not?
Stage 4: What the hero or heroine actually does to overcome the obstacles.
Stage 5: The happy or unhappy ending.

The order of the stages may be different – for instance, the storyteller may start at the end and work backwards. The storyteller may play with the structure, mixing flashback with here-and-now narrative. The emphasis may be different – for instance, Stage 1 may be drawn out and Stage 2 hurtled into the end. Most thriller and adventure stories concentrate their emphasis on Stage 4 – the killings, car chases or fights. Some concentrate on Stage 3 with the emphasis on the psychological aspects of the protagonist's struggles. You will find your own format. You might, for instance, be able to use storytelling to make it personal – for instance, describing your own history as you struggled to understand/come to terms with whatever your theme is. Tell other people's stories and describe the human conflict that your topic creates – for example, any associated moral dilemmas.

Conveying confidence and authority

However wonderful your content, you will capture people's attention more readily if you convey confidence and authority. To give a talk well, you need to understand the differences between high- and low-status behaviour. Naturally you will be aiming for high-status, conveyed with relaxed authority.

Low-status behaviour is suggested by any or all of these:

- leaning on one foot;
- crossing one leg over the other;
- cocking your head to one side like a bird listening for worms, something that we women are particularly prone to doing;
- hopping;
- nervous little movements;
- darting eye contact;
- turning slightly away from the audience with one shoulder;
- touching your hair, ears or face – especially covering your mouth with your hand. This suggests lack of belief in what you are saying;
- fig leaf (hands covering genital area) or pious preacher (hands steepled);
- nervous little coughs;
- jingling change or keys in your pocket;
- scratching;
- pushing glasses up your nose;
- pushing or tossing hair away from your face;
- frowning;
- remaining unnaturally rooted to a few centimetres of space.

All of these convey lack of authority. Ask someone you trust to give you feedback about any mannerisms you might have which could distract while giving your lecture or demonstration. They all come from nervousness and you may not be aware of them.

High-status behaviour includes the following:

Always stand – you cannot convey authority so easily if you are sitting down. Stand with your body in a straight but not rigid line facing your audience straight on. Speak slowly and deliberately and make clean breaks in eye contact.

Keep your hands lightly together or straight at your sides with the fingers pointing loosely down. Use your notes judiciously – try not to get fixated by them; never hide behind them. Mentally stake out several metres of your space and use it to take a few well-paced and deliberate steps backwards, sideways and forwards while you are speaking. This conveys, 'This is my space and I am happy and confident to occupy it'.

High-status behaviour should be reinforced by high-status clothing. Informal may be fine but if it edges into sloppy it will not be. Aim to dress a little more formally than the dress you anticipate your group wearing. Fastening the buttons on a jacket can sometimes make the difference between seeming up-together and looking a mess. Whatever the style of clothing, the grooming should be immaculate: people will notice your shoes, I promise. If your self-presentation generally is not smart, reasonably contemporary, clean and in good condition people may assume that the same is true about the rest of you, including your thinking.

Voice, style, vocabulary

Slow, steady breathing will help you calm down and will prevent the nervous speaker's obvious problem – gulping for breath because you are only using the upper part of your lungs. Keeping your shoulders down and your chest open conveys relaxation and is actually relaxing. Check that everyone can hear you before you get going properly and pause for two or three seconds before starting your presentation – this gives a little added drama and allows you to get your thoughts together. Remember to use pauses to add impact and use the whole of your mouth to speak. If you know you have difficulties with volume, it can help to visit the actual room and to try out your first few sentences, though bear in mind that a room full of people has a different acoustic from an empty one. For set-piece lectures to large numbers, ask for a microphone. They are easy and cheap to hire.

Some people acquire the habit of gaining time for thinking by adding verbal mannerisms: *um, er, sort of, you know, kind of, I mean ...* Extreme offenders may use all of these constructions in the same sentence. If you are one of them, you may not know. Record one of your set pieces or ask a sympathetic colleague to observe you to find out. Rehearsal, practice, feedback and determination are the best ways to overcome this problem. Others have the opposite difficulty – gabbling. The best speed at which to deliver a lecture is to speak at a significantly slower pace than you do in normal conversation but not so slowly that it sounds ponderous. Study any television or radio news broadcast to see how steadily a news bulletin is read: often the speed is little more than 120 words a minute. The gabbling lecturer can often reach speeds of 300 words per minute – or more. If you do this, people will switch off.

Research consistently shows that a conversational style is far more popular with listeners than anything formal. Keep your vocabulary simple and encourage your group to challenge if they catch you using jargon. Jargon is specialist vocabulary which only those in the know are likely to understand. Its effect is instantly alienating to those who are still on the outside.

Keeping in touch with the group

It can feel scary to be the focus of all those eyes. This alarm is often well justified. The longer you continue your solo performance, the more opportunity you are giving the group for critical appraisal of your mannerisms, dress and voice:

> It's almost like coming into a room naked. You know they can see every tremor in your hands, hear every shake in your voice, observe every change of colour, notice only too well when you're not completely master of your material. After all, what else have they got to look at?

> It was his voice that got me in the end ... it just ground on and on. And he always had stains on his tie!

One of the best ways to keep people's attention is to use the *lighthouse effect* – raking your audience slowly from one side to the other throughout your presentation. This means that you are engaging everyone in a few seconds of regular eye contact. It retains their interest and creates the impression that you are talking to each person individually. It also gives you immediate feedback – who is looking bored, asleep, fidgety?

Beware of talking to any of these: only one side of the room; the ceiling; your notes; your graphics; the flipchart; your feet; one or two smiley people in the audience; the tops of the chairs; the spaces between people's chairs.

The other important rule to remember is to *smile*. If you look too serious people will lose interest. Show passion and enthusiasm. If you are not enthusiastic about your subject why should anyone else be?

Handouts

You can reduce some of the disadvantages of the lecture or demonstration by making sure that people have handouts. There are some simple, commonsense rules which will help make your handouts as useful as possible. First, don't attempt to give people every word you intend to say: no one will read anything lengthy. Try to limit handout material to no more than two pages of well laid out text per hour of spoken material. Restrict yourself to your main points. Write clearly and unambiguously – ask yourself whether the handout will make sense to someone who has not been present at your session. If not, think again; it probably lacks clarity.

We are surrounded by excellence in graphic design all day every day, so a sloppily prepared page will convey a poor impression. If you are using colour, stick to no more than two unless it is essential for the sake of clarity to use more. Use cross-headings and a reasonable type size – nothing smaller than 12 point. Keep the page uncluttered with wide margins and also keep to lower case type – all capitals makes for a hard read. Look at any motorway sign for a good example of clever use of lower case letters easily read at a glance even by a speeding motorist. If you are using diagrams, keep the lettering horizontal – it's not pleasant to have to turn a page upside down in order to read the labels. Where you have to present figures, use bar or pie charts – they are much easier to read. Put your contact details as the footer if you want to encourage people to get in touch with you later if they have queries. Finally, avoid clipart drawings because everyone has seen them hundreds of times and they are clichéd.

If you are using PowerPoint for your presentation, you can produce a small-scale version of each slide without having to waste huge quantities of paper on photocopying.

Tell people that you have produced a handout and encourage them to make their own choice about whether to make their own notes or not, but always give people any printed material *after* you have spoken, unless there is a case for offering them the chance to make notes on your handout while you speak.

Notes and visual aids

With experience you will be able to give a lecture or presentation without any notes – the best option of all because you can engage fully with your group. If you are less experienced, you will need notes for the reassurance they give against 'drying' – usually the inexperienced tutor's ultimate nightmare. There is no note-taking or audio-visual method which is 100 per cent reliable. Even the simplest can let you down – a sheaf of notes can fall to the floor, the bulb on the overhead projector can blow with no replacement available. I once saw a distinguished speaker at a grand awards ceremony watch in disbelief and horror as his paper notes caught fire, thanks to the lighted candle on the table in front of him. So always have a Plan B. Work out what you would do if all your aids and props failed.

The various options for notes are shown in Table 10.2

Handling questions and comments

Encouraging questions, discussion and comments can do a lot to mitigate the disadvantages of a lecture. Invite people to add their own gloss on the subject, to challenge you or to ask you for clarification on anything they have not understood. It goes without saying that it is important to demonstrate respect for the questioner at all times. Keep eye contact throughout the entire

Table 10.2 Making and using notes

Method	*Comments*
Writing out in full.	Reassuring, but stultifying – it always sounds as if you are reading and you have to keep your eyes down, thus losing contact with your audience.
Writing out a précis of the full version.	Better, but A4 sheets can be bulky.
Reducing the content to cards with key words only. *Tip*: punch a hole in the corner and put a treasury tag or ring through them so that they cannot get out of order even if you drop them.	Best if you need notes. Cards are easily handled and make a smaller barrier than sheets of paper.
Using PowerPoint or an overhead projector (OHP). *Tip* : don't overdo it – the audience will keep looking at the screen and not at you. Restrict yourself to no more than seven slides in a 20-minute presentation and turn the projector off between slides to reduce distraction.	Useful if you can remember not to keep looking behind you at the screen. Use a pointer which enables you to keep facing the audience. Check that both you and the venue can cope with the technology. OHPs can look dated but the low-tech method may mean that they are easier to manage. Keep the number of characters on a slide to no more than 50, ideally fewer.
Using flip charts made on the spot or prepared in advance. *Tip*: resist the temptation to keep turning to the flipchart and talking to it rather than to the audience.	Flexible because you can add as you go. Bulky if you have to carry them around from one event to another. Looks informal and also gives the audience something to look at other than you. Can look amateurish or old-fashioned, especially if your flip chart writing is scruffy.

question and answer sequence and listen to the complete question carefully. You can probably anticipate obvious questions and come prepared.

Keep your answers short – there will probably be others in the group who want to have their say. Conclude with 'Did I answer your question?' to make sure that the questioner is satisfied. Where you get challenging or apparently aggressive questions, beware of the trap of answering at the questioner's expense – you're not at the hustings or dealing with hecklers. Self-deprecating humour often works, so does stating the obvious – 'That's a difficult question.' Where you have a long-winded questioner, wait until they pause for breath and break in quickly with 'I believe I can answer that...'

Playing for time is often important. For instance, you may need a few seconds to make sure you've understood the question or to consider your answer. You can try any of these tactics:

- staying deliberately cool;
- repeating the question;
- asking the questioner to repeat the question;
- asking for clarification;
- asking the questioner to answer their own question – for instance, 'That's a good question. Before answering, I'd like to hear your answer'.

Sometimes a challenging question is actually a statement in disguise. The give-away here is 'Wouldn't you agree that . . .' There may be no need to reply at all, other than to say something like 'That's a very interesting contribution to the debate. Thanks for making that point'.

Demonstrations

A demonstration is a lecture with actions. The same basic principles apply as to lectures. You may need to think about whether you face the group or find some way for them to see the action from the operator's point of view. If you make no provision for this, your learners will always have to reverse your hand movements, which is confusing, to say the least. Cookery schools solve this problem with large mirrors. My dance teachers do it by having a radio mike and keeping their backs to the group so that their right or left legs and ours are facing the same way.

I learnt a lot about demonstrations from directing cookery programmes for television. It was always vital to have everything the presenter needed laid out as if for a medical operation. This meant that utensils and ingredients were set out in the order that they would be used and all containers were made of transparent materials as far as possible, to increase the chances that the details would be easy to see even on a poor-quality home monitor. No one ever wants to see an onion being chopped every time a recipe included one, so these and other ingredients would be pre-prepared. The principles apply to anything where there is a natural sequence to the demonstration. If it's a complicated one, have a dry run at home – this will usually reveal what you have forgotten.

Demonstration also has a useful role to play where behavioural skill is the focus. For instance, you might want to show how to handle the first stages of negotiation in a course on conflict-resolution. Demonstration is useful where the skill is one that demands a high level of emotional intelligence – for instance, the skill of how to give bad news, something that all doctors need to have but may want to avoid. Some form of demonstration is used to introduce or follow up skill practice on all our own courses at Management Futures. The way we do it is to limit the demonstration to a few minutes, stopping frequently to comment on what we are doing, drawing attention to features and behaviours which we think the group needs to note and following this immediately with opportunities for practice and feedback.

The tempting dangers of demonstrations are of over-simplifying and going too fast. As an expert, you will probably have forgotten what it feels like, if you ever knew, to be a complete beginner or to have little natural aptitude for a skill. It is all too easy to make unwarranted assumptions about what people already know, to go too fast and, it must be said, to see the demo as a place where you show off. If you know this applies to you, slow down and check your assumptions with your group. Aim to give a few minutes of demo followed immediately by opportunities for the group to practise the sequence. A demonstration for purposes of learning is not a *performance*; it's a way of showing what a skilled performance looks like when broken down into learnable bits – a different emphasis.

As with every other type of teaching method, you need to arrange the room and its furniture carefully in advance. Spare chairs are best removed altogether. Curved rows will give a greater feeling of belonging and therefore more chance of participation than straight ones. A hollow square around a table will encourage more questioning than rows. A large room may offer poor acoustics for a quiet voice and encourages the development of vast spaces between individuals. If your subject demands extensive note-taking, there may be a case for chairs with hinged tables which provide a firm surface to rest on.

In general, lectures and demonstrations are probably best used in short bursts, with frequent recourse to alternative methods of learning like discussion, individual practice, projects or reading. Far too many lecturers and demonstrators assume that their listeners have some hole in the head into which information can conveniently be poured. As Thomas Carlyle wisely said, 'Too much faith is commonly placed in oral lessons and lectures. To be poured into like a bucket is not exhilarating to any soul'.

Blended learning

Blended learning has come to be the phrase used to describe combinations of e-learning with other means of delivery. Vaguer definitions have suggested that it describes any situation where learners are disconnected for at least some part of the course in time and space from each other and from the course tutors. If this is so, then you could say that an awful lot of learning is *blended* and has been for many years. When I studied for my qualification in the Myers Briggs Type Indicator (see page 28) seventeen years ago, the provider sent me a fat manual, including self-tests, in advance of the five-day course and emphasized that it was essential to spend at least 60 hours on this material before attending. Correspondence courses have been around for over a century and the Open University has spent many decades perfecting combinations of print with many other forms of easily distributed audio-visual media. I include blended learning in this chapter because its most useful application seems to be in the way it can replace lecturing with other ways of delivering information.

The difference – an enormous one – is the increased potential for instant access to large numbers of people and immediate opportunities to update the material either by learners themselves or by course designers. Other advantages include the possibility of working 'own place, own pace', and for building in immediate assessment so that learners can see for themselves whether they have understood an idea or not. Face-to-face contact time can be reduced with potentially large savings on venues, travel and tutor time. Large organizations have delivered material to huge numbers of people worldwide. For instance, Cisco trained 860,000 field salespeople using electronic means, thus ensuring consistency and speedy access to their message. By using electronic media you can also avoid the bottlenecks that can build up when there is only a small number of suitable teaching and training personnel available.

Like so many other technological innovations, enthusiasts for blended learning have sometimes claimed more for it than it can really deliver. E-learning often turns out to mean *e-reading* or *e-listening/watching* in reality. A client of mine kindly gave me access to one university's course, a rival provider of coach-training. She had not been impressed with the quality of her course, describing it as 'a low-energy experience'. The university is proud to boast that much of the material is 'delivered online'. In practice this meant *modules* which consisted of a few pages of electronically delivered text with exhortations to read particular chapters of five or six books, on which essays were set. There was also a Bulletin Board for questions and the occasional podcast. The fact that the modules were reached via a website and the essays had to be sent by email did not disguise the fact that the whole experience was perfectly recognizable as a rather dull kind of traditional course. The only difference was that the students sat at their home computers, sent in their questions by email and read the material that would otherwise have been delivered as a lecture. All of this saves the university money but I think it is dubious whether it adds to the quality of the student experience.

In an interesting web-posted piece,[5] Bersin Associates, who have been in the field for more than twenty years, also analyse why e-learning solutions may fail. First, it may not always save money because development can be enormously expensive, though simple authoring tools can now reduce a lot of this cost. Installing an efficient Learning Management System to track who is doing what and who has successfully completed the various assessments can be pricey. Success can depend on all learners having high bandwidth connectivity and this is not always the case, nor can you assume that people have standard browsers. If you don't have a fully operational help-desk available around the clock, non-IT literate people may simply give up and not come back. Large corporations, as in any other kind of training, may assume that they can just shuffle off the whole process on to the training professionals without the active endorsement and integration into business processes that are so vital to success. The technological hurdles can be a lot more complex than they first seem.

As with lecturing, e-materials probably work best for conceptually less complex material that also lends itself to relatively simple testing and assessment. As with any other form of turning words into material that has to be read and watched or listened to, the same rules apply as they always have: accessible vocabulary, simplicity that does not betray the integrity of the material, imaginative treatment, excellent structure and high-quality illustrations. A podcast given by an untalented lecturer will only have the advantage that the watcher can switch him or her off. The quality principles are the same, whatever the medium. The old rule of GIGO – garbage in, garbage out – applies here. Creativity and flair in communication skills and learning design are relatively rare.

For more complex material it is probably hard to beat print. Bear in mind, though, that where actual behavioural or motor skills are involved, it is impossible to acquire these effectively from reading or watching. Practice and feedback in a live environment are essential.

However, where you do have simple information to convey, it is essential to consider not *whether* you can deliver it electronically, but *how*. Assuming your learners all have access to the technology, a big assumption, and depending on the amount of time, skill and money available, then you could choose from podcasts, wikis, audio-books, CD-ROM courseware, virtual classes run live, web pages, websites, blogs, discussion and chat-rooms, conference calls, DVDs – and many more.

How to choose which approach will work best is a subject I deal with in the next chapter.

Further reading

There are many books on lecturing. The three listed here are both useful and practical; Donald Bligh's book is a classic first published in the early 1970s and reissued in an American edition. The Edwards, Smith and Webb book is both amusing and instructive, containing a number of case studies showing where and how things can go wrong and how to retrieve the situation when they do. Phil Race has devoted a career to teaching and writing. His advice is always sound.

Bligh, D.A. (2000) *What's the Use of Lectures?* New York: Jossey-Bass.

Edwards, H., Smith, B. and Webb, G. (eds) *Lecturing: Case Studies, Experience and Practice*. London: Kogan Page.

Race, P. (2006) *The Lecturer's Tool Kit: A Practical Guide to Learning, Teaching and Assessment* 3rd edition. London: Routledge.

For a crisp guide to the art of storytelling, read McKee, R. and Fryer, B. (2003) Storytelling that moves people, *Harvard Business Review*, June.

These are all useful books on blended learning written by hands-on practitioners:

Bersin, J. (2004) *The Blended Learning Book: Best Practices, Proven Methodologies and Lessons Learned*. San Francisco, CA: John Wiley.

Salmon, G. (2003) E-moderating: The Key to Teaching and Learning Online, 2nd edition. London: Taylor & Francis Books.

Thorne, K. (2004) *How to Integrate Online and Traditional Teaching*. London: Kogan Page.

Notes

1 Zander, A. (1951) Student motives and teaching methods in four informal adult classes, *Adult Education USA*, 2.

2 Whithall, J. (1956) An objective measure of a teacher's classroom interactions, *Journal of Educational Research*, 47.

3 Hoggart, R. (1969) The role of the teacher, in J. Rogers, *Teaching on Equal Terms*. London: BBC Publications.

4 Meyler-Campbell Annual Lecture (2006) *Positive Psychology in Coaching*, unpublished.

5 *Blended Learning: What Works?* www.bersin.com

11 Design for learning

Musing about what to include in this chapter I typed *lesson plans* into Google. What a dispiriting experience. After the first few of many hundreds of off-the-peg lessons for teachers in every conceivable subject, I gave up. Why would anyone but the most nervous and inexperienced young teacher need so much ready-made help? My aim here is different. It is about explaining how to design learning so that it meets the needs both of your learners and of any other opinion formers in your system.

However, I do acknowledge that starting with a blank sheet can feel daunting. There is so much material that you might include – too much probably for the time you have available. There is so much that interests you – but will it interest your group? There are so many possible methods, but which ones will produce the best results? When you have never met the group, there are additional concerns: how can you be certain that what you are planning will meet their needs? Most learning groups will contain people of varying ability, so how can you ensure that everyone is involved and that everyone learns at the pace that is right for them? How do you cater for the many possibilities for self-directed learning that could happen outside the domains of the formal sessions in any learning event?

In this chapter I cover the essential preliminaries which may at first seem to have little to do with the practicalities of how to design a learning event, then how to identify the objectives for the learning, and only then how to consider all the other variables which will affect what you can actually do in the class or training room.

Designing learning falls naturally into a six-phase process. In practice they may overlap:

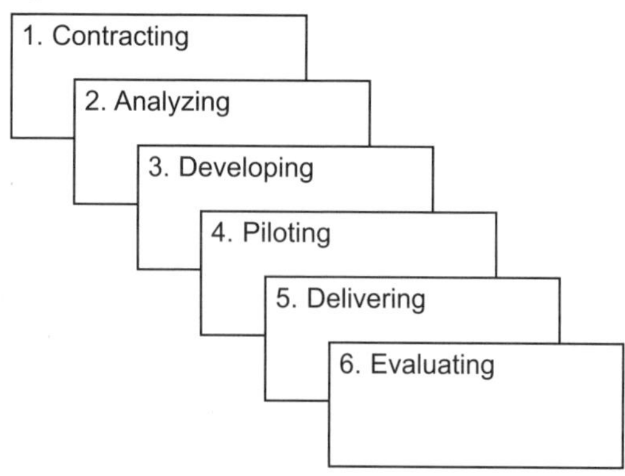

This chapter is about the first four of these phases.

1 Contracting

Inexperienced tutors may be tempted to start at Phase 3, *Developing*, then to jump straight to Phase 5, *Delivering*. But the work starts long before you get to the classroom – by contracting unambiguously with whoever is commissioning you about what they expect and what it is possible for you to deliver. This process will vary enormously in its importance and complexity and will depend on the sector and its customs. If you work in higher education the syllabus and methods may already have been laid out for you so the need to contract may be modest. In adult education there may sometimes be a charming vagueness about what is expected and it may be implied that you can do whatever you like, give or take a few notional swipes in the direction of writing something down which will impress any passing inspector. In the world of corporate training your commissioners are likely to take a keen interest in your plans, knowing that their own reputation depends to at least some extent on your success.

Journalists like to mock what they see as management jargon, and perhaps they are right, but one such word that is useful here is *stakeholder*. A stakeholder is anyone whose opinion can affect the outcome of an enterprise. In an educational institution it will probably include senior management, heads of departments, examination authorities, students, funders, co-tutors, and anyone whose function is to measure quality. The point about stakeholders is that their individual wishes are often at odds. For instance, the Prime Minister of the day has us, the electorate, as stakeholders, plus party members, cabinet colleagues, MPs, commentators and civil servants, but it is unlikely that these stakeholder groups will ever be in agreement about what he or she should do; in fact their wishes may be diametrically opposed.

Within this group of stakeholders there will be someone who is the *real client* for your proposed course or event. Finding out who this is may be more difficult than it seems. For instance, in our firm, we are often approached by someone who has been charged with procuring the work but, when probed, turns out to know only the headlines about why it is being commissioned or what need it is intended to meet. The actual budget-holder may be someone different and the person who really wants the work is someone different again. To complicate it still further, the person who really wants the work may not be in the close touch that they need to be with the target participants.

To cut through all of this, ask the three questions recommended by Reg Revans (page 144), the developer of action learning:

1. *Who knows?* Who has the information about the issues? Often the person who knows most is the target learner. Or there may be colleagues who have taught similar groups in the past whom it would be worth consulting.
2. *Who cares?* Who is most concerned about the issue? Why is the course being run at all? What does he or she hope to achieve through it? What changes is the event supposed to deliver? Whose reputation will be at risk if nothing happens, or if it all goes wrong?
3. *Who can?* Who has the clout, the administrative systems, the money or other resources – and the passion – to make something happen?

My advice about this stage of designing for learning is never to assume that talking to one person will give you the answers to these three questions. You are dealing with a system and systems are often more complicated than they seem. The more you can explore, the more you will get underneath the presenting issues to the true needs.

Let's assume that you do know who your commissioning client is. He or she may be straightforwardly your line manager – for instance a head of department, or, in the corporate world, a training manager acting as broker on behalf of his or her internal client. Whichever the variant, you now need to contract with him or her. I use the word *contracting* not in its legal but in its social and moral sense, though you may wish to follow up a contracting conversation with a written confirmation or even with a formal contract, depending on the circumstances. This process is about getting mutual expectations clear. To do this you will need to set up a meeting where the specific purpose is to flush out assumptions on both sides, thus reducing the chances of misunderstanding and disappointment later. Ideally you want a reliably strong, mutually enjoyable relationship where there is a high degree of frankness and trust. Prepare for the meeting by thinking through your own must-haves. At the same time, remind yourself of what you are offering, both technically and in personal terms.

For your part, these are the questions to ask the client:

Objectives for the learning

What do you hope to achieve from this course/event?
What will have changed if it is successful?
What is already going well in terms of the changes the event is designed to deliver?
How could we build on what is going well?
How will you measure success?
Who are the target participants?
What do you see as their needs?
What motivation will they bring?

Resources

How much time is available, not only for the event itself but also for planning?

What access can I have to essential information – for instance to records of previous events?

What rooms will be available?

What equipment is available?

What internet or intranet support is possible?

What systems are there for producing and distributing handouts or other supporting materials?

What administrative support is there – for instance to send out joining instructions or suggestions about pre-event work?

Budget

Fees?

Expenses? Travel time?

Is there a budget for a co-trainer/tutor?

Is there is a budget for meals, tea and coffee?

The answers to these questions may come as a shock. You may agree on the objectives but discover that the commissioner has what to you is a totally unrealistic idea about what can be achieved within the time and budget available – normally far too optimistic. Or the commissioner may have little idea of what the target participants already know and may claim to have no means of finding out. Alternatively, what the commissioner wants in the way of subject matter and what you can offer are wildly different. Or you and the commissioner may agree about objectives and the amount of time available for the event, but the budget available may seem too small. Anything is possible. The point is that now is the time to find out, not later when the chances of toxic misunderstanding increase in direct proportion to the diminution of your chances of influencing the outcome.

Ideally this is a mutually respectful relationship where power is shared 50–50. Be prepared to compromise and also to say no or to ask straightforwardly for what you want in order to do your best work. At the most extreme, but only at the most extreme, be prepared to walk away if what you think you need and can offer and what the commissioner needs and can offer are not reconcilable. Don't sit on any reservations; express them courteously and ask your commissioner whether he or she has concerns which it would be useful to explore at this early stage.

The benefits of good contracting are immense:

You create an honest relationship which can withstand the inevitable ups and downs of the project.

You have a supporter who will be prepared to give you feedback and help.

Misunderstandings are minimized from the outset.
Your self-respect is enhanced.
The chances of designing learning which will meet everyone's needs are hugely increased.

2 Analysing

Gathering data

You know what your brief is and have agreed that it is achievable. You have a pleasant and professionally rewarding relationship with your commissioner. The task now is to scope the project. This starts with the target learners. Who are they and what do they want? The more you and any colleagues can investigate this at first hand, the better the data you will obtain. Ask your commissioner for help here. How might you access your learners? How willing is he or she to give you email addresses and phone numbers? (The answer should be *very willing* as the institution will gain from the work you are proposing to do on its behalf.) The key questions are these:

- What is their motivation for signing up?
- What do they expect to be different as a result of attending?
- What do they already know about the subject? Or, what skills do they believe they already possess?
- What might stand in the way of their learning?
- What are they expecting from you?
- What supporting skills do they have – for instance IT?
- What other resources can they access easily – for instance the internet?
- Do they have any special needs that you should know about – for instance mobility problems?

The simplest and most direct way to do this research is through brief telephone interviews with a selection of participants, but you could also consider questionnaires by mail or email. A lot will depend on the time available – including the amount you are personally prepared to invest, the length of the event you are planning and the budget. If you are running a single two-hour session such intricate research might seem over-elaborate, but it might also look skimpy if you are designing a year-long piece of substantial academic learning.

Armed with the data that this process reveals, I have frequently returned to my commissioner for another contracting meeting. Essentially I am asking to recontract with him or her. This will be because through the process of research into the learners, I will have discovered that the original hopes for the event have to be modified. For instance, the learners may know less or more than anyone thought. They may turn out to be less motivated than my commissioner had hoped, or they may be expecting even more than is feasible given the time and budget available.

Finally, I often write myself an identikit portrait of the typical learner. For instance, let's imagine I am mulling over how to fulfil a commission to run a series of courses for junior staff on how to run meetings. The ultimate answers to my research in this case may run something like this:

> *Typical participant for course on Managing Meetings*
> Age about 30, woman, senior secretary or junior researcher. Wants more confidence to speak up at internal and external meetings; for the future, needs to know how to chair, plan agenda and write up minutes or action points. Standing in the way currently: lack of assertiveness, lack of practice in leadership. Plenty of previous knowledge of attending meetings, very little of running them. Wants this training because she can see that it is necessary for career advancement.

Writing this analysis helps both me and my commissioner to be clear about what the event will aim to do.

Objectives

> I just have an idea in my head of where I want to get to by the end of the course . . . no, I never write it down.
>
> (Catering tutor)

> My aim is to turn them into critical, sensitive readers.
>
> (Literature tutor)

> Turn them into better managers!
>
> (Management development tutor)

These vague and hopeful statements could well have described my own actual practice in my early days as a teacher, though of course I would have been as capable as anyone of writing down fine-sounding words had one of Her Majesty's Inspectors happened to call.

Today I am a reformed character. I would not dream of planning a piece of teaching or training without first making a proper list of objectives. The reasons are that making such a list helps me plan the syllabus and choose appropriate teaching methods, and usefully reminds me of how little it is actually possible to achieve in the limited time available to me for the course.

It also helps me to define who the course is *for*, thus again anticipating and perhaps deflecting any problems of gross extremes in the abilities of my students.

It is useful to distinguish between 'aims' and 'objectives'. 'Aims' tends to describe the pious hopes that some teachers have of their learners, or that principals often claim for their institutions:

> Our aim is to produce the leaders of tomorrow.

> We aim to produce young adults who can reach their full potential intellectually, socially and physically.

'Objectives' are much more precise because they list the intended *outcomes* of the learning by stating what a person who completes the course should be able to do.

Everyone in the business of learning today owes a debt to one of the outstanding educational thinkers of the twentieth century, Benjamin Bloom, who first offered an analysis of what educational objectives were in 1956.[1] Although others have refined and fiddled with his list, usually known as Bloom's Taxonomy, it remains a towering achievement. Bloom suggests that learning objectives fall into three categories or *domains:*

1. *Cognitive:* the knowledge area. This means recalling, analysing, applying, synthesizing and evaluating.
2. *Affective:* the underpinning attitudes and values including the values which keep us responsive and open to challenge and willing to consider changing deeply held attitudes and beliefs.
3. *Psychomotor:* originally developed to cover purely manual skills, this domain now includes social skills relating to behaviour – for instance, communication and networking or giving a presentation. This domain is particularly useful for teaching adults because in the version developed by one of Bloom's colleagues, R.H. Dave, it includes a number of levels, from the simplest, Imitation and Manipulation, to the most complex – what Dave calls Naturalization, where the learner has mastered the skill to a high level and can create their own version of it.

So if I use Bloom's approach, I might list the knowledge, attitudes and skills that my target learner will need to have after attending my event. It might be something like this:

Knowledge: the learner will be able to
describe the effect of group size on participation patterns;

predict how seating will affect the flow of discussion;
identify differences between chairing and other types of meeting role;
describe the standard customs and formalities of meetings;
identify the differences between high- and low-status behaviour and its connections with ability to influence affectively.

Attitudes: learners will demonstrate

willingness to assume the role, especially its more assertive elements;
willingness to accept and listen to a wide variety of points of view.

Skills: learners will be able to

plan agenda;
present themselves confidently;
demonstrate verbal fluency when addressing the meeting;
create the appropriate degree of participation in the discussion;
summarize accurately;
interrupt courteously;
demonstrate negotiation skills;
demonstrate the ability to create consensus;
demonstrate how to use problem-solving techniques with a group;
write simple, accurate action points in straightforward English for distribution after the meeting.

This exercise will help clarify my thoughts, because I have asked myself what I want my learners to be able to do by the time they have completed the course. The key word here is 'do'. The ideal objective is one where the learner could *demonstrate competence to somebody else*. This is why it is better to stick to objectives where the learner's achievements by the end of the course begin with words like:

Table 11.1

Adapt	Analyse	Construct
Compare	Create	Define
Discriminate	Evaluate	Execute
Facilitate	Guide	Identify
Judge	Lead	List
Make	Manage	Plan
Produce	Quantify	Write

Ideally, objectives also need to state in what circumstances the objective is being applied. For instance, for my learners, it would not be fair to expect them to chair a large and tricky negotiating meeting involving outsiders, so my objectives should probably also contain a conditional phrase such as 'Given a routine internal meeting of not more than ten people, could ...' (then describing the objectives).

Finally, who else needs to be consulted? Once you have an outline list of objectives, it is always a good idea to return to your commissioning clients. Is this what they want their people to learn? Ask the learners too – is this what they think they want and need? Ask people who have done the same kind of course in the past. Most objectives have to be modified at least a little in the light of this exercise.

Writing objectives is effort well spent. It forces you to focus on what it is actually possible for people to learn in the time available, and will help you decide where you should put the boundaries on previous experience or ability in your learners. It will also help you choose the most appropriate teaching method and how much time to allocate to it. If one of my objectives is that people should be able to negotiate their way through the disagreements that typically surface during a meeting, then clearly I must spend large chunks of the course giving everyone practice at doing just that.

3 Developing

The questions here are about which approaches and techniques you are going to employ to reach the objectives you have agreed. These are the criteria to consider:

The purpose of the event

Purpose influences style. A conference for senior nuclear physicists will most probably not be the right place to introduce role play. A class of fencing enthusiasts will want to get on with their fencing and is unlikely to welcome an extended lecture on great fencers of the past and present.

The prejudices, quirks, wishes and existing knowledge or skills of the learners

Researching what these are will have given you vital information about what you can and can't risk in the design of the event. People may have told you firmly how much they love or hate a particular method, but you will need to measure this against what your own professional judgement tells you about the real learning need. Some years ago I was one of a faculty charged with delivering a leadership development event for a well-known British organization. Pre-event research revealed that most of the target participants were highly qualified academically, indeed many were former academics, and had a strong preference for what they tended to call *intellectual robustness*. Probing this phrase suggested that what they wanted was star speakers who could deliver a series of charismatic lectures on leadership. However, our research into what the organization actually needed, and what our corporate client wanted, suggested the opposite: an entirely experiential workshop on leadership behaviour. What we came to call *intellectualizing,* something everyone in this organization was already extremely good at, was discouraged. A five-day experiential event was what we delivered, even though it meant weathering an enormous degree of bewilderment and fear (a lot of it presented as hostility) during the first thirty-six hours of the course.

Part of what you uncover may be that you have a wide range of ability and experience in your learner population. This may be an asset rather than an intractable problem. Most of the leadership development courses my company now runs inevitably have people of very mixed ability and it is rarely if ever an issue. Experience and skill needs to be acknowledged and used: the question at the design stage is more usually how you can do this, not whether you can eliminate such differences through selection and streaming. As a learner myself, I had a vivid experience of how little difference it can make. I put myself on a course about coaching run in a horrible hotel just off the Ml. I had very low expectations of the course. Since at the stage I did the course I had been doing coaching for ten years or more, I felt it was unlikely that I would learn very much. When the first round of introductions was in full swing I began to feel even more disappointed and prepared to depart early. Probably about half the people on the course had no coaching experience whatsoever and the majority of the others were counsellors or therapists – a related but different skill (see Chapter 8). However, I stayed, soon realizing how much it had to offer me. The reasons were that the course was entirely participative. It allowed people to enter at their own level. It mattered not a jot that some people had no experience and some had a lot. Where it covered ground I already knew well, I simply felt affirmed. Where it covered unfamiliar ground I felt stretched and challenged.

All groups of learners are of mixed ability to some extent. Even members of an apparently homogeneous group will still actually vary a good deal in their individual talents and interests. Sometimes, this really will matter, as this learner's experience suggests:

> When it was clear that my marriage was over, I decided that I had to update my skills, so I went on a computer course. I was just about able to type with two fingers, but I'd never had any proper typing training. The brochure said this didn't matter. Unfortunately it did. There were 11 other people on the course. Some of them were very fast, skilled typists whose companies had sent them for updating in the particular program we were learning – I don't know why, as quite a few seemed to be pretty expert already. One was a freelance journalist who'd just bought a new laptop and couldn't work out how to use it, then there were two or three people like me. The tutor's method was to give a lot of instructions all at once at the beginning

> of each section, then to set us all the same exercise. It was hopeless. The experienced people rattled away. Because they could type accurately they made fewer mistakes and finished first. She timed the exercises by these fast people and just said 'Oh never mind, just do what you can' to the rest of us. It was very discouraging: I felt very stupid. Since I was paying, I stuck it out, but really it was a waste of money.

Giving in to the deadly attraction of gearing everything to the needs of the most able learners was only one of the traps this tutor dug for herself. The other traps included a failure to recognize that a group of mixed ability means a need for a completely different approach. This tutor at least kept her group with her to the end, perhaps because they were desperate to learn and had all parted with good money. They clung to the hope that there might be an improvement, in spite of evidence to the contrary. Where courses are cheap, or the learners' needs are not so great, it is often simpler for them just to melt away.

Sequencing the content

This will be more complex where you have groups of widely mixed skill and previous knowledge. Where you already know that this is the case, consider filling gaps with pre-course reading and exercises so that everyone starts in the same place. In general proceed from the known to the unknown, with frequent opportunities to reinforce earlier learning by incorporating it into new areas. An example is the coaching courses we run in my company where we send people pre-course work, asking them to identify their existing skills and self-knowledge. On the course, one of our key topics is teaching people how to ask the powerful open questions which distinguish coaching from giving advice. We start by asking people to recognize their existing assumptions and actual practice. This usually reveals how often people are giving advice rather than asking genuinely open questions. We then show them a simple, brief protocol which they use in pairs, and then ask them to apply their own versions of the protocol in a bigger group, proceeding to even more complex tests of skill with a more elaborate protocol as the week goes on, but always building step by step on what people have already learnt. To achieve the Diploma in Coaching they then have to make another leap by demonstrating the use of the same questioning skills through submitting recorded sessions with their own clients over a one-year period.

Introducing pace and variety

Listen to any successful music station to see how important this principle is. A slow dreamy ballad in a minor key is invariably followed by something upbeat with a fast tempo. A learning event is no different. Anything that proceeds at one pace, whether fast or slow, will be a lot less gripping than one where there is variety. A course where there is only one mood, whether of laughter or of quiet reflection, is likely to fail. Similarly, relying on one pattern is likely to induce boredom. At a one-day professional development event that I attended recently, the format was the following: five minutes of input from the tutor followed by thirty minutes of activity in trios – the same trios throughout the day. In effect this meant we only worked with two other people from the course. This was not merely tedious in its predictability but also a chronic waste of all the expertise available in the rest of the room. Equally, it was a misjudgement of our motives for attending, the dominant one of which was to get updated on our practice in a particular area from a leading exponent in the field. In practice, she contributed little to the day.

Chapter 4 has more on this, but the size of the group has a profound effect on what you can do to introduce variety and differences in pace. You may be able to influence the number of participants at the contracting and commissioning stage, but remember that commissioners may want to squeeze as many people as they can into one event in order to save or make money. If so, it may be useful to point out, politely of course, that cost and value are two different concepts. I like to work with groups of 12. It is just about possible to observe individuals with a group this size but big enough to have a range of views and experience and not so big as to intimidate the shyer people. A group of 12 also gives six design possibilities:

Solo
Six pairs
Four trios
Three quartets
Two sextets
One group of 12

You may also be able to introduce a so-called *fishbowl*, where an inner group works with you on, say, a skill practice, observed and surrounded by the rest of the group. A further refinement of this approach is for each member of the inner circle to observe a particular person during the activity, offering them feedback later. The observer can gain almost as much as the people doing the actual practice.

Variety is important again here. By mixing the size and composition of working groups you enable people to get to know each other better and to experience a wider range of ideas.

The larger the ratio of learner to tutor the fewer the chances of offering tutor feedback. Participants may resist small group work if they perceive that it is pointless without feedback or input from you and other tutors and view it as merely a device for giving you a bit of a rest.

It usually makes sense to start and finish the day with a plenary session – that is, the whole group together. This is your chance to ask for feedback on the day and to discuss how people are going to apply the learning. A day where people drift off after finishing a small-group activity can feel incomplete and ragged, though sometimes the circumstances justify it.

The possibilities for introducing pace and variety will also be affected by room layout (page 101). One of the reasons that I prefer to work without desks or tables whenever I can is that a room where the furniture is just chairs can be quickly rearranged, whereas it may be too daunting or actually physically unachievable to get rid of tables.

The time available

A five-day event has a different rhythm from a five-hour event. People will be more tolerant of depth and reflection in a five-day event than they are in a five-hour event but in a long event there is the danger of loping along at too slow a pace, especially on the first day. A course run in two-hour weekly segments over a term will feel different again. The art with a short course is to keep the content to what can reasonably be accomplished in the time, remembering that the temptation to over-fill the agenda is always there. Going for the easy option of transmitting information through lectures is another danger, as is the risk of producing an over-busy design where learners never have time to reinforce learning or to ask questions.

Be especially aware of the time implications of the design decisions you make. For instance, if you build in small-group work, you need to have some way of reviewing it. If you give each group the same task, there is serious risk of asking each group for lengthy 'report-backs' which can eat up enormous amounts of time and can also become repetitious, but if you ignore what went on in the groups you may imply that this had no value. Asking each group for a headline sentence to sum up their learning, soliciting a few questions from the whole group or adding comments from your own observations – these are all ways of acknowledging the work. Another is to ask each group in turn for one point then to ask the others in turn for a different point, rotating in this way until everything that can usefully be said has been said. Sometimes it is better to set each group a different task so that the report-back at least has difference in subject-matter. The point is, however, that, even when kept brief, this all takes time. The design stage is the place to calculate how much.

Minimizing dependence on verbally given information

Adults do not do well with techniques that depend on everyone absorbing the same information at the same pace (see Chapter 1). Alternative methods usually get better results and also allow for people of mixed ability to work within the same group successfully.

Catering for all four learning styles (page 26)

Learning style theory has immediate relevance to course design and is one of the most central elements to consider. Not only do you need to cater for the differences in dominant preferences among learners, but to maximize the chances that learners will learn you need to design activities that touch all four places on the learning cycle: activity, reflection, theory and application.

Here is a simple example. Let's suppose that your objective is to introduce your group to the Alexander technique: a decades-old method of learning how to use the body more effectively. For the first ten minutes of the class you may briefly establish what people already know and review what they want to learn, assuming that this has already been made clear in pre-event material. You then move on to a short history of the Alexander technique, including the contribution of its founders. This is the theory part of the learning cycle. You invite five minutes of questions about its applications in everyday life. This is the applied learning or pragmatic part of the cycle. You then introduce a simple activity which you know everyone will be able to do – an observed walk a few paces long, paying particular attention to the position of the neck relative to the head. This is the action part of the cycle. In giving people feedback you invite thoughtful comparison with people's everyday habits – the reflective part of the cycle. The whole cycle starts again when you demonstrate correct usage, offering yourself and one volunteer learner as examples. Then you invite the group to do the same, this time in pairs – activity again – and so on. In this way you can cycle through all four parts of the learning cycle, not necessarily in any particular order, several times in any ninety-minute session. As a principle I have noticed that this often gets better results than extended periods of one type of learning activity followed by extended periods of another.

Accommodating the likely psychological state of learners and group at any given point

Look back to previous chapters on learners (Chapter 1) and group states (Chapter 4) for a reminder of how important this element is. For instance, a group which is meeting again after a long break will need to reconnect through an Inclusion activity. A group of anxious new learners will need an ice-breaker which will calm them down.

Accommodating physical needs for breaks and refreshment

Be realistic. You can only fight human physiology to some extent. The time of day will affect what you can do. For instance, a series of seminars run between eleven and twelve o'clock will feel and be different from the same seminars run between three and four in the afternoon.

Adults fidget after more than ninety minutes in one place. Many people have back problems and much standard seating is uncomfortable. People used to roaming around freely during the day may hate sitting down for extended periods. An unusually early start may mean that they have skipped breakfast so that by eleven o'clock they are ready to snarl with the irritability caused by low blood sugar. Never assume that a break for drinks can be accomplished in ten minutes. If the service is slow, if the coffee is too hot, if people have to queue for the lavatories, if they are smokers, if they find that they enjoy chatting ... then you will be lucky to get them back in less than twenty minutes. Similarly, meal breaks rarely take less than the full hour. One useful tip here: if you can influence the choice of lunch food, choose light, easily digestible snacks and ban alcohol. I still cringe to remember a day I ran for a bar chain where the excellent buffet lunch was supplemented by lavish quantities of free wine and beer. Needless to say, little work was done that afternoon.

Even if a meal can be eaten quickly, it is a good idea for everyone, including you, to have some kind of rest for reflection and maybe also the reinvigoration that some mild exercise and fresh air can bring. Plan this in to your design. Note also that you must design some kind of lively activity to follow immediately after lunch when human beings seem to have been designed to have a nap. This is not the place in the timetable to drone your way through a lecture.

Where you are running a whole day event, be alert to this and to other biological rhythms and work with them wherever you can. Bear in mind that they affect you as much as they affect your participants. Early to mid-morning is the best place for heavyweight theoretical input. Reflection can fit well with the pre-lunch dip in energy. Mid-afternoon is a good place for extended skill practice. Days which extend into the early evening, thus making potentially a ten-hour learning day, are doomed. People are normally just too tired to concentrate.

The best match of methodology to all of the above

Here is an at-a-glance table which sums up how you might match objectives to the methods that are possible, most of which I have discussed earlier in this book.

Table 11.2

Objective	*Possible methods to consider*
Acquiring information	Reading, delivered through reading list or via website and other media Quizzes, tests, questionnaires, delivered as above Lecture/talk given in person or through the Web or other media Problem-based learning Facilitated discussion
Acquiring a skill	Demonstration – live or recorded Observation Skill practice solo or in small groups with feedback Role play Coaching
Discrimination, diagnosis and problem-solving	Reading Guided observation Problem-based learning Case studies Simulation Role play Facilitated discussion Project work Coaching Action learning
Changing attitudes	Facilitated discussion Case studies Role play Coaching Project work Simulations and games

Designing a piece of learning is a creative process. It needs a playful, confident, optimistic mood. If you are lucky enough to have a co-tutor, or, even luckier, a whole faculty of colleagues, you will get best results from a discussion that begins by encouraging any idea, however outrageous. I have always liked the management guru Tom Peters's phrase about 'throwing some spaghetti at the wall and seeing what sticks'.

Start by listing or reminding yourself of all the givens: objectives, length of event, numbers of participants, rooms and other resources. Now take a large sheet of paper – flip-chart size is ideal. Let's assume you are designing a day-long workshop due to run from 09.30 until 17.00. In the light of what you now know about your target participants, you may want to consider what work you need them to do ahead of the actual meeting, and, if so, how you will deliver it – for instance through a website or a specially designed set of worksheets sent through the post. So for my putative course on running meetings, I might consider sending my learners an observation sheet and asking them to use it to assess a meeting that they are attending. This sheet will contain the criteria that we will be working from on the course, so the exercise will begin the process of awareness-raising on which we will be working during the course itself. Similarly, a recent training event that a colleague and I ran for trainee assessors on our coaching course was preceded by distributing a copy of a taped coaching session. We asked our trainees to assess this tape exactly as they would if they were doing it for real. Starting the day by sharing the results gave us a pacey and purposeful beginning to the event.

Given the short time the group will be meeting, you may also want to consider what follow-up activity may be necessary – for instance some kind of assessment.

In the day itself, although you can flex the precise length of each session, you can only really have four substantial blocks of working time. You already know that you are going to have to spend at least a little time at the outset welcoming people and reminding them of the objectives for the day and some matching time at the end on action-planning and asking them for feedback. You are bound to want to have some kind of ice-breaker. There will be breaks for refreshments and for a meal in the middle of the day. So your grid will look something like Table 11.3.

Put your favourite ideas for the design on post-it notes and attach them to the vacant slots. The post-it approach helps to avoid getting too fixed in your ideas at this stage. You will probably have too many ideas for the time available. Realism and ruthless editing is the only solution here. For my course on running meetings, I have a short simulation that is a favourite because of the opportunities it gives people to get some feedback by seeing their own meetings behaviour under the microscope, and people usually enjoy it as an activity. However, I know that it will take at least forty minutes to run and another half hour to debrief. In arguing for its inclusion, I may have to sacrifice other activities that seem equally attractive and important. Don't succumb to the tempting fantasy, a particular weakness of my own, of thinking that somehow the time will magically expand so that all your ideas can find a home.

When you have what looks like a reasonable draft, stand back and review

Table 11.3

Pre-work	*Purpose/Objective*	*How delivered – media, materials etc.*
Time	*Purpose/Objective*	*Activity, materials, group format (pairs, trios etc.)*
09.00–09.30	Social, meet people as they arrive, reduce anxiety	Make tea and coffee available
09.30–09.40	Inclusion: help get people fully present	Introduce self, reiterate objectives
09.40–10.00	Inclusion, as before	Ice-breaker
10.00 – 11.10 Session 1		
11.10–11.30 Break		
11.30–13.00 Session 2		
13.00–14.00 Lunch		
14.00–15.25 Session 3		

15.25–15.45 Break		
15.45–16.54 Session 4		
16.45–17.00	Action-planning, feedback and wrap up	
Post-course work	*Purpose/Objective*	*How delivered*

it against the starting point and then against basic principles of design by asking yourself and colleagues, if you are working with them, the questions in Table 11.4 and scoring yourself on a 5–1 scale. 5 = excellent, 1 = poor.

Going public

Part of the job of designing learning is to take sensible action before the event by making it perfectly clear to prospective participants what is on offer. Once you have clarified in your own and your commissioner's mind what the objectives and design for the event are, this becomes a relatively easy task.

I don't want to clutter my course description on running meetings with what might look to potential participants like educational jargon, so what is sent to the participants might look something like this:

- How can you ensure that you feel confident and in control during a meeting that you chair?
- How do you keep everyone involved?
- How do you deal with the problems that can happen in any meeting with people who are too dominant or too silent?
- How can you run meetings that are productive and enjoyable?
- How can you leave a positive impression of your chairing skills?

  This course is designed for people who need to chair meetings but may have little experience. The course offers a highly practical set of

Table 11.4

How far does this design	*5*	*4*	*3*	*2*	*1*
Build on people's existing knowledge and skill?					
Vary the pace?					
Give opportunities for people to work in a variety of group sizes and formats?					
Minimize dependence on verbally given information?					
Contain cycles of activities within each session which allow for Activity? Reflection? Theory? Practical application?					
Allow people of mixed ability to work together?					
Cater for the likely psychological state of the group and its individual members?					
Cater for the likely physiological state of the group and its members at any one time?					
Sequence the learning, building from simple to more complex, reinforcing earlier learning?					
Meet the agreed learning objectives through all of the above?					

Anything you or colleagues mark below 4 should prompt a rethink.

tools and techniques, and the opportunity to practise and gain feedback on the core skills of chairing. It also invites you to think about the overall purpose and structure of meetings and the conditions that support successful action after the meeting.

Let's take a language course as another example. The briefer the description, the more likely it is to raise unrealistic hopes or to encourage a reader to read whatever assumptions they care to into vague words:

French for Near-Beginners: two-hour class, weekly

Compare this with:

> French, Stage Two. This is the level for you if you have already studied French for at least sixty hours and can hold a simple conversation in French – for instance, give straightforward personal information such as your name, age and address, ask for directions and order a meal. You will already be able to use the present, basic past tenses and future tense and will be able to write a short, simple letter in French. You will be able to read and understand a French newspaper on everyday topics. By attending this class you will be able to understand a wider range of conversations in French, take part in a discussion, justifying your opinions and asking relevant questions and also produce an accurate summary of a piece of given text. You will be able to use a wide range of grammatical structures such as the conditional and subjunctive tenses. The class meets weekly for two hours of concentrated work. Places are at a premium and in joining we expect you to commit yourself to regular attendance. The course prepares you to take the exam of the Diplome d'Etudes en Langue Française (DELF), A2 Level. The fee includes non-refundable exam costs payable in advance. If in doubt about whether this is the right course for you, please ring the Languages Tutor on <telephone number> for an informal interview.

The first entry tells a prospective learner little. It gives no indication of the previous experience expected and no hint of the pace, style and final accomplishments of its graduates. It is the type of description written by people who want to hedge their bets: they are afraid enrolment will go down if they are too specific.

The second entry is a good deal more helpful. It identifies the entry level expected, is specific about objectives and makes it clear that there will be a brisk and businesslike pace to the proceedings. This realistic approach will certainly discourage the people for whom the course is not intended, but then if they did enrol they would quickly find out for themselves that the course was unsuitable. 'Enrolment at any price' in practice means enrolment at the cost of learner achievement and satisfaction and a high price also paid in tutor frustration.

So when your client circulates the details through a brochure or website, the objectives of the course and the person it is typically aimed at will be as clear as possible to potential attendees. If, for instance, you are aiming your course at beginners, and bogus beginners come forward (this is people whom you discover or know have quite a lot of experience already) you have various options: to discourage them or arrange a more suitable piece of training; to find out what lies underneath this apparent miscasting; to accept them and use them as deliberate sources of advice and experience during the course. The point is that you can make the choice: there might be something to be said for any of these tactics. If you end up with a group of wildly mixed ability and startlingly varied motivation, then it is because you have weighed up the advantages and disadvantages yourself: you are not helplessly accepting someone else's judgement.

Finally, once you have designed your event, think carefully about how prospective learners make further decisions as to whether it is for them or not. How you contact them is vital. If you are running one-off events, all your communications will be telling them something about you. Make sure it is the message you want to convey. For instance, if they have to wait weeks to hear whether or not they have a place, this will not give an efficient or friendly impression. If it's clear that someone is over- or under-qualified for an event, always discuss it thoroughly with them, suggesting an alternative event if you feel that only disappointment could result from attending your event. Similarly, when you send out joining instructions, encourage people to contact you with their queries or worries. A surprising number may do so. Even where the question is something like, 'I've got to go to a meeting on the second day; is that all right?', take the opportunity to confirm that this person fits the profile of your target learner.

Once your learners have decided that this is indeed the course for them, it is good practice to let them have as much information in advance as possible. At a minimum this should include:

- the objectives for the event described in a way that makes them sound attractive;
- pre-work; whether it is essential and, if so, why; how it will reach them and by when; how much time it will take to complete; what support will be available to complete it;
- an invitation to contact you if there is anything they do not understand or want to discuss;
- your expectations about attendance – for instance, the importance of not missing sessions and the consequences if people do;
- an outline programme;
- your CV;
- the kinds of method you will be using so that there are no surprises on the day;
- dress code;
- telephone number of the venue and directions about how to get there;
- any equipment or other materials they need to bring with them;
- links of the event with any examination requirements;
- follow-up activity, if any.

4 Piloting

However careful your preparation, it is unlikely to have produced the perfect course. Essentially the first run is a trial. Ask the group for their support by telling them that they are guinea pigs and actively soliciting their feedback, remembering that sometimes this feedback contains irreconcilable opposites or else counsel of perfection that cannot be acted on in its entirety. Similarly, review the event with any colleagues and agree what changes you can and should make to the course to improve it. Your commissioner also needs to be involved at this stage. He or she may have access to other useful comments but the more you are proactive in leading the process of gathering feedback, the less likely you are to be at the mercy of rumour and scuttlebutt.

In practice, any long-running event, much repeated, will evolve continuously, responding to modifications in the learner population, developments in knowledge, technological change and, with all of this, changes in demand. Like any product, a course has a limited life cycle and the secret is knowing when to call it a day.

Phase 5, *Delivering*, is what all the preceding chapters in this book have been about. Phase 6, the final stage in any piece of learning, is to assess how far your objectives have been met. Understanding how to evaluate what people have actually learnt is the subject of the next chapter.

Further reading

I have not been able to find a good selection of up-to-date books on curriculum design that relate specifically to adult learning. (If you know of such, please contact me.)

There is a useful section, *Teaching: Content and Methods*, in Chapter 9 of Alan Rogers's comprehensive book *Teaching Adults*, see page 42.

Forsythe, I., Joliffe, A. and Stevens, D. (1999) Planning a Course: Practical Strategies for Teachers, Lecturers and Trainers, 2nd edition. London: Kogan Page.

Sork, T.J. (ed.) (1983) *Designing and Implementing Effective Workshops*. San Francisco, CA: Jossey-Bass.

The internet is the best source of commercially available curriculum-planning tools and also of ready-made designs – if you are desperate and stuck. Type your subject area together with the words *curriculum design* into a search engine to see what might be available. Many university education departments around the world have helpful sites on curriculum planning but the emphasis tends to be on school education. In the UK, the *Higher Education*

Academy, whose purpose is to improve the quality of experience for students, has a number of useful pages devoted to curriculum design. Although specifically for higher education, these pages also have broad, general application: www.heacademy.ac.uk

Note

1 Bloom, B.S. (1956) *Taxonomy of Educational Objectives*. New York: David McKay Co. Inc.

12 Evaluating

School education is now clotted with attempts to measure the progress of learning. One recent estimate suggested that by the time he or she leaves full-time education, the average child will have been subjected to no fewer than 76 different tests, with all the stress and misery that these events can generate.

SATs (standard assessment tasks) and their like were probably an inevitable reaction to the nebulous claims of a let-it-all-hang-out-everything-is-creative approach of the 1960s and 1970s. Before that, the only measures of success in education were the notorious eleven-plus, largely abandoned after the mid-1960s, and public examinations at 16 and 18. Now, there are not only SATs but league tables comparing one school with another and tables that will compare success rates at GCSE and A level in one year with those in another, plus debate about whether these exams are getting easier. Adult, further and university education organizations are, in their turn, rigorously inspected and asked to justify the public money they receive.

Depending on where you teach adults, you may be feeling the back-draught from all of this, too. Certainly, in the work that I do, exclusively now with people in organizations, many of my company's clients are interested to know how we will evaluate success. They are spending a lot of money and they want reassurance that their investment is likely to be realized.

Why evaluate?

I don't believe you can be serious as a teacher of adults without being interested in this question. Even in my very early days as a tutor I wanted to know the answer to the question: *Is it working?* At the simplest level, I took falling or rising numbers of attendees at voluntary classes to be a reflection of how well I was doing, and I was right to do so, even though there can be many reasons for changes in attendance patterns other than your own prowess.

At the same time, you do also have to take a reasonably relaxed view. Anxiously awaiting my first-ever batch of A level students' results, I remember a cynical colleague telling me that if the pass rate was high then the college would credit the students, whereas if it was low then it was my fault. Alas, we can see the same churlish syndrome at work today. If exam pass rates go down, then it is the responsibility of the teachers. If pass rates continue to rise, then it must because the standard is declining.

In spite of the review-by-newspaper that oppresses education, there are sound reasons for evaluating:

- No learning is ever undertaken unless it is to change and improve something. If it is worth doing at all, then you or your sponsor will want to know that improvement is likely.
- All training costs money. This is true where it is the 'wooden pounds' that are involved when the training is done internally by an organization using its own staff and premises. It is also true when both trainers and trainees are volunteers. I donate a small percentage of my time as a trainer, designating it 'gift work', but I make it a principle to let the recipient organization or person know what the value of that gift is. There is an opportunity cost for me in doing free work and an opportunity cost for the client, too.
- All teachers, trainers and tutors worth their salt want to know how they compare with others doing similar work. When I was working in colleges of further education, it was very clear to me that some of my colleagues were effective and some, dealing with the same students and in the same subject, were not so effective. I wanted to know why and how this difference happened. Similarly, when I ran a training department at the BBC, we delivered many apparently identical courses for similar participants. But some courses got positive evaluations from participants and some did not. Patterns soon emerged when we tracked the same courses over time. It was crystal clear that the differentiating factor was the tutor. If you are that tutor, unless you know where you stand, you can't improve.
- If you are searching for a new job as a trainer or tutor, anticipate being asked the question, 'How do you know that what you do works?' If you have never thought about it before, expect to fail the interview.

A word of caution: anyone who is serious about their teaching or training will already be evaluating constantly, for instance by asking people formally and informally how they are doing and what they are learning; asking people what they think and feel about the quality of the event; observing who is looking happy, unhappy, bored or tired and investigating what is going on through discussion. You do not necessarily need forms to do evaluation. It's a bit like finding out that you are speaking prose all the time.

Evaluation is challenging

You want to evaluate the success of your efforts. You want to improve the quality of what you do. Yet there are many difficulties in doing this. For instance, you may have no control over who enters your course even though a close match between participant ability and eventual results is clearly critical to success. But who defines *success?* I would take as an example one of the dance classes I attend. This class for over-fifties is subsidized by Sadlers Wells Theatre as part of its community outreach programme. How does the theatre assess its investment? If our progress were to be evaluated by the most obvious external criterion – how well we dance as a result of the teaching – then the results would probably not be impressive. A good quarter of the class makes no discernible improvement from one week to the next. One or two of our members simply sway about in a vague way and make the same mistakes repeatedly. If our teacher were worried by ruthless assessment of our eventual skills as a condition of continued funding, he would probably need to insist on audition at entry, rejecting those who had no aptitude and concentrating instead on the minority who are naturally talented dancers, several of them former professionals. This control at entry-point is what is happening to many schools, caught up in the toxic competition of league tables. Fortunately, Sadlers Wells is a lot more forward thinking. They clearly see that participation in exercise and dance is valuable in itself and that the social inclusion of older people through dance is an aim that is worth supporting. My guess is that they are assessing success through the simple metric of attendance and would be worried if numbers dropped significantly, though, in fact, the numbers keep growing.

Then there is the problem of how to assess whether or not people have made progress against the stated aims of the course. This is going to be much easier in some subjects than others. I take two at random from a recent prospectus of a well-known London Adult Education Institute:

> *HTML for beginners*. Learn the formatting language used to write web pages, how to apply it and how to structure a website in which various pages are linked together. Knowledge required: basic computing.

How do you evaluate the success of this course? This might be relatively easy. Assuming people really do have knowledge of basic computing, a big assumption in itself, you could readily assess a few weeks after the event whether its participants have actually built a simple website using the knowledge they have acquired. But even here, it might be trickier than it looks. If they haven't built a website, then what would explain it? There could be any number of reasons, some of them more to do with life circumstances, with initial motivation, existing knowledge or access to equipment than with the skill of the tutor.

And how about this one?

> *Achieving Emotional Literacy.* Your success at work and in your personal life requires 'EQ' as well as IQ. Learn the language of emotions to know what you feel, get what you need and have the relationships you desire.

Here we are in more difficult territory. It is unlikely that the Institute can or would wish to screen potential participants for their emotional stability and it is possible that the course will attract at least some people whose psychological state is a little flaky. After the course, how would you assess whether or not its members had raised their EQ? Would you administer an EQ questionnaire before and after the course? Who would decide what constituted improvement? Would self-assessment be valid? What might seem like a marginal improvement to one course member might be a giant step for another and the tutor might take a different view again. Standardizing would be difficult, if not impossible.

Some of the results that a tutor obtains are notoriously difficult to measure because they depend to a large extent on the subjective impressions of the learners. Not only will these vary from one learner to another but they may also vary according to when and how you ask the same learner. When you try to correlate results with some kind of measurable outcome it often proves difficult. For instance, if your organization sponsors a course on *Managing Stress*, how would you prove that the event had any impact on the bottom line results of the organization? The individuals attending may feel better in the sense that they are more relaxed after the course than they were before it, but how long does this effect last? If the rate of absenteeism, a proper bottom line metric, subsequently drops among those who attended the course, can we be certain that there is a correlation? Probably not, because so many other factors are likely to be involved, the size of the sample group is likely to be too small to give reliable results and it is unlikely that anyone thought, 'Hang on, let's set up a control group and see what comparisons we can make . . .'.

Then there is the issue of how to assess what people have actually learnt, even when you have a robust before and after assessment process in place. What is to say that learners do not take away pieces of learning which are the perverse opposite of what you have intended? A friend of mine, sent by her organization on a negotiation skills course, returned convinced that the allegedly ethical approach offered by the course tutors was simply manipulation in disguise and decided that, in this case, negotiation was code for

Might is Right. I think that her tutors would undoubtedly have been in despair had they heard this.

Evaluation is time-consuming. To do it seriously involves skill, time, dedication and therefore money. You have to be clear that the benefits of any evaluation will justify the costs involved. The truth is that the wish to evaluate needs to be stronger than the inertia which results from just assuming that everything is more or less OK as it is. In the case of schools, the compulsion to evaluate arises mostly from political pressure dressed up as social justice.

Useful terms

There are a number of different terms in this arena that it is useful to define:

- *Evaluation* means a system of judging the benefit of teaching or training to participants or to the sponsoring organization.
- *Validation* means judging whether the training met the objectives set for it, regardless of whether the participants liked or enjoyed the training.
- *Assessment* means judging whether the teaching or training meets a national or international standard – for instance, the baccalaureate, A level, NVQ.

Who does the evaluating?

There is no proof that I know of which will show that a so-called 'independent' evaluation is any 'better' than one carried out by the tutor or institution itself. What is true is that you will get a different result, depending on who carries out the evaluation. No evaluation of one human being by another can be 'objective'. The opinions, bias, assumptions and knowledge of the observer inevitably get in the way.

Also, I believe it is a basic scientific principle that you cannot measure anything without altering it. So, for instance, if you press a ruler against paper to measure a distance, you will have altered the surface of the paper, however minimally. If you count the number of blackbird nests in a field as part of an ecological study, you may disturb the birds and thus alter the number of chicks they rear successfully.

This principle is even more obviously true of evaluating human learning. The presence of an observer changes the process, putting both participants and tutors on their guard, thus altering their behaviour. Sometimes this can produce gross distortions. There are many accounts from schools of how an approaching Ofsted (Office for Standards in Education) inspection means that children and lessons are rehearsed, that teachers can have nervous breakdowns and that an air of anxious despair can hang over the whole school, particularly if it has already been designated as 'failing'. The sense of indignation that this can create has led some schools to fight back by instituting an informal process for evaluating the evaluators, thus swallowing up yet more energy and effort.

A colleague and I ran a particular course over many years and suggested that one of our sponsors might like to evaluate it. We insisted that an independent third party should do the evaluating. However, our faith in the process was dented by a number of events during the evaluation itself. First, our evaluator appeared only sporadically during the course, so she missed large chunks of key activity. She also told us that she had only just had a baby and so was feeling 'a bit dippy'. Then, instead of remaining outside various group discussions as an observer, to our amazement and horror she actually joined in, excusing herself by saying 'This is a subject I'm really interested in!' Finally, the consultancy hired by our commissioning client was a competitor. Our participants realized this and told us that their loyalty was to us. When the evaluator rang them several months later for comments about how far they had carried the learning into their everyday activity, several people told us that they had given guarded replies, for this reason. We might also have suspected that our evaluator had every reason to downplay our success, though to be fair her eventual report was enthusiastic. As a final twist to possibly mixed motives, we learnt that six months later her company was offering an event that looked remarkably like a copy-cat reflection of ours.

However, there is certainly a case for someone other than the tutor asking the questions. When you as the tutor ask the questions, you may get vague, or softer answers, as people don't want to be horrible and may dress up their criticisms to avoid hurting you. Alternatively, if for some reason they have taken a violent dislike to you, their negative comments may be more extreme than is really justified by whatever offence they believe you have caused.

Also, you may find it difficult to hear the comments of participants, especially if they are not put tactfully. I worked some years ago with a distinguished consultant, a world leader in his field. He told me that he had no interest whatsoever in hearing what participants had to say about him or his events because he was his own harshest critic and always knew when he was on form and when he was not. I attended a course he ran and found him shamelessly open about this in what he said to us at the opening session. 'Don't bother to think that you can redesign this event', he announced calmly to the assembled participants – also people in the consulting and training business. 'I've been running it for twelve years and I've already heard any comment you are likely to make'.

For all these reasons, think carefully about who does the evaluation and put the answers you get into a cautious perspective.

What do you evaluate against?

Preparation for evaluation starts with a careful analysis of learning needs and of objectives (see page 243). If you don't have objectives for learning, then you have no prospect of evaluating anything.

It also starts with an analysis of what your learners already know. If you have no baseline, then you can't evaluate. Blended and e-learning may come into their own here. Where large organizations are making major investments in training programmes and delivering substantial parts of it through electronic means, such programmes do often begin with an assessment of initial knowledge. A module may also end with a set of multiple-choice questions designed to assess how much information learners have gained as a result of their efforts. For most tutors, however, the evaluation process will apparently fail at this point. Most of us cannot sit our learners down and subject them to tests of their existing knowledge and attitudes. The process is particularly vulnerable when it comes to assessment of skills. Unless others have been involved in some kind of 360-degree feedback process, you will be relying on self-assessment – notoriously unreliable.

In general the pre-course process is usually loose and informal. Most probably, you will have to do this impressionistically on the basis of what participants tell you about their existing knowledge or skill and on your own observation in any activities you set them at the outset.

All of us in the training and teaching field owe a debt to two men: the US expert Donald Kirkpatrick and a British counterpart, Leslie Rae. Kirkpatrick first put forward his ideas as long ago as 1959 and has updated them constantly since.[1] Others have offered alternative frameworks, but these are the ones to which we constantly return. Kirkpatrick's ideas about the four levels of evaluation have entered the bloodstream of debate about how to evaluate. Leslie Rae has written extensively about evaluating training and his work is invariably accessible, wise and informative. I have drawn on the ideas of both men in this chapter, though the interpretation is down to me.

The four levels

Kirkpatrick's framework suggests that it is useful to look at evaluation in four stages. These are usually described as Levels 1, 2, 3 and 4. Each succeeding level builds on information obtained at the preceding stage to build a full picture:

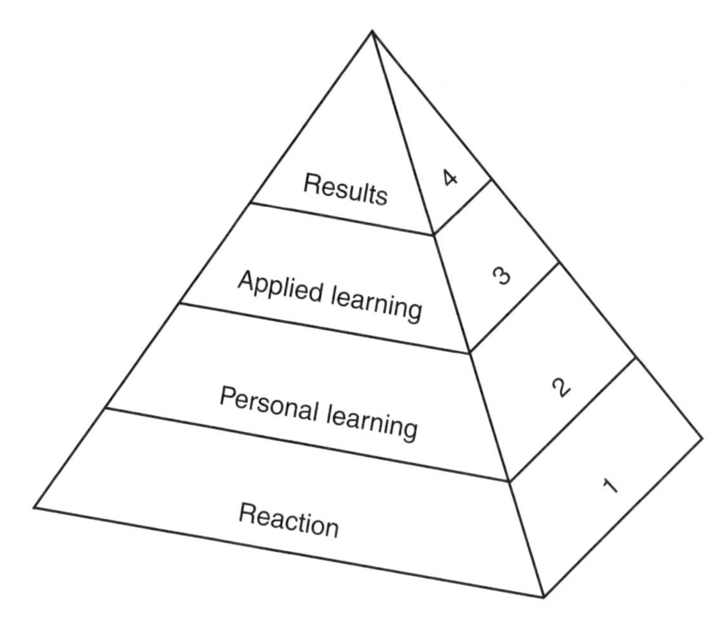

Figure 12.1

Level 1: Reaction

Level 1 is about the event. This level looks at what is happening during and at the end of an event. You are looking at it in its own setting, not afterwards. This level is really about how the participants enjoyed it and found it useful. They are evaluating the *teaching*, not the *learning*. To a large extent, they are evaluating *you*. At Level 1, you are asking for opinions on areas such as:

- Did you enjoy it?
- Was it useful?
- What do you think you have learnt?
- What comments do you have on the tutor(s)?
- How was the level of participation for you?
- What did you feel about the training methods?
- What do you think of the venue?
- How did you feel about the joining instructions?

These questions, and others like them, are the foundations of the so-called 'Happy Sheet', distributed to participants at the end of an event. The down-putting phrase *Happy Sheet* is misleading. It suggests that this information is of no importance; participants' minds are on going home and they don't care; people will write anything just to get away and that all their remarks will be skewed to the 'happy' – i.e. to the positive.

I don't agree with the generally dismissive view of end-of-course evaluations. They do give pricelessly useful information as long as you put it into context. For a start, if you are running the same learning event more than once, you can benchmark one event against another. If you are running the same event but with different tutors, you can do the same. Where you ask people to give a numerical score for an event, you can average the scores, turn them into a percentage 'satisfaction score' and track them over weeks or even years. I have found that they are remarkably sensitive ways to look at participant satisfaction.

Giving people a 1–7 scale is a useful way to look at how they feel about the event. Using such a scale, questions you should consider including at Level 1 are:

- How far did this course meet your objectives?
- How far did the course content meet your needs?
- How relevant to your objectives did you find the course?
- What major pieces of learning did you accomplish on this event?
- How do you rate the tutors?
- How do you rate the venue?
- How do you rate the admin?
- What overall satisfaction score would you give this event?

You might also like to consider some open-ended questions such as:

- Which sessions do you think might be added, lengthened or shortened? What are your reasons here?
- What could we or should we do to improve this event?

Alan Chapman's free and useful website on business topics, Business balls,[2] offers several ready-made evaluation forms designed by Leslie Rae which you can download and adapt. At the very least, these will offer you some excellent templates against which to compare the forms you already use.

There are a number of other, more informal ways in which you can do Level 1 evaluation. One that I like is the 'Graffiti Wall'. Stick several pieces of flip-chart paper together so that they join up along a wall. Draw a huge 'wall' with large 'bricks' and invite participants to write their comments in a 'brick' (as many per person as they like) in felt-tip pen.

The evaluators at Level 1 are the participants. Like any of us, they will have their preconceptions, prejudices and concerns. They may rate you high or low on the basis of impression, not reality, whatever that is. You may be the 'wrong' age, gender, sexual orientation, profession, race, religion or nationality, and have the 'wrong' appearance or credentials. Several well-known experiments have shown, for instance, that the same 'lecturer' (actually an actor) could be introduced to different groups of matched students in a variety of guises. The more gilded and impressive his apparent credentials, the more highly the students rated him, even though he gave the same performance each time.

It is perfectly possible to dislike an event, but also to learn from it. The most unsatisfying course I ever attended as a participant involved qualifying to administer a particular psychometric questionnaire. The trainer had been to California and had, as he thought, learnt there from a master. He had us lying on the floor, holding hands, visualizing, 'doing personal work' and 'group process'. I have no objection to these approaches, indeed I use some of them myself, but they need to be used in the right place and at the right time and also need to be carried out with flair and conviction. My view was that these methods were inappropriate for the subject and that the tutor was fumbling for the right tone. I was there to learn about the construction of the questionnaire, its aims and how to administer it. I did in fact learn some of this, in spite of the tutor and his course. I went away fuming with frustration, but I now use that questionnaire all the time.

You can also really enjoy an event but fail to learn from it. All experienced tutors will have encountered the participant who loves courses, goes on them all the time, gives them rave reviews, but appears not to have done much learning in spite of innumerable opportunities to do so during the events.

Level 2: Personal learning

Level 2 is about learning. It happens during the event, at the end and sometimes immediately after it. Essentially, Level 2 moves from whether or not people have enjoyed the event (Level 1) to whether they believe they have learnt from it. The formal way to assess learning is to apply some kind of test of achievement. Can participants now do something they couldn't do before? In practical subjects this will be easy to judge. Can people sew a straight seam, or build a strong wall or make a non-collapsing cake? In areas where physical prowess in involved, again it will be relatively easy to see. Can participants do yoga positions that defeated them when they began? Can they run a mile in ten minutes when previously they were out of breath after thirty seconds? Have they reached their target in a weight-loss programme? Once again, where evaluation is concerned, it is easy for this process to become a mere tiresome ritual or open to manipulation of all sorts, for instance to meet externally imposed targets. Even the apparent rigour of the SATS process can be perverted by teachers anxious to inflate the scores of their schools with the implied reflection on their own performance.

Where your subject is more about attitudes than about skills, you will have to be more ingenious. Apart from the informal ways of assessing, there are, again, a number of written forms you can use. A useful one is the so-called 'tea bag' technique. The name comes from the way 'the flavour just floods out'. Give each person a piece of paper where they have to complete these phrases:

Table 12.1

I've learnt...	I'm puzzled...
I've discovered...	I can develop...
I've understood...	I'm disappointed...

You can do this at the end of each day, or at the end of the course. Vengeful participants can still use this format to tell you some unpleasant truths as they see them, but essentially the onus here is on participants to identify their learning, not to pass judgement on the tutor.

Another excellent idea is to introduce a *Learning Log* where people write a brief account of their learning for each day, with a copy for the tutor. These journals are often remarkable documents, which amaze both their authors and the tutor. They chart a learning journey in a way that is difficult to trap by other means, though you can also design a questionnaire specifically aimed at asking people to identify their learning.

Action Plans, where appropriate, are another way of capturing learning by asking people to identify how they are going to build on whatever they have achieved during the course. The act of writing it down increases the chance that they will carry it out. Offer participants a simple five-column format something Table 12.2. Five goals are usually enough.

Table 12.2

Goal	Purpose of goal	Who/what can help	How to be achieved	By when
1				
2				
3				
4				
5				

You may also be able to include a formal assessment as a Level 2 method. We do this on the final day of Module One of our Diploma in Coaching course. We introduce 'real' clients and ask the participants to coach them with a trained assessor in the room. The assessor marks them against a detailed competency framework, ending with a summary of strengths and weaknesses as he or she sees the candidate, followed by verbal feedback. There are similar assessments or tests at the end of most programmes where licensing or a qualification is involved. These may include written tests, perhaps with multiple-choice questionnaires, interviews, role-played assignments to test behaviour, performing tasks under time and resource constraints, or some mix of all of these. When it is appropriate, these assessments are powerful for both tutors and participants. They form a permanent record for the participant and can be read calmly after all the immediate excitement of the assessment. Tutors get a reliable way of seeing what people have learnt and what their struggles have been. Where innumerable people seem to be having the same difficulty, it points unerringly to a deficit in your training. You will have misjudged what people can learn and do, given the time and methods you have used with them.

To undertake formal assessments it is essential to be explicit about negative and positive indicators, listing them clearly, to standardize your scoring and therefore to train your assessors. Inconsistent assessment is unfair to learners and exasperating to administrators.

Unless you are running formal assessments, most evaluation at this level is impressionistic and probably has to be. It assumes, for instance, that participants will know how much they have learnt, whereas this may not be the case. People may have done some significant learning but may not realize it. They may claim to have learnt something when they haven't.

Unless you can actually observe performance and see how and in what ways it has changed, you will be working mostly on intuition. Even when you can observe performance, observer bias will come into the frame. For instance, one of my colleagues specializes in training people in presentation skills. This is one of the areas of our work where it is possible to make dramatic improvements in a very short time. But who says what constitutes an 'improvement'? Most comment on 'improvement' amounts to phrases such as 'I thought your opening sentence was much punchier', or 'You strike me as a lot more confident.' In other words, such comments are subjective rather than objective because they are going through the sieve of the observer's brain.

Level 3: Applied learning

At Level 3 you are looking at the longer term. Can people actually transfer what they have learnt to the 'real world'? Does their knowledge and skill stay with them after the course is over? Was there some kind of measurable change in what they can do? Could this person reliably train someone else in the skills they have now acquired?

At Level 3 you are acknowledging that knowledge and skill has a half-life, or even a quarter-life. It decays unless it is reinforced and many things can get in the way of reinforcement. For instance, in my field, coaching and leadership development, the most obvious way in which knowledge and skill are destroyed is that the organization is indifferent or actively hostile to what people have learnt on a course. A recently returned course member may be trying really hard to apply and use her new-found skill, only to be greeted with phrases like, 'Oh she's been on a course. Never mind. She'll soon get over it.'

Less obviously, other interests and commitments press their claims. People may lack access to equipment and situations where they can use what they have learnt. For instance, if you go on a computer course, but lack a computer on which to practise, you will soon find that you have forgotten most of what you learnt.

One way to track Level 3 learning is to return to participants six months or so after the event and ask them questions such as:

- What stays with you about the course?
- What are you doing differently as a result of what you learnt?
- How important are these differences to you?
- What is the impact of what you are doing differently on your colleagues/family?
- What bottom line improvements have resulted from your training?

Where you are working with people from organizations and the organization is paying for your expertise as a trainer, then the participants' colleagues ideally need to be included in the evaluation. It is especially useful if their line manager is involved. Ask, 'What changes have you seen in this person's behaviour?' 'Which of these changes might you attribute directly to the training?' 'How do these changes affect the bottom line?'

There are a number of ways in which you can ask these questions. Choose from questionnaires such as 360-degree reviews, individual interviews and focus groups. All have their pluses and minuses.

Level 4: Results

At this level, you are looking for the longest-term impact – on people's lives, and in work settings on the organization. This kind of evaluation is rarely attempted because it is difficult if not impossible to disentangle the effects of learning from many other factors.

An example from our own practice is a major project we did for a public sector client. The focus of the intervention was customer care. The need was acute: the organization was losing its customers and a survey showed the abysmally low opinion held about them by the majority of customers. The organization was also rapidly losing its customers to external competitors. So we had some valid pre-intervention data. We ran innumerable workshops and trained more than 3500 staff. At these workshops we administered Level 1 evaluations and were able to track the satisfaction of participants with the training they had received: mostly it was high or very high. After a year, a new customer survey was carried out by the same agency that had administered the first one. This showed that customer satisfaction had risen significantly. It also showed that the decline in business had been halted.

Naturally we were pleased with this data. However, we also had to accept that many factors other than our training were at play here. For instance, there was a major internal reorganization, a new managing director had been appointed, market conditions had changed, and so on. Also it was possible that the units attracted to the training were better run, so might have improved anyway. We still believe that our training was a significant factor in enhanced organizational performance, but it was hard to prove conclusively that this was so.

Remember, also, that as at Level 1 people can dislike the intervention but still learn from it. An example was a series of workshops run in one organization with the aim of breaking through widespread complacency about its market position. It was mandatory to attend. Non-compliance was a way of life in this organization, and many staff found reasons to wriggle out of going. Those who did go described the day as 'brainwashing', and told colleagues who had not yet attended that the only good thing about the day was the lunch. However, it was remarkable that very soon afterwards, opinion in the organization about its financial position and about competitors was notably better informed and a number of business units began talking about doing 'competitor analysis' and 'strategic alliances' with other businesses, phrases they would previously have scorned as *management gobbledygook*. How far this could be attributed to the workshops and how far to other elements remains open to question. However, the department that ran the workshops has no doubt that it was an important trigger to greater realism, followed by action and change for the better.

It is common now for organizations to ask, 'What is the Return on Investment (ROI)?' Essentially they are asking for Level 4 evaluation. Requests for ROI are to be welcomed. They suggest that the questioner has a keen interest in training. Some trainers and tutors feel attacked and vulnerable when the question is asked because they know how hard it is to answer it convincingly. They interpret it as an assault on the training profession generally. However, it seems obvious to me that all human societies accept that training works. Its value is self-evident in professions like medicine and the law. Requests for information on ROI should be seen, rather, as asking, 'Could we organize this more efficiently?' 'Could there be other ways to achieve the same or similar results in a shorter time and at less cost?' Or even, 'Do we need to be spending more money on this in order to achieve what we want?'

ROI goes back to the reason that training was commissioned in the first place. What were the drivers? Invariably, in organizations, these will be to do with bottom line performance. Organizations do not commission training just to be nice. Going back to the original commission will usually reveal what sort of measures you should be looking at. Usually these will be elements such as

volume – e.g. of sales, of turnover, or profit;
percentages of complaints;
numbers of 'adverse incidents';
rework and wastage rates;
achievements against national standards such as Investors in People;
key staff retention;
prizes and awards.

The quintet

Leslie Rae suggests that where training in organizations is concerned there needs to be a 'quintet' involved in evaluation. The principle is important because it is basic to the validity of any assessment that the more raters are involved the more reliable and valid the assessment will be. Rae's quintet is:

The senior management of the organization: the people who set the overall objectives and commission the training.
The trainer or tutor who delivers it.
The line manager who manages the performance of the participant and whose duty must include at the very least a preparation with the learner about what the organization expects, a debrief on the event and subsequent follow-up on performance, usually as part of the normal performance-management processes of the organization.
The training manager who manages the budget of the training department and matches trainer to trainee and whose duty must include overall monitoring of training quality.
The learner – on the receiving end of all of the above.

If you work in education rather than in other kinds of organizations, then it might be fruitful to consider who your own equivalents of the quintet are.

Precision in evaluation

Little precision is possible in evaluating learning. If you think about the different levels, there is a steep decline in reliability and validity as you progress from Level 1 to Level 4. At Level 1 you have relatively complete information because you are isolating the learning event from everything else and asking people to give an opinion while the experience is fresh in their minds. By the time you get to Level 4, time will have passed and many other elements will have come into play, most of them things over which your learners have no control. Unfortunately, this is precisely the opposite of the equation that organizations wish to prove. Organizations and governments invest in learning because they want long-term impact, but the further away you get from the learning event, the harder it is to say for certain that the learning was the cause of change. At Levels 1 and 2 the importance of the learning to the individual may be high while the importance to the organization is probably low, whereas the opposite is true at Levels 3 and 4.

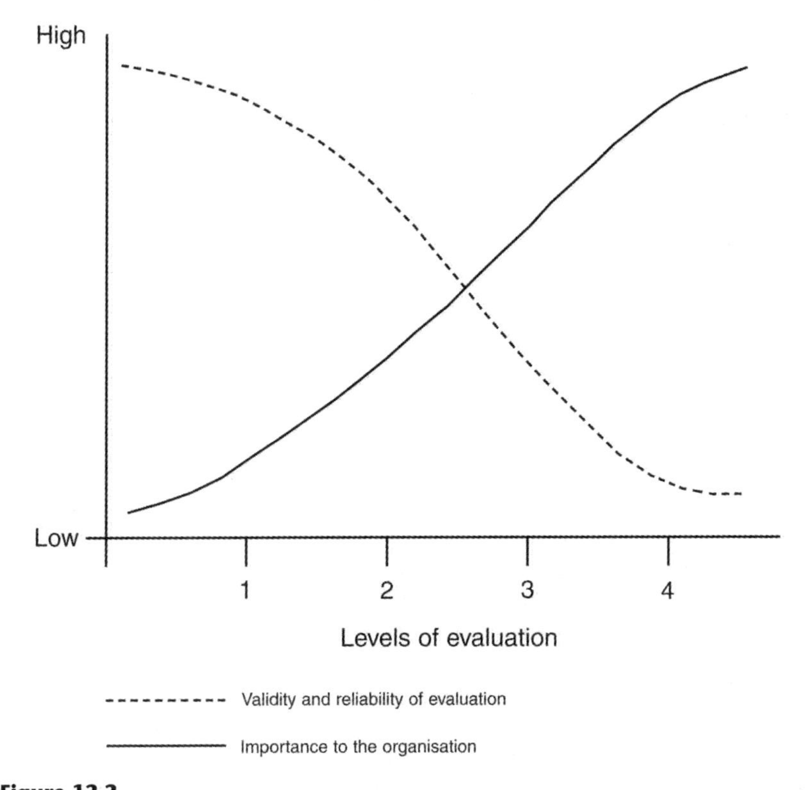

Figure 12.2

You can try to put precision into evaluation, and just because it is difficult does not mean we should not try. However, remember:

- Much wasted effort can be spent on trying to measure and evaluate. Always ask if the effort spent on evaluation is justified by the quality of the information obtained. Leslie Rae comments in his interesting article on the Businessballs website[3] that 'Jack Philips, an American ROI guru, recently commented about training ROI: Organizations should be considering implementing ROI impact studies very selectively on only 5 to 10 percent of their training programs, otherwise it becomes incredibly expensive and resource intensive.'
- People can dislike an event (Level 1) but still learn from it.
- People can enjoy an event (Level 1) but fail to learn from it (Level 2).
- There is always a tendency to measure the things that can be measured. For instance, you can readily measure the cost of a training programme and numbers of participants. But neither of these measures will tell you what people have learnt.
- Sometimes the most important things are intangible and cannot be measured. For instance, you cannot truly measure the pleasure of achievement, the delight in acquiring knowledge for its own sake, or the satisfaction of solving a long-standing problem. Yet these may be as important to individuals as anything to do with passing a test. An example is a conversation I had recently with someone who had been on an event I ran some years back with a colleague. 'I don't remember anything else about the course', said this person, 'except a blinding revelation: that *I was responsible for me.* This meant I couldn't be a victim, couldn't blame anyone, was responsible for my own moods and actions and couldn't be *made* to do anything. That piece of learning has literally changed my life.' I barely remembered the person or the event, but I recognized the passion and sincerity of these comments.

Much teaching and training comes down to acts of faith. We offer them and undertake them in the belief that they will be beneficial. There is also the argument that training, especially in organizations, is no longer an option – it is an investment. Employees see it as a right and as a privilege. The more talented people are seen to be or perceive themselves to be, the bigger the sum they expect to have spent on their development. The most successful organizations in the UK generally spend about 3 per cent of their payroll costs on training. If you fail to make the investment there could be a high price to pay. *Aha!* say the cynics. You cannot say that organizations are successful because of their training activity – perhaps these are successful organizations anyway. They have spare pre-tax money to spend, so they put it into training.

I personally believe this to be nonsense. At its best, learning is about flexibility. It is about learning how to learn. It is about problem-solving. It is about development. People and organizations investing in this process are bound to benefit. But it is difficult to prove it unequivocally.

In the end there are no simple answers to these challenges. Learning is about change and change in human beings is hard to track. A small change may have a huge effect and apparently big changes may have little effect. As people charged with shaping learning, we have to hope that we are producing the biggest change with the least possible cost and effort and that time will show that we made a significant difference.

Further reading

I have not attempted to consider formal assessments and inspections in this chapter. If this interests you, this book is a comprehensive starting point:

Reece, I. and Walker, S. (2006) *Teaching, Training and Learning*, 6th edition. Sunderland: Business Education Publishers. A detailed guide to formal professional assessment for qualifications, including Continuous Professional Development, plus advice on building portfolios, preparing for inspections.

For useful guidelines of the whole subject of evaluation, I suggest these books:

Bee, R. and Bee, F. (2003) *Learning Needs Analysis and Evaluation*. London: CIPD.

Kirkpatrick, D.L. (1996) *Evaluating Training Programs: The Four Levels*. San Francisco, CA: Berrett-Koehler.

Rae, L. (2002) *Assessing the Value of Your Training: The Evaluation Process from Training Needs to the Report to the Board*. Aldershot: Gower.

The Businessballs website contains a useful summary of current thinking on training evaluation: www.businessballs.com

There is a brief timeline of approaches to evaluation on the Campaign for Learning website: www.campaign-for-learning.org.uk

Notes

1 See Further Reading for references to both Kirkpatrick and Rae.
2 See Further Reading.
3 See Further Reading.

Index